Blood at the Root

Blood at the Root
Lynching as American Cultural Nucleus

Jennie Lightweis-Goff

An earlier version of the Introduction appeared as " 'Blood at the Root': Lynching, Memory, and Freudian Group Psychology" in *Journal for Psychoanalysis of Culture and Society* 12, no. 3 (September 2007): 288–95.

Published by State University of New York Press, Albany

© 2011 State University of New York

All rights reserved

Printed in the United States of America

No part of this book may be used or reproduced in any manner whatsoever without written permission. No part of this book may be stored in a retrieval system or transmitted in any form or by any means including electronic, electrostatic, magnetic tape, mechanical, photocopying, recording, or otherwise without the prior permission in writing of the publisher.

For information, contact State University of New York Press, Albany, NY
www.sunypress.edu

Production by Kelli W. LeRoux
Marketing by Anne M. Valentine

Library of Congress Cataloging-in-Publication Data

Lightweis-Goff, Jennie.
   Blood at the root : lynching as American cultural nucleus / Jennie Lightweis-Goff.
      p. cm.
   Includes bibliographical references and index.
   ISBN 978-1-4384-3629-6 (hardcover : alk. paper)
   ISBN 978-1-4384-3628-9 (pbk. : alk. paper)
   1. Lynching—United States—History. 2. United States—Race relations.
3. Race relations in literature. I. Title.

HV6457.L54 2011
364.1'34—dc22
                                      2010032064

10 9 8 7 6 5 4 3 2 1

For Frank Embree's Eyes: See Again
For Leo Frank's Throat: Speak Again
For Laura Nelson's Body: Live Again

Contents

List of Illustrations — ix

Love, Debt, Collaboration, and Thanks — xi

Introduction
Self and State: Lynching's Intimate Violence — 1

Chapter 1
"America is Mississippi Now": The Portable South and the Exile of Richard Wright — 31

Chapter 2
Beneath the Skin: George Schuyler and the Fantasy of Race — 59

Chapter 3
"Peaceful and Unfathomable and Unbearable Eyes": William Faulkner's Elisions of Witness — 83

Chapter 4
The Lynched Woman: Kara Walker, Laura Nelson, and the Question of Agency — 113

Conclusion
Vacant Lots: Public Memory and the Practice of Forgetting — 145

Notes — 179

Bibliography — 189

Index — 207

List of Illustrations

Figure 1	A noose covers the photograph of the execution of Haas Butler in the Pickens County Museum.	147
Figure 2	The intersection of Gethsemane and Old Bramlett Roads in Greenville, South Carolina	149
Figure 3	Under kudzu vines and new-growth white pines is the abattoir where Willie Earle's body was found.	150
Figure 4	The First Baptist Church in Port Jervis, New York. Robert Jackson Lewis was lynched near the church's current location in 1892.	159
Figure 5	The Grant County Security Center in Marion, Indiana	166
Figure 6	The courthouse in Marion, Indiana	167
Figure 7	"You are not forgotten," reads the Vietnam POW/MIA memorial on the courthouse lawn where Shipp and Smith were lynched in 1930.	173

Love, Debt, Collaboration, and Thanks

In May 2003, Andy Doolen—then an assistant professor at Clemson University—lent me his copy of *Without Sanctuary: Lynching Photography in America*. At the time, I was writing *Reconstructing Hitler's Body in Cinema*, an examination of the relationship between Axis propaganda and the "heroic comedies" of the Allied countries, a study subsequently submitted as a thesis for the Masters of Arts at Clemson University. After three months of reading, researching, screening, writing, and arguing about Leni Riefenstahl's *Triumph des Willens*, I was astonished at the distinction between the modes of propaganda I knew and the one with which Doolen had forced an encounter. In the length of Riefenstahl's film, neither Hitler nor his lieutenants use the word *Jew*, and words like *race* and *religion* are studiously avoided, though *blood* is mentioned once. Gazing at Laura Nelson's raped and mutilated corpse, Leo Frank's slashed throat, and Jesse Washington's charred flesh made it impossible for me to look across an ocean for modes of racist propaganda, when citizens of my own nation had created forms of propaganda that placed neither racism's violence nor virulence under erasure, but displayed both as proudly as its politicians wave its flag. I dedicated myself to the completion of *"Blood at the Root": Lynching as American Cultural Nucleus* on that day in 2003. Though I have lived with this violence, I acknowledge, like James Allen, the curator of *Without Sanctuary*, that it has given me purpose and, in the pursuit of that purpose, a hunger that will not be sated until "justice rolls down like waters, and righteousness like a mighty stream" (Amos 5:24).

I must thank a remarkable group of scholars at the institutions at which I have made my homes, most especially Jeffrey Tucker, Stephanie Li, David Bleich, Joan Saab, Greta Niu, and Genevieve Guenther at the University of Rochester, as well as Catherine Paul, Martin Jacobi, and Beth Daniell at Clemson, and Greg Forter, Ed Madden, and Pamela Barnett at University of South Carolina. Two professors at Clemson—Lee Morrissey and the late Fred Shilstone—trained me as a stylist, relieving me of the misguided sense that academic writing ought to be sapped of rhetorical beauty. I am grateful to both, and wish that I could thank Fred once again. The faculty and staff of the Susan B. Anthony Institute for Gender and Women's Studies at University of Rochester—Professors Jeffrey Runner and Honey Meconi, as well as administrators Aimee Senise Bohn and Angela Clark-Taylor—have made the writing of this project much more comfortable than it would have been without them. At the University of Rochester, I learned much from my peers—particularly Russell Sbriglia, Kristi Castleberry, Jessie Crabill, and Rachel Lee—who have been patient, kind, and attentive readers of this project and loving readers of this strange animal. All of them are very dear to me.

Hobart and William Smith Colleges, which hired me the morning of my dissertation defense, were willing to take a risk on a scholar and teacher who had already shown herself to be the bastard child of her discipline of study. Little did I know that my illegitimacy would prove a boon in an institutional setting where interdisciplinarity is a given, rather than a goal to be striven for. Though I was hired to teach Women's Studies, I feel almost as though I discovered feminism under the tutelage of the women I met there: my students as well as the tenured women I began to think of (lovingly) as the Coven. Betty Bayer and Susanne McNally were patient and remarkable guides in the first year of my academic career; anyone would be lucky to experience the intellectual vitality and power that I observed in their presence. Surrounded by Susan Henking's books in our shared office, I attained my second education in both feminism and psychoanalysis; I am grateful that she trusted me with the knowledge. Anna Creadick offered comfort and kindness more than once.

I would be remiss not to thank a number of students who have inspired me. In no particular order: Libby Greene, Patricia Bamonti, Gina Ragusa, Molly DiStefano, David Weisberg, Kyle Roe, Jess McCue, Jamie Frank, Amanda Fleming, Kyvaughn Henry, Julia O'Halloran, Mr. President J. David Schlink, Julianne Nigro, Catherine Yee, George-Tom Rogers (who has nothing to lose but his chains), Joshua Reynolds, Ellie Adair, Leah Swenson, Angela Stoutenburgh, Erin Cunningham, Erin Laskey, Anna Grushevksy, David Benavidez, Michela Paniccia, Susan Storey, Glenn Buchberger, John Kowalcyzk, Heather O'Riordan, Campbell Garland, and Roger Arnold. This list concludes with Roger's name because he is a Hobart man for all seasons, and a gift to me as a teacher and an author. I am grateful for his attentive reading of this manuscript in his senior semester, when he was writing his own thesis. One day, I will return the favor with *his* first book.

※

On the day that my first year of graduate school ended, I packed a bag, rushed to the side of my then-boyfriend, Chip, and spent a year off the grid, but not without connection. In our house in Central, South Carolina, painted with stars and sunflowers, with a fine mat of moss on the shingled roof, I met Keith Wayne Davis, Bethany Purdin, and Mark Theiling. Flung to the far corners of a continent though we may be, I love them. They move my heart, I assure them, *every damn time.* In New York, I am reminded of Mark in the company of his brother Dale, who lives, mercifully, much closer. Holly Norton can argue circles around me, and I am grateful when she does. During our years in Western New York, Dale and Holly have often given Chip and me access to nature at their farm in Skaneateles. The waterfall, the fields, and the chickens were always precisely what we needed.

On the subject of friends of the heart, I eat best in parties of four. In my childhood, Bryan, Bonnie, and Karen sustained me; I could have not have asked for better siblings, and am grateful to Phillip Schmidt for increasing our number. I think of Beth Marie Lightweis—our missing fifth—everyday, imagining what her foreshortened life might have been like and how the addition might have changed the equation. When I dine with Allyson Hallman, Joseph Whitehurst, and Kayce Weatherford, I am grateful for the ways they animated me and taught me to say "I love you" without hesitation or shame—and free from the bonds of blood—in the years I lived in Columbia, South Carolina. When in Rochester, New York, I'd rather cook for Chip Lightweis-Goff, Katie Van Wert, and Burke Scarbrough than dine at the tables of kings.

My parents, Alan and Patricia Lightweis, have sustained me in ways that I cannot account for in this or any project. They have been there to pick me up off the floor and assure me that I am loved without the language of debt. ("Save it for the bean-counters," my father once said.) Such generosity is too rare in this world. They won't be at all interested in the reference, but I'm reminded of my favorite television show, *Buffy the Vampire Slayer*, when I try to describe how I love them. When Buffy fights the super-android Adam, she goes to battle animated by her mentor Giles's mind, her friend Willow's spirit, and her friend Xander's heart; she herself is the hand. When I think of the people who made me, I am assured that I am the hand, animated by the pieces of themselves they have given me. I cannot throw a punch, teach a class, pick *myself* up off the floor, love another person, comb my hair, write these words, or print these pages without their animating force (and their hard-earned approval). To my husband's family—especially Carole Morgan, David Blagg, and Phil Goff—I extend the metaphor and my love.

Before I lavish praise on my husband, I return to Katie Van Wert and Burke Scarbrough. Last year, I recommended Katie for a job with an unreserved outpouring of affection. "This woman," I told her prospective employer, "can fill a room with love." This sentiment is one that I also extend to Burke who, as Katie says, is the part of her that loves. After our sojourn in Port Jervis, I think of him as the part of me that forgives in constant rememory of the effect Port Jervis had on his face, which I describe in my final chapter as possessing a "prelapsarian fairness." I repeat it here, because I'd like him to read it twice if he's scanning for his name. Every word from Katie reminds me of why I love language. Every word from Burke reminds me to give as much as I can while still sustaining myself, to commit myself to the world most near as well as the one so far. . . .

Which is the world that Chip Lightweis-Goff has given to me: stars, mountains, syllables, sunflowers, waterfalls. During my winter break from Rochester in my first year of study, I met the man who changed me utterly—from a beast that worshipped the work of its own hands to an animal attentive to the motion of world and water. We met on my way out and his way in to Nick's Tavern on Sloan Street in Clemson, South Carolina, a place whose tawdriness is redeemed for me by the event. The years with him have revealed the nature of love: he knew me as much on that first night as he does today, but we must be revealed, not discovered, and build our lives in the recursive and gradual nature of the unveiling. I knew I loved him at the moment I saw him at a crowded diner: sensitive to the moods and desires of the crowd, to his responsibility for each and every soul in it, from the loudest child to the most harried waitress. That profound connection to the world has travelled with us to London, to Budapest, to Indiana, to Prague, to Vienna, to Paris, to Dublin, to New York, to Chicago, to New Orleans, to Philadelphia, to Atlanta, to Alabama, and to Bluefield, West Virginia. He never wavers in his principles, never compromises his remarkable heart. Because he is the opposite of death, I cannot dedicate this project to him. I can only offer my life.

INTRODUCTION

Self and State

Lynching's Intimate Violence

The Color

When I was six years old, I moved to South Carolina from suburban New Jersey. My father worked as a platinum broker for Engelhard Corporation, which had branches in Ann Arbor, Michigan; Seneca, South Carolina; and various international locations. When offered a transfer, my parents narrowed their options by omitting the coldest locales and the foreign ones. They were remarkably gentle; the worst slight they ever perpetrated against their children was declining the option of moving to Rome. Their worst punishment was a rap on the knuckles with a wooden spoon, so one can imagine the surprise when I began public school in South Carolina where, as my classmates gleefully relayed, teachers hit. A teacup paddle—a wooden plank with a depression and drilled holes designed to land with the *thwack* of phenomenal velocity on the posterior of the unlucky—would emerge to punish me for the frenetic humming sound that I make—quite unwittingly—as I work, or the more significant crime of having come from somewhere else.

I told my mother I was afraid to return, but she could not believe my story. After all, she had gone to parochial school in New York City in the 1950s, and had never been subject to corporal punishment. Thirty years later, ensconced in the halls of a more democratic public institution, children's bodies ought to have been inviolable. But my classmates had spoken the truth; when the day of my primal scene arrived, it was not my unlucky ass on the receiving end of the paddle, though I became a witness to the pain of another. While the rest of us lined up for lunch, our teacher positioned the punished child ten feet away. He placed his hands against the wall; she hit him four times with thunderous *thwacks* against his flesh. His thin shoulders convulsed, blood pooled in his bitten lips, and the rest of us did nothing. He was small and dark-skinned, but I am not certain I knew that at the time; in the liminal and undifferentiated space of childhood resided a pleasurable androgyny that I recall with much nostalgia for the days before, as W. E. B. DuBois wrote about race, "it dawned upon me with a certain suddenness that I was different from the others; or like, mayhap, in heart and life and longing, but shut out from their world by a vast veil" (DuBois 1999, 10).

What account I gave of his suffering to my mother has also disappeared into the memory hole, but it certainly impressed her. She did not drop me off the next day, but parked the car and walked me in to school. While I went alone to my classroom, my mother kept her appointment with the principal. She wanted to know that I was safe, that no hostile hand would touch me while I was away from her; she undoubtedly hoped that my story was false. The principal, who retired at the end of that year and died at the end of the subsequent one, told her not to worry.

"Mrs. Lightweis, we use the paddle to control the color."

The words they exchanged—his casual racism, her confusion and anger—were ones I was not privy to that day, or for years afterwards. Nevertheless, I did not have to be told what the paddle was used for, or what color it controlled. Over the next ten years, I saw its damage—not often, but often enough—and always against children who grew up to be African-American men, a population uniquely vulnerable to containment and discipline because—in part—of targeted enforcement, discretionary arrests, and strategies of surveillance that would, if enacted on the college campuses of the Ivy League, fill American prisons with young white men. My place also felt fixed and determined: I was always the audience and never acted. Never moved to defend, never interposed with my body, never felt pushed toward resistance. I suspected that the school was run by bigots; insidious racial separation prevailed in the demographics of our tracked classes and the segregated lunch tables, but I responded to it with detachment and withdrawal rather than heroism. When I graduated from high school, my transcripts were unremarkable, save for the juxtaposition of two earned Fs with maximum scores on advanced placement exams, so I felt lucky when I was accepted to University of South Carolina, located in what passed for a city inside the state's borders. Though I remember little of what I was taught in Seneca and refused any authority asserted there, I had attained one lesson perfectly: *we use the paddle to control the color*. Of all the wisdom imparted in the childhood I lived in public space, my role as a voyeur to racial violence is all that I can recall.

Twenty-five years later, with a multiracial president of the United States, I still feel the weight of this expectation. In the emergency dental clinic where I went for treatment as a cash-strapped graduate student, I saw the casual racism with which women of color and their children are treated by nurses who gatekeep access to doctors, treatment, and, most vigorously, drugs. Local news stations in Rochester, New York refer to a predominantly black neighborhood as the "Murder Crescent"; when acquaintances echo the phrase in conversation, I offer no correction. Life is nasty, brutish, and short, as Hobbes observed, but nastier, more brutal, and shorter for people of color. The system that sustains inequality trains "whites" to regard the "premature death of the Other" as their natural lot (Gilmore 2007, 27). These violent erasures and metaphors of invisibility bequeathed to American rhetorics of difference by Ralph Ellison shape the problematic of racism.

Long before I witnessed the paddling, racism had been imagined by Ellison and others as a structure of looking, a strategy of surveillance, and a quality of vision. The public sites of American democracy—the courthouse lawns, churchyards, main streets, and, indeed, school hallways—had been militarized for white supremacy, though private spheres were permeable to this violence. Whether or not my fate was sealed at the moment I saw the other child paddled is unclear to me. In a town as small as mine, few people leave. When I return to visit my parents, I sometimes encounter one of the classmates who lined the walls with me—always the white ones, since the town's public spaces remain remarkably segregated and too many of my childhood friends who were subject to the paddle now reside with a number for a name in Afghanistan, Iraq, or Turbeville Correctional Institute. The rest are unremarkable—neither firebrands for equality nor hooded Klansmen. We and the spectacle we witnessed are mundane. What marked me as different—as a person who would one day write a book about lynching, rather than buy a Toby Keith album with a song that valorizes lynching—is as yet unknown.[1] Can I attribute it to feeling always like an outsider—a Northern child from a family of recent immigrants? The fact that I looked like no one else in school, since it was full of towheads and freckled faces whose worst insult for other so-called "white" people was "nigger lips?" I cannot answer, though I cannot stop asking the question.

What I saw in Seneca was no lynching, but it nonetheless offered a pedagogy of racialized citizenship. For theorist Lauren Berlant, the interventions of women of color who have offered testimony against sexual and racial violence constitute "diva citizenship," public claims that create an optimistic intimacy between speaking subjects, wherein the "member of a stigmatized population" transforms the public sphere "into a scene of teaching and an act of heroic pedagogy" (Berlant 1997, 222). In watching the paddle control the color, I experienced public space as the site of my most painful lessons. Rather than watching a "risky dramatic persuasion" that enabled me to respond "to the sublimity of reason" in agitation against inequality, I encountered a stunning silence, a shocking lack of testimony on the role of race in identity formation (Berlant 1997, 223). Had a white student said, "only black children are paddled," the likely response would have been "don't be *racial*," a curious substitution in the language for the more value-laden term *racist*. It was nonetheless the response I heard to every intervention about race in South Carolina public schools. "I don't mean to be *racial*; I don't want to be *racial*; stop me if this sounds *racial*." All were common refrains in the admittedly limited vernacular theorizations of race I heard as a child and young adult. The substitution would have enabled an identical response to a white or black student who said, "only black children are paddled"; the sentence asserts parity between any statements—pernicious or liberatory—in which race is acknowledged as a lived reality.

Witnesses to this discipline nonetheless experienced a form of citizenship contiguous to and inherited from American mob violence. The practice of lynching, as Ken Gonzales Day has argued, began earlier than most histories of black-white lynching, on the Western frontier (Day 2006, 27). As white settlers moved west, lynching moved east—migrating from its uses against Latinos, Native Americans, and Chinese immigrants on the West Coast and the frontier—to the East, where it was deployed against African-Americans. A thirty-year history of mob violence in the West precedes what many scholars have offered as an origin point for lynching—1862, the first year listed in Ralph Ginzburg's influential *One Hundred Years of Lynching* (1962), but I nonetheless focus on the problematic of white-black racism in almost exclusively Eastern contexts. The acceleration of lynching against African-Americans at the end of Reconstruction indicates a changing value of black life that alters the commodity status of enslaved peoples into the degraded status of the "Fourth World" populations, against whom white settlers exercised their violence on the frontier. Spectacle that lynchings became, they also had the function of vernacular pedagogy; moving eastward in the years of the Civil War (1861–1865) and the Reconstruction Amendments (1865–1870), they delineated a form of citizenship that neither manumission nor legislation could racially "corrupt" in the metaphoric miscegenation of integration. Just as the incomplete project of black citizenship sparked the civil disobedience of the Freedom Movement in the 1960s, the "uncivil disobedience" of American lynch mobs disregarded "power-conferring rules" of multiracial citizenship for a form that was "participatory and public" (Kirkpatrick 2008, 14). Of course, it was also exclusionary and violent; its publicness cannot be mistaken for an ideology or an ethic. Once codifications of citizenship were no longer exclusively white, lynch mobs offered a vision of mob citizenship to replace them, a vision that staged a drama of intrusion by and protection from external enemies.[2] Mobs lost their war with history and were supplanted by citizenships of inclusion offered by civil rights reforms of the mid-twentieth century, yet the strategies of violence, vision, and exclusion that constituted their political inheritance to American political life did not disappear.

Studying that patrimony reveals that its terms remain under contestation. In the early days of the NAACP, a black banner with white letters that read "a man was lynched yesterday" hanged over a busy block in New York City, echoing the "strange fruit" of Billie Holliday's song. The banner, which appeared after reports of lynching, would have been hung at a rate of twice a week had it counted every lynching (Dray 2002, 257). Though the history is recent and the memory historically accessible, nothing in American culture memorializes lynching the way that the black banner marked its living presence. Constructing a genealogy of the act evinces the entrenched cultural repression that silences memory. To investigate lynching, I have set aside the study of pathological individuals and begun the study of pathological cultural formations, though my introduction to this chapter—with its attention to subjectivity under white supremacy—reveals something of the permeability of the two categories.

The constitutive feature of lynching is not only violence, but the collapse of the boundary between private prejudice and public punishment. The replacement of the crime of lynching with the juridical model of the hate crime enables forgetting of its collective, public face, substituting the crowded public square of the lynching with the murderer's lair—the darkened, private spaces where Matthew Shephard and James Byrd were murdered by men in pairs. While the murderers' bigotry emerges from an American lineage of violence, their crimes did not have the explicit community approval that lynching did—evinced by the crowds surrounding the lynched bodies in James Allen's *Without Sanctuary: Lynching Photography in America*. Influenced by Nietzschean formations of subjectivity, Judith Butler has argued that selfhood is "fabricated as a prior and causal origin of a painful effect that is cast as injury"; therefore, the self comes into being as a juridical convenience to punish criminality (Butler 1997, 45). The visceral truth of her formulation is revealed by the fact that, while there is federal anti-hate crime legislation, the quest for federal anti-lynching legislation failed spectacularly. Seemingly, the law has no tools by which to imagine group psychology or prosecute collective accountability.

Because of these erasures, my book undertakes the project of recuperating group identity and collective accountability from American hagiographies of selfhood that would occlude both in favor of a national innocence that renders its citizens unimplicated in structures of racial violence. Each chapter considers an element in these practices of forgetting. The first chapter complicates the replacement of the racist nation with the pathological South in accounts of racism and political retrogression—with recourse to Richard Wright's theorization of the state as seamless and portable within the migrant who flees the "night" of Southern oppression for a dawn presumed to arrive in the Northern metropolis. Through readings of Jean Toomer's "Portrait in Georgia" and George Schuyler's *Black No More*, the second chapter complicates the assumption of antiracist politics that have offered the private sphere as salvation from the racist American public, despite the permeability of the body and subjectivity of the oppressed to the forces of racism. The third chapter traces the deployment of the prevailing logics of American racism—the pathology (rather than normativity) of lynch mobs, the innocence of the passive witness, and the aberration of racial violence—in the lynching narratives of William Faulkner, locating his refusal to provide eyewitness accounts of lynching in his short stories in the Western tradition of privileging sight over other senses. My fourth chapter reads critical responses to lynching photography, which have located agentic resistance in the frozen instant before the subject's death, positing narratives of agency as attempts to virilize the dead men by casting them as heroic resisters. I offer contemporary artist Kara Walker's images of suicidal, self-injuring black subjects as complications to prevailing narratives of agency. Ultimately, my conclusion locates the impetus for erasures and refusals that characterize both critical and literary narratives in the public sphere of American lynching towns, where the locations of violence are left naked with neither memorial nor memory. Each chapter considers abdications of collectivity and publicity as present in both dominant narratives of lynching practices and antiracist resistance to them—arguing for an intervention against racism that reclaims and reforms the public sphere, rather than retreating to the imagined sancticities of (respectable) privacy and individual (unmarked) subjectivities.

Modes of Memory, Nodes of Forgetting

Until recently, one could follow the twisting path of lynching's genealogy to encounter a four-headed creature guarding the term's discursive deployment. The four heads belonged to Matthew Shephard, James Byrd, O. J. Simpson, and Clarence Thomas. The relationship of lynching to the first two men is evident; unspeakable hate crimes penetrated their bodies with particular ferocity. The Simpson and Thomas cases are more nebulous; both men invoked the specter of lynching to contest the public conviction of their guilt and, in Thomas's case, to reconnect the events of the "high-tech lynching" of his Supreme Court confirmation hearings—nearly derailed by an accusation of sexual harassoment—to the cultural surveillance of black male sexuality. The public, sexualized spectacle is what both Thomas and Simpson evoke. Though they were wrong about their victimhood, they had some knowledge of how publicity constructs blackness; the racialized spectacle of violence is elided when lynching is fused with the juridical model of the hate crime.

From the mid-century to the millennium, the assumptions that undergirded these comparisons—notions of lynching as "anomalous, aberrant, local, and anti-modern"—predominated in the limited inquiry that the subject had attracted (Goldsby 2006, 27). But the publication of Jacqueline Goldsby's *Spectacular Secret: Lynching in American Life and Literature* profoundly reshaped the field, changing the language with which we narrate the cultural practice with more force than any writer or activist since the initial anti-lynching campaigns of the early twentieth century. Alongside the publication and exhibition of lynching photographs, Goldsby's study has initiated something of a renaissance in examining American mob violence. Our studies share more than an analysand; her language has so infiltrated the field that I find myself using her phrase *cultural logic* almost reflexively throughout this project. Indeed, her influential thesis bears restatement here:

> Lynching thrived at the turn of the new century not because violence was endemic to the South's presumably retrograde relation to the developments that constituted modernity in America. Rather, I contend that anti-black mob murders flourished as registers

of the nation's ambivalences attending its nascent modernism. (Goldsby 2006, 24)

Because of the force of Goldby's claim, I take the association of modernity and lynching as a presupposition within this study, which attempts to consider cultural forces that rendered lynching illegible before Goldsby's intervention. The four terms—*anomalous, aberrant, local*, and *anti-modern*—are ones that inform my study, which emphasizes the construction of the lynching spectacle as secret, Southern, and fundamentally individual. Goldsby's list of adjectives have cumulative effects; they add to a longstanding cultural refusal to offer systemic critiques of lynching. After Goldsby's critique of this logic, it becomes necessary to consider *why* lynching was rendered anti-modern and anomalous to the history of the United States; therefore, I spend the rest of this section offering reasons for the erasure of lynching from the middle of the twentieth century to the millennium.

Within the primary sites of cultural mythmaking—from public schools to the miniseries *Roots*—the defining experience of African-American history is presumed to be slavery. While I do not contest the importance of slavery, emphasis on the practice enables anti–antiracist arguments, in which whites self-righteously swear that they have never owned slaves and, thus, have no stake in racial politics. Yet, Jim Crow has had no official end. Because many Americans believe that racial justice has moved in a linear progressive fashion since Emancipation, the national conversation about race is woefully incomplete. This cultural conversation is, as I argue in my fourth chapter, enabled by the new social history of the 1960s, which made slavery the central issue of racism in American because of its agentic potential in contrast to the seemingly total victimization that lynching offers. By excluding Jim Crow from the cultural conversation, Americans disavow the nearness of racism and the potential for continued vulnerability to its discipline.

In those contemporary conversations, racism is a linguistic pose, a singular utterance. Consider the case of comic Michael Richards, *Seinfeld*'s Cosmo Kramer (or, for that matter, any prominent celebrity racist from John Mayer to Don Imus). Media attention focused on his repeated use of racial epithets; *The New York Post* referred to him as "the n-word comic" in a headline, associating him with discursive rather than physical violence (Johnson 2007, 12). The verbal threat of lynching, in which he told an African-American audience member that "fifty years ago, we would have you upside down with a fucking fork up your ass," went unmentioned in the *Post*. Similarly, former Virginia Senator George Allen was repeatedly called upon to swear that he had never used "the n-word" during the 2006 election (Shear and Craig, B01). The accusation that he stuffed a severed deer head in a black family's mailbox when he was a college athlete at University of Virginia was relegated to the final sentences of a brief news article about his habitual use of racial slurs (Scherer 2006, 2). Enthroning the word over the deed promotes manners and restraint as the ideal relationship between interracial communities; thus, discursive violence supplants the mortification of the flesh.

That discursive shift replaces pathological *racism* with the pathologist *racist* in accordance with the paradigm that elevates the individual, rather than the collective, as the prized unit of American capitalism. Hagiographies of selfhood emerge in narratives of self-actualization and fulfillment that dominate American culture. As I have previously argued, narratives of the self and the related concepts of agency and will are omnipresent in academic chatter and frequently obscure the issues of coercion, violence, and force that are inseparable from lynching (Lightweis-Goff 2006). Frankly, I cannot imagine what bell hooks would find to write about at the scene of the lynching and its circumscription of black subjectivity, since she defines *agency* as the power to resist by acting in "one's best interest" (hooks 1990, 206). What about Haiping Yan, who argued in a 2006 address to Cornell School for Criticism and Theory, that agency enables subjects to choose what they feel about prior trauma (Yan 2006)? Certainly, I hope contemporary spectators of lynching photography "choose" well what they feel about their trauma; otherwise, I fear critics would accuse them of not exercising their personal responsibility.

Contingent upon the tendency to study, isolate, and pathologize racism within the individual subject is the likelihood of quarantining racism with the American South, whose "dangerous territory" serves as the national id (Ladd 1996, xii). At rare moments when collective responsibility is assessed, it is located in the traditional Confederacy, despite the fact that racism is a fifty-state phenomenon. Sociologist James Loewen, in his study of whites-only "sundown" towns across the United States, writes that audiences frequently refer to his research as located in the South, despite the fact that the majority of sundown towns were in border states and around cities to which African-Americans migrated in the 1920s (Loewen 2006, 23). Surrounding a multi-racial city was, inevitably, a ring of all-white suburbs. This spatial metaphor can easily be transposed onto the cultural use of the South. Like racism, racial difference is quarantined in the South. Such a discursive deployment of the South is seldom labeled racist, but I would argue—influenced by Houston Baker's *Turning South Again*—that uses of the word *Southern* to mean David Duke but not Medgar Evers, Margaret Mitchell but not Alice Walker, Lester Maddox but not Martin Luther King, Strom Thurmond but not Louis Armstrong are collaborations with white supremacy. However ardently speakers may wish it, such language does not divest them of "the possessive investment in whiteness," the title of George Lipsitz's seminal work on white privilege (Lipsitz 1998).

This critique does not deny the racism of the South; it nationalizes it, resisting narratives of American exceptionalism that posit violence as an aberration in the history of a largely moral nation. In so doing, I attempt to break the chain of displacements and denials that James Allen warns of in his epilogue to *Without Sanctuary: Lynching Photography in America*:

> Studying [lynching] photographs has engendered in me a caution of whites, of the majority, of the young, of religion, of the accepted of the accepted. . . . I believe the photographer was more than a perceptive spectator at lynchings . . . the photographic art played as significant a role in the ritual as torture or souvenir grabbing . . . a sort of two-dimensional biblical swine, a receptacle for a collective sinful self. Lust propelled the commercial reproduction and distribution of the images, facilitating the endless replay of anguish. Even dead, the victims were without sanctuary. (Allen et al. 2000, 203)

This admonition speaks to the necessity of remembering the collective. Forgetting public spectacle and widespread cultural collusion means forgetting the perpetrators (the community) and the weapon (white supremacy), and recollecting the victim—in the most sanitary memory—with no crowds, no mob and, thus, no crime. In the section that follows, I attempt to explore this forgotten collectivity with recourse to Freudian group psychology.

Collective Violence

Using two "artificial" organizations as paradigms for group psychology, Freud argues that collective action is motivated by forces distinct from the drives of the individual psyche. The church and the armed services, regardless of their apparent function of sublimation, aid a process by which "individual inhibitions fall away and all the cruel, brutal and destructive instincts, which lie dormant in individuals as relics of a primitive epoch" replace them (Freud 1959, 11). Freud illuminates how the trappings of these groups transform individual racism into the punitive violence of the lynch mob. His classification of these group structures as artificial, while accurate, neglects to explain how both structures become naturalized within society and thereby posits exclusionary practices as intrinsic to human nature. The church reproduces an organic and spiritual allegation about the origins of the universe, while the nation's simultaneous prevention and preparation for war reinforce the illusion of the naturalness of national boundaries. Both organizational structures enabled the violence of Reconstruction-era domestic terrorism by the Ku Klux Klan, founded by Confederate General Nathan Bedford Forrest to extend the violence of his early massacre at Fort Pillow to the postwar political climate, during which he supported the use of violence to control miscegenation between black men and white women (Dray 2002, 44). The prevalence of lynching in the nation's most religious regions made its violence synonymous with "American Christianity," a headline the Chicago Defender used as a caption for Lawrence Beitler's iconic image of the 1930 lynching of Thomas Shipp and Abram Smith. The lynch mob seizes the brotherly, pseudo-democratic structure of both the church and the army to police the borders of the nation within a nation—the inner sanctum of patriarchy: the white woman's body.

By the end of federal occupation of the American South, many whites felt as though they were living post-apocalyptically and seized on the church's structure to punish African-American overreaching. As Leon Litwack argues, "The closer the black man got to the ballot box . . . the more he looked like a rapist" (Allen et al. 2000, 30). Though an accusation of rape preceded fewer than a quarter of all lynchings, the white mobs posited themselves as defenders of religious and sexual virtue, restituting the rape of the white woman's body as well as the postwar national body. Indeed, a popular name for the post-Reconstruction period was the "Redemption," which ultimately came for white supremacy in the form of Jim Crow (Dray 2000, 80). The crusade waged by whites against African-Americans cannot be separated from religion. American fundamentalism is, as Philip Dray notes, marked with a radically delineated line between good and evil that reproduced the linguistic frame of evil blackness and pure whiteness (Dray 2000, 78). The sheer medievalism of American Christianity led to the most archaic of all religious trappings—the collection and enshrinement of relics. Souveniring and relic-hunting were standard features of lynchcraft. After the lynching of Sam Hose in Newnan, Georgia, W. E. B. DuBois heard that Hose's knuckles were preserved in the window of a butcher shop in Atlanta. James Allen, curator of the Without Sanctuary project, found a framed photograph of the lynching of Thomas Shipp and Abram Smith with hair trapped between the matting and glass—representing a simultaneous memorial and fetish (Allen et al. 2000, 84, frame 32). The preservation of the souvenir reveals the "oblatory, efficacious goal of giving up something valuable" that is inherent to the act of collective violence; a presumptive brutal, degraded physical power transforms the lynched person into an object of veneration who could be overcome and contained to shore up the social power of the lynchers (Pizzato 2005, 8).

Freud's reading of religion accommodates violent and democratic principles, as well as fetishistic tendencies. As in the lynch mob, a libidinal economy binds the group. Desire for the woman's purity calls the fantasy of the black rapist into being, and the act of looking at and policing the black male body obliterates it—according to Frantz Fanon, replacing it, with a penis: the "black man has been occulted" by assumptions about his hypersexual body (Fanon 2008, 147). Such religious exclusivity relied on the artificial parallel between blackness and evil, but Jewish victims of lynchings were pariahs because of a tangible religious difference. According to the fantasies of the lynchers of Leo Frank, the immigration of European-born Jews into the Protestant South would result in the "usury" of African-Americans as automatons. Controlled by "Jewish money," these automatons would agitate for civil rights and violate Christian womanhood (Dray 2002, 436). The message was devastatingly clear; Christian love extended only to white Christians. The outsider was not tolerated, despite the "equal share" of Christ's love that each human subject allegedly receives. White Christians delineated the boundary of what Freud calls "the community of believers, who do not love [Christ], and whom he does not love" (Freud 1959, 26). Lynch victims "stand outside the tie" of herrenvolk democracy and are exterminated for their deviance. Their suffering does not "cause sympathy or make torture unacceptable," as Slavoj Zizek has argued of the tortured, because it is not the "physical proximity [of the body] . . . but the proximity of the Neighbor"—in religious conceptions of loving and privileging the subjectivity of one's culturally similar neighbor—that causes a shudder in the presence of pain (Zizek 2008, 45).

Martial group character mimes that of the religious group within Freud's model, though the terms one might use to describe lynch mobs—*murderers, terrorists*—were subsumed to the martial language of *warriors* and, in the case of both the KKK and the lynchers of Leo Frank, *knights*. In 1921, the white citizens of Tulsa, Oklahoma commandeered planes from the local army base to firebomb the city's black neighborhood. The fact that 9/11 rather than the Tulsa riots is remembered as the first terrorist air attack on American soil indicates how deeply the term *terrorist* is raced, since white communities are so often protected from the stigma of its application.[3] By mixing elements of the conventionally martial and the paramilitary, racists established constant racial warfare in the American South and Midwest, the region into which white supremacist groups later branched out with far greater power. The martial intensity and structure of their organizations are a symptom of the "group panic" that Freud observed in the paramilitary system. Pathological racism is dedicated to perpetuating the lie that empowered racial others constitute a "common danger" that will infiltrate and destroy the community via sexual and cultural miscegenation.

Because ideological constructions of race and community find locations of contestation in the public spaces of the late nineteenth and early twentieth century, much of my book's polemic force emerges in critiques of nationalism, citizenship, and publicness, as well as the institutions that undergirded them. And yet, private spheres are not analytically abandoned by the project—because, for minority communities, the private sphere was particularly permeable. As Elizabeth Schneider has argued, there is "violence" inherent in figurations of privacy. "There is no realm of personal and family life that exists totally separate from the reach of the state. . . . 'Private' and 'public' exist on a continuum," she writes. "Thus, in the so-called private sphere . . . which is purportedly immune from law, there is always the selective application of law [which] invokes 'privacy' as a rationale for immunity in order to protect male domination" (Schneider 1990, 977). Comparable formations of racial privilege enabled the unique benefits of both privacy and publicness to accrue exclusively to the white male subject, who was guaranteed full participation in American democratic spheres, as well as an impermeable private sphere that protected his privilege. Insofar as contemporary memory of racism considers it private—manifest only in the invisible "heart" and intention of the subject—rather than public speech acts and outcomes foundational to democratic structures and theorizations of citizenship, the invisibility of lynching in American public space collaborates with practices of forgetting and evasion that have become hallmarks of white male identity politics.

Forgetting the collectivity of violence indicts the pathological individual at the cost of forgetting a pathological culture; it obliterates the continuity of lynching with racial violence occurring in the shadow of its history. Eleven decades ago, Ida B. Wells-Barnett argued for lynching as a distinctly national crime at a moment when reunion between the defeated Confederacy and the victorious Union required precisely this nostalgia, one accomplished by bringing the assumptions of white innocence and black pathology into stark relief. Rather than enable this erasure by retreating to the politics of respectability found in the women's club movements, she staged a spectacular coup, by demonstrating a commitment to resist and declaim lynching in the public sphere that the practice had claimed for itself.[4]

Though a recent explosion of work on Wells-Barnett's activism and exile has told her story, she has seldom been placed within the literary and political nexus of twentieth century migration narratives. Even the bravura statement on literature and migration, Farah Jasmine Griffin's *"Who Set you Flowin'?": The African-American Migration Narrative* (1996) offers two scant references to Wells-Barnett's writing. Her work is treated as offering historical verification of American lynching practices, rather than new creations of meaning associated with African-American literary and cultural production. As Anthony Bogues has argued, "Her essays on lynching are interventionist texts in which the issues about the referential functions of language are replaced with notions about language and writing as truth claims" (Bogues 2003, 48). Though Bogues' work on Wells-Barnett is laudatory, reading her work as "sociological excursions" makes little room for inventions of meaning that she bequeaths to migrants like Richard Wright, who offered his own vernacular theorization of the national crime of lynching.

Influential readings of her polemics by Gail Bederman and Jeffory A. Clymer have located Wells-Barnett's claims in discourses of nation and citizenship, terms that I treat extensively in the reading of *Southern Horrors* that follows. Bederman suggests that Wells-Barnett's speaking tour in Great Britain in opposition to lynching enabled her to deploy the terms of *citizenship* against the nation, inspiring the Northern metropolitan to militate against Southern lynching practices by warning that "Southern men's unrestrained lust had spread north and corrupted Northern men's manliness" (Bederman 1995, 59). Taking from Bederman the terms of both *civilization* and *nationhood*, Clymer argues that Wells-Barnett "ground[s] her rhetoric in an argument of civilization and patriotic nationhood in which the North and South are equally accountable for the era's racial terrorism" (Clymer 2003, 104). I do not disagree with either critic that our shared analysand overturns assignations of primitivism and civilization, nor do I contest the discourses of national accountability that characterize both interpretations. Instead, I argue that Wells-Barnett concretizes geographies and borders to locate lynching, rather than legal accountability, in the American nation rather than its Southern region. Formal strategies in her pamphlets foreground Northern lynchings despite her claim to treat only *Southern* horrors. Though her title anticipates twentieth-century attempts to discursively quarantine racial violence in the South, her theorizations of the nation and region lay claim to citizenship in both geographical categories—thereby, enacting national reunion (and collective accountability) without the sacrifice of black citizenship that such practices often demanded. Those sacrifices—and the disappointments that attended them in communities of freedmen—are resisted by Wells-Barnett's rhetorical immediacy; her pamphlets seem to be written in transit and motion that delay the horrors of the migrant's discovery of racial violence in the Northern city. Though her title foregrounds the South, her argument resists its isolation.

Sanguinary Banners of the Sunny South

In his germinal definition of the relationship of racial violence to American culture, Southern historian Fitzhugh Brundage writes that the remarkable thing about lynching is not that it happened at all—not that cities like Atlanta, Georgia; Marion, Indiana; the District of Columbia; and Port Jervis, New York tortured and murdered African-Americans convicted of no crime and often accused of only minor violations of Jim Crow etiquette—but that it has receded from its once foundational place in American life and public space (Brundage 1993, 258). Despite years of agitation by moderate groups like the National Association for the Advancement of Colored People and the Association of Southern Women for the Prevention of Lynching, and radical ones like the Communist Party, lynching continued into the 1930s—with a major spike in the Red Summer of 1919, when more than thirty race riots hazarded the lives of new Northward migrants as well as those who had stayed in the South. Though federal anti-lynching legislation failed, the practice slowed considerably after World War II, when the 1946 lynching of two married couples in Moore's Ford, Georgia raised public outrage against the treatment of returning black GIs (Wexler 2003, 90). The last known spectacle lynching was in 1981 in Mobile, Alabama, where white supremacists kidnapped, stabbed, and hanged Michael Donald in a well-traveled public space—to the relative indifference of local authorities. Despite the Southern locations I have listed in this introduction, the practice of lynching was a national one—a claim that Wells-Barnett anticipates—so much so that I cannot walk down the street of any American city without imagining how violence constitutes its very architecture. Even Manhattan—that safe harbor from American "flyover country"—is a mere eighty-three miles from Port Jervis, the site of the spectacle lynching of Robert Jackson Lewis in 1892.

While lynching was one form of public spectacle, counter-hegemonic protests of the practice adapted its publicness for the purposes of resistance. A decade before DuBois's black banner and, indeed, the most ardent anti-lynching campaigns of the NAACP, journalist Ida B. Wells-Barnett located her acts of resistance—her guerilla theatre—in the urban South, the primary sites of lynching in the period following Reconstruction. Indeed, her resistance began close to home. When Thomas Moss, Calvin McDowell, and William Stewart—three men who operated a grocery in Memphis—were lynched in March 1892 for "commit[ing] no crime other than to open a store that challenged a nearby white-owned business," Wells-Barnett began a political campaign informed and motivated by her ties of friendship and community to the dead men (Bay 2010, 5). The violence and economic motive for the triple lynching led her to flee Memphis (as Moss urged his fellow African-Americans in his last words to the assembled mob) and to challenge and complicate the politics of respectability and racial uplift for which both Southern whites and moderate blacks advocated (Ibid., 87–88).

In the months after the lynching at the "Curve"—a black neighborhood in Memphis—the economic motive for the violence was forgotten and the white press began to "invoke . . . rape as a justification for the killings," in response to condemnatory media coverage of the lynching in the liberal press (Ibid., 99). Despite the risk of violence and ostracism vicariously acquired in her friendships with the three lynched men, Wells-Barnett forced her voice into the public dialogue on lynching in an act of speech so incendiary that it led to her exile in Chicago. Published in a journal called *Free Speech* on May 21, 1892, and reprinted in her subsequent broadside *Southern Horrors*, Wells-Barnett's protest took the form of a brief editorial letter:

> Eight negroes lynched since last issue of the 'Free Speech' one at Little Rock, Ark. [sic], last Saturday morning where the citizens broke (?) [sic] into the penitentiary and got their man; three near Anniston, Ala., one near New Orleans; and three at Clarksville, Ga., the last three for killing a white man, and five on the same old racket—the new alarm about raping white women. . . . Nobody in this section believes the old threadbare lie that Negro men rape white women. If Southern white men are not careful, they will over-reach themselves and public sentiment will have a reaction; a conclusion will then be reached which will be very damning to the moral reputation of their women. (51–52)

The response to the editorial was immediate and violent. *The Daily Commercial* newspaper argued that the "wonderful patience of Southern whites" was tested by such calumny and libel against the flower of Southern womanhood, which ought to be protected because of the editorialist's testing of the "very outermost limits of public patience" (52). *The Evening Scimitar* demanded that the author, who they assumed to be a man, be "brand[ed] . . . in the forehead with a hot iron" and castrated, a practice euphemistically described as a "surgical operation with a pair of tailor's shears" (52). Rushing to the offices of Wells-Barnett's newspaper, the mob found her missing and lynched her printing press as a proxy for her body (Goldsby 2006, 46).

The "threadbare" editorial offers two interventions against the lynch mob that correspond with the deprivileged intersectionalities of Wells-Barnett's identity as a woman of color, negotiating the rhetoric of "manhood rights" and "woman's suffrage" in a culture where, as a trio of black feminists have more recently titled a polemic, dominant rhetoric asserts that "all the women are white [and] all the blacks are men" (Hull, Scott, and Smith 2003). Wells-Barnett first provides the voice and testimony of the white female subject who was silenced by the lynch mob and, ultimately, lays claim to citizenship in the American nation, the Southern region, and the city of Memphis. The gendered dimension of the first claim is felt in her reprinting of the testimony of "Mrs. Underwood," a white woman whose black lover was imprisoned when she accused him of rape to disguise their consensual adultery:

> I met Offett at the Post Office. It was raining. He was polite to me, and as I had several bundles in my arms he offered to carry them home for me. . . . He had a strange fascination for me, and I invited him to call. . . . He called, bringing chestnuts and candy for the children. By this means we got them to leave us alone in the room. Then I sat on his lap. He made a proposal to me and I readily consented. . . . He visited me several times after that and each time I was indiscreet. I did not care after the first time. In fact I could not have resisted, and had no desire to resist. (Wells-Barnett 1997, 54–55)

Emerging in a chapter called "The Black and White of It," which catalogs consensual relationships between black men and white women, this testimony is a powerful statement of female desire. As Wells-Barnett later argued in *A Red Record: Lynching in the United States of America*, an accusation of rape was the initiating cause in fewer than a quarter of all lynchings. Even in those cases when rape was alleged, there was often no woman offering testimony, since the lynched men were sometimes their lovers—named "rapists" by the prevailing logic that structured rape as a crime not against a class of people (women) by another class (men), but committed by a race of people (black rapists) against another race (white victims). Wells-Barnett's intervention concretes the female subject, often evoked abstractly by pro-lynching rhetorics that refer to white women as "the flowers of Southern womanhood," "virtuous Southern belles." and "honorable white virgins," staples of propaganda that Wells-Barnett parodies by spelling honor "honah," in a mockery of the moonlight-and-magnolias Southern accent."

The history of lynching evinces that it was not white women but white mobs that most often alleged rape. They policed interracial desire and the public sphere, and therefore eschewed the possibility of white women's engagement with either. Wells-Barnett attests to the mob's disregard for actual women's testimony in favor of abstract notions of white womanhood—noting a Maryland lynching in which a woman who had been assaulted swore that the African-American man captured by the mob had never touched her (Wells-Barnett 1997, 61) as well as a Mississippi lynching in which a mob lynched a man with whom the town sheriff's daughter had been having a consensual affair (Ibid., 65) and a Memphis case in which a woman who bore a biracial child refused to give the father's name; the press nonetheless reported the cause of the child's conception as rape (Ibid., 56). Lynch mobs went without female verification, often avoiding testimonies of consent to avoid complicating notions of white women's sexual purity.

The long citation of Mrs. Underwood's testimony replaces the archetypal black Jezebel with the white Delilah, who lied about her own desires to save her reputation and virtue. Sandra Gunning argues, "With a white, not black female voice referencing sexual misconduct, the return to the female body—the site of sexual transgression—is approached by a white narrator, through the tabooed discussion of white female lust" (Gunning 1996, 86). Wells-Barnett affirms, Gunning argues, that the desire for miscegenation is "white not black." Subverting the unspeakability of interracial desire might be the function of Wells-Barnett's citation. By disavowing Mrs. Underwood, she delineates black women's chastity in a culture that made no space for it; yet, in giving the testimony so much narrative room, Wells-Barnett remarks on the sexual desirability of black men, whose rising social and educational statuses between manumission and the fin de siècle, are offered as primary reasons for white women's sexual attraction. Wells-Barnett thereby "afford[s] a woman's desire some respect" absent in lynchers who valorized sexual chastity (Davis 1995, 90). The rigid sexual restrictions of the intra-racial community of Memphis, as well as the opprobrium of the white press, delimited Wells-

Barnett's own sexual freedom; because of her feelings of restriction, she uses Mrs. Underwood's voice as a testament to both female sexual desire and imminent white betrayal. Conventions of black sexual pathology as espoused by white supremacists and the politics of respectability that sprung up in response to those claims shape Wells-Barnett's representation of eroticism.[5]

Though Mrs. Underwood's confession of lust and love might have given Wells-Barnett space for identification with her own sexual longings, she rhetorically pairs white female desire with black female resistance, attesting to sexual exploitation of black women that had its roots in slavery. As Jacqueline Goldsby notes:

> The evidence Wells[-Barnett] marshals to document the rape of black girls or women by white men best measures th[e] effect of *Southern Horror*'s parodic force: disturbingly, there is none. Wells[-Barnett] lists no newspaper accounts of the four cases she discusses, not even from the black press. Nor does she claim personal relationships to the victim as authority for her statements. Refusing to disclose her sources, [she] lets these elisions stand as testimony to the stunt's power to mediate how acts of racial violence were archived as public history in the first place. (Goldsby 2006, 79)

When juxtaposed to the voices of white women earlier in Wells-Barnett's text, this ommision is notable. Sexual desire is locatable in the public and legal testimony of white women, but is not expressible expressible for women of color. Indeed, biographer Mia Bay reads these representations as models of "Victorian discretion," which resist identifying black victims in an anticipation of contemporary rape shield laws (Bay 2010, 126). All but one of the women's names are hidden; all of the rapists' names are revealed. The anonymity of even the white women underscores the lynch mob's indifference to the identities and experiences of the women they claimed to protect; Wells-Barnett reveals that the mob preferred the abstract woman to actual women.

Just as profoundly as she gives voice to desire and resistance, Wells-Barnett claims Southern citizenship, counting herself as a regional citizen of "this section," the South, and "this city," Memphis. By deploying the language of national honor and public consensus, lynch mobs delineated national citizenship as *mob* citizenship, participation in violent retribution against black subjects, and belief in the bestiality of African-Americans. Refusing the logic that attributes whiteness and maleness to the unmarked "American" or "Southern," Wells-Barnett's intervention in the public sphere asserts her national and regional identity in resistance to mob citizenship—jettisoning a logic that I assail in my next chapter, in which *Southern* delineates whiteness and the South is imagined as a sectional quarantine for racial violence.

As Tara McPherson argues in *Reconstructing Dixie*, the displacement of American racism is achieved by "lenticular logic," which she defines as a "schema by which histories or images that are actually copresent get presented (structurally, ideologically) so that only one of these images can be seen at a time" (McPherson 2003, 7). Though lenticular logics of vision have been the guiding modes by which the South has constituted race, America suffers from its own lenticular vision with regards to the South. The commodification of Southern culture through PBS documentaries, the marketing of Scarlett O'Hara, and plantation tours in Natchez and New Orleans have enabled white Americans to "connect imaginatively to Old South traditions of grandeur and elegance" in a "lost world of white dominance and beauty . . . [un]complicated by race or racism" (Ibid., 253). Outside of this culturally approved game of dress-up, Americans are less eager to claim Southernness; in fact, the discourse of American exceptionalism requires a disavowal of the region. Wells-Barnett's *Southern Horrors*, in which the "threadbare lie" editorial was later interwoven, contests the logic of quarantine—slyly alluding to it in the title but asserting that contemporaneous gestures toward post-Reconstruction national reformation achieved reconciliation with the bloody sacrifice of black bodies.

Written in the anthologizing style of the troubadour's travelogue—from the Grand Coolie Dam to the Capital in Bob Dylan's "Idiot Wind" (1971), from Pascagoula to Ottawa in Lucky Starr's "I've Been Everywhere" (1962), and from the redwood forests to the gulf stream waters in Woody Guthrie's "This Land is Your Land" (1931)—*Southern Horrors* crosses the nation to assemble the "red record" of mob violence. Though the title delineates regional boundaries, it is bookended with two distinctly un-Southern lynchings. Near Cleveland, Ohio—the antebellum contact zone between North and South, slave and free—an African-American man is jailed when his white lover accuses him of rape to save herself from her husband's wrath at her infidelity (Wells-Barnett 1997, 54). In Port Jervis, New York, the apparently cosmopolitan Northeast, a white man hires a black man to rape his former girlfriend as revenge for her rejection. The black man is lynched, but the white man goes free (Ibid., 71).

Though the majority of Wells-Barnett's cases take place in the urban South, the text's slippages are not limited to two. Lawrence, Kansas, a hotbed of progressive racial politics since the Free-Soil Revolt, also makes an appearance. And yet it is "Southern hate and prejudice" and "Southern horrors" that eviscerate, kill, and disarticulate black men (Ibid.). Her consciously-styled polemic saves the introduction and conclusion to recount *Northern* horrors, thereby positing an explicitly seamless national body through which the Southern disease of lynching circulates. With purposeful language suggestive of contagion and penetration, Wells-Barnett claims that the South triumphed in the ideological civil war. She argues that the nation is the South, though the South must not be its own nation, considering its previous national foundations were "laid . . . upon the great truth that the negro is not equal to the white man" (Stephens 1861). Narrative motion offers the reader a shifting regional perspective from which to view American racial violence. The revelation of lynching's national character offers a political solution: since the nation will not act against mob violence, the race must.

In a chapter called "The South's Position," Wells-Barnett stakes out the national character of lynch law, suggesting that the South is the origin point, but not the destination, of lynching's spread:

> The result [of Jim Crow] is a growing disregard for human life. Lynch law has spread its insidious influence till men in New York State, Pennsylvania, and on the free Western plains feel they can take the law in their own hands with impunity, especially where an Afro-American is concerned. The South is brutalized to a degree not realized by its own inhabitants, and the very foundation of government, law and order, are imperiled. (Wells-Barnett 1997, 66)

As lynching spread throughout the national body, Wells-Barnett recognized that the resistant strategy of migration would no longer be viable. It is not enough to withdraw capital when the places to withdraw it are fewer and fewer; in Jacksonville, Florida and Paducah, Kentucky—both absent from the Confederate map—effective resistance was only possible when the African-American lynch target "had a gun and used it in self-defense" (Ibid., 70).

With the growth of racial violence, Wells-Barnett argues, racial resistance must grow as well—not only by means of civil disobedience, but also by the violent resistance of antebellum figures like John Brown and Nat Turner:

> Nothing is more definitely settled than [the Afro-American] must act for himself. I have shown how he may employ the boycott, emigration, and the press, and I feel that by a combination of all these agencies can be effectively stamped out lynch law, that last relic of barbarism and slavery. "The gods help those who help themselves." (Ibid., 72)

The rhetorical figures of the singular African-American standing in for his community and the proverb that ensures his success suggest how citizenship and legal action can halt lynching. Unlike the civil rights movement that followed, Wells-Barnett does not demand that state intervention precede black citizenship; in fact, it cannot do so. The codification of African-American citizenship must follow from black political agitation and energy.

The intra-national migratory impulse is geared toward escape and resistance, yet the spatial shift, with its attendant illusion of personal agency, offer only maddening psychic effects. Moving from one place to another indicates the seamlessness of borders, as the mechanism of escape carves a path on which violence follows. American literature is created by the kind of journey that Wells-Barnett took from the delta to Chicago, but lighting out to the territory is another American trope: the belief that a change in location creates a new identity. Born into slavery in Holly Springs, Mississippi in 1862, Wells-Barnett likely knew the potential of fleeing North. Yet, the landscape of America had changed dramatically between slavery and Reconstruction, indicating the South's most powerful victory: as surely as there were no slave states, there were no free states, either. Gentlemanly handshakes between former enemies at Appomattox, Antietam, and Gettysburg were, by Wells-Barnett's time, familiar public spectacles celebrating memorial days and Civil War anniversaries (Blight 2002, 14). When white hands met, they crafted an exclusionary gentleman's agreement that denied full citizenship for African-Americans, a denial that Wells-Barnett's discursive interventions resist. Though the South lost the War in 1865, Wells-Barnett lived to see it win. This victory did not foreclose black resistance any more than Appomattox constituted surrender by Confederates. Wells-Barnett registers resistance to this victory by demanding inclusion in the category of national and regional citizenship.

In Lauren Berlant's terminology, this is diva citizenship, an act of witness that "stages a dramatic coup in a public sphere in which [the subaltern speaker] does not have privilege" (Berlant 1997, 222–23). The risk of this coup is that a "willful and memorable rhetorical performance" can be mistaken for "sustained social change" on the part of an already rights-bearing citizen, rather than a plea for justice by a deprivileged subject (Ibid., 223). Though the connection between Berlant and Wells-Barnett was first noted by Alison Piepmeier in her bravura reading of Wells-Barnett's "The Supreme Right of America Citizenship," I differ with the reading in the unabashed and unmitigated optimism that Piepmeier assigns to Wells-Barnett's publicity and coup. Diva citizenship, Piepmeier argues, "flashes up, challenges, and invokes change," thereby offering an "alternative to the current models" of citizenship (Piepmeier 2004, 164–65). The distinction between my use of Berlant and Piepmeier's rests in our differing conception of agency. While Piepmeier attaches Wells-Barnett to the successful creation of new space and alternative visions of corporeality, I read agency as less willful and more desirous: an attempt, though not always a successful one, to find space for oneself within a language of rights and authority. Moreover, I do not think that this coup can only be accomplished in the sphere of *American* citizenship, when Southern particularity—imagined as attachment to honor, home, and community—was so often deployed as a justification for lynching. Wells-Barnett's reclamation of region and home, as well as her self-described status as an "exile" contest these narratives (Wells-Barnett 1997, 50).

The publicity of diva citizenship was particularly fraught in the nineteenth century, when American narratives of progress and reunion staged spectacular public interventions of their own. James C. Davis writes of Wells-Barnett's collaborative counterprotest with Frederick Douglass at the World's Columbia Exposition, where they shared space with Nancy Green—the ex-slave hired by Quaker Oats to play Aunt Jemima in a live-action advertising tableau—and Dahomey natives, narrated by the fair officials as savages and throwbacks who "depict[ed] a perversion of gender roles" (Davis 2007, 80). The " 'sham' public sphere" of the fair "enact[ed] and naturalize[d] a mode of social segregation and economic and political subordination as much as to reflect an existing one," Davis writes (Ibid., 78). Rather than buy entry to the public sphere with the "restrained mode of address" of respectable civil rights leaders or with a willingness to "identify . . . her own body with a commercial trademark," as Green did, Wells-Barnett negotiated this imaginary public—and indeed, the presumptive whiteness of the Southern citizen by attaching citizenship to acts of traumatic witness rooted in her identity as a black woman (Ibid., 82).

In more contemporary accounts of Southern identity, the desire to claim that white and black Southerners share in regional citizenship is sometimes accompanied by claims of moral equivalency and racial romanticism. Consider the lyrical, pastoral introduction to David R. Goldfield's *Black, White, and Southern*:

> There were two races, one black and one white. They shared a common history: they had suffered together through defeat and

> oppression, each in its own way . . . They shared the land—the land overworked by cotton or tobacco, rutted and ragged and abandoned to scrub and gullies. . . . They shared a faith that God had chosen them as modern-day Hebrews to lead them to a promised land of better times, if not here and now, then assuredly in the by-and-by. (Goldfield 1990, 1)

Operating on the factual premise that white and black Southerners share a land and history, Goldfield offers too simple an equivalency between the experiences of black and white Southerners, refusing differences in both experience and condition. While slavery and Jim Crow were legal and civil oppressions, he attempts to extend the experience of oppression to white Southerners in Reconstruction and the Depression, despite the conditions of white supremacy that existed with greater violence in those epochs. And, while the intellectual and spiritual connections between the enslavement of diasporic Hebrews and Africans is accounted in dozens of sorrow songs and intellectual histories from W. E. B. DuBois to Paul Gilroy, no one has yet convincingly argued that white Southerners shared the experience of diaspora or enslavement that the metaphor of connection between African-American and Jewish conditions suggests. To accomplish the aim of defining crossracial Southern citizenship, Goldfield elides difference in history and condition.

Running counter to this logic is the antiracist tradition among both white and black Southerners that demands inclusion in the category of Southernness—resisting the homogenizing narratives of red states and blue, of whiteness as precondition for regional identity, and of political retrogression as the only true heritage of the South. This countertradition can be found in Medgar Evers, who didn't care if he went to heaven or hell, as long as he went from Mississippi; Richard Wright, whose *American Hunger* was so blistering an account of *Northern* racism that editors cut his memoirs in half to craft a narrative of triumph; and in Paul Robeson, who testified to the House Un-American Activities Committee that he would stay in America because he inherited it from the labor of enslaved ancestors. As Judith Butler writes of Rosa Parks's arrest, civil disobedience "lays . . . claim to . . . right[s] for which . . . no *prior* authorization" exists, asserting a sense of home even when the privileges of citizenship are denied (Butler 1997, 147). Within this tradition, and similarly resisting both racialist and romantic conceptions of nationhood and regionalism, Wells-Barnett demands that nation and region rise anew, rather than rise again.

A Genealogy of Lynching

When James Allen, a self-described "picker" who salvages history's forgotten materials, first exhibited a collection of lynching photographs culled from flea markets, family photo albums, and newspapers in the Roth Horowitz Gallery in New York City in 2000, responses to the exhibition ranged from the exhortatory to the excoriating. Since the exhibition, subsequently named *Without Sanctuary: Lynching Photography in America*, scholarly responses have explored the endless facets of this historical tragedy with a flood of case studies, memoirs, and literary and historical analyses that attempt to rescue lynching from the aporia of memory. The interlocking discourses of psychoanalysis, critical race theory, body studies, and the emerging scholarship on citizenship and the public/private binary enable me to examine the privileged legal and psychological constructions of white selfhood—while investigating the oppression of black subjects forced to relinquish personhood in the American public sphere, where the privileges of white nationalism were preserved by extending exclusively to whites the power to touch with both curiosity and violence the body of the Other. For African-Americans, the public spaces valorized by American exceptionalism became "stages of sufferance," as Saidiya Hartman has argued (Hartman 1997, 17)—as well as places of political lack, conditions to which black writers responded by recuperating citizenship outside the demarcations of the white mob.

As I argue in my earlier reading of Ida Wells-Barnett, Americans discursively quarantine racial violence in the American South, thereby exempting the nation from the charge of racism. In the first chapter, "America is Mississippi Now: The Portable South and the Exile of Richard Wright," I examine the construction of the South as a byword for racism despite its constitutive role in African diasporic culture formation. In contemporary debates, the South is a stand-in for and distillation of American political problematics. Contemporary liberal punditry uses the South to signify political corruption and pathology, while academic discourses conceive of the region as post-national diasporic space. Within contemporary conversations about race, the South is figured as the location of violence and racism; though mid-century publishers and editors present Richard Wright's memoir *Black Boy* to affirm that logic, and he complicates it by rendering the borders of the South as transportable within the wounded psyche of the migrant. Just as Wells-Barnett nationalized the crime of lynching, Richard Wright paradoxically broadened the sites of racism—from the South to Chicago—and reduced them in size to the intangible horrors that the exile carried with him away from the site of trauma. These figurations highlight key relationships between binaries that my book complicates—public/private, nation/region, individual/collective—and reveal the fundamental violability of the spheres and spaces in which the migrant seeks sanctuary.

By analyzing George Schuyler's *Black No More* and Jean Toomer's "A Portrait in Georgia" from *Cane*—the second chapter, "Beneath the Skin: George Schuyler and the Fantasy of Race," considers the uses of fantasy and dreaming in representations of lynching. Toomer's poem describes the beauty of a white woman, but is interrupted by lynching's violent interventions. Within Schuyler's novel, Max Disher finds, after being rejected by a white woman, that his fantasy of consummating his desire is interrupted by nightmare lynchers. Beginning with a review of psychoanalytic conceptions of *fantasy*, I read sexual fantasy within these texts as regulated and policed by invisible white lynchers. The grim success of white racism is its ability to produce a burdened subject that self-polices pleasure and internalizes discourses of responsibility and guilt, shifting accountability for lynching from the mob to the victim. Between Reconstruction and modernism, the character of fantasy is not substantively transformed; crossracial affiliation—figured as utopian fantasy—violates the body of the race-crosser and criminalizes sexual desire. Penetrating acts of violence—fire, flaying, stabbing—are strategies that lynching shares with essential, pseudoscientific models of race. Since at least Thomas Jefferson's *Notes on the State of Virginia*, racially essentialist claims have been deployed to regulate the bodies of people without privilege. How deep is black? Can it be located in the body as well as the burdened psyche? These are the ontological questions that racial science shared with the dominant lynching culture. In Schuyler's novel, which takes place in an America cosmetically changed by a machine that bleached the skin of nonwhites, race does not disappear. Instead, the means of accessing it travel from the visual to the genealogical—and finally, to the visceral when the bodies of lynch victims are torn open in a quest to find the source of racial difference underneath the skin.

Like Schuyler's *Black No More*, William Faulkner's short stories "Dry September" and "Pantaloon in Black" examine what can and cannot be seen, but they are more concerned with the trauma of the witness. As I argue in the third chapter, " 'Peaceful and Unfathomable and Unbearable Eyes': William Faulkner and the Elision of Witness," the author foreclosed traumatic witness as the model from which to write about race, refusing to write a lynching story for *Vanity Fair* because, as he told Morton Goldman, he "never saw a lynching and could not describe one" (Blotner 1977, 89). By the time he made this claim, he had already written "Dry September," a short story that prominently features lynching but refuses a present-tense narration of that violence with rhetorical strategies that shift to unseeing witnesses—people who hear lynchings or hear of them secondhand. These strategies preserve the veracity of Faulkner's claim of never having *seen* a lynching, despite the spectacle lynchings of Nelse Patton (1908) and Ellwood Higginbotham (1935) in his hometown of Oxford, Mississippi. I consider this refusal to see violence as a constitutive feature of the role of spectators at the scene of lynchings. Those who witnessed lynching recognized their privilege and the violence that sustained it within the spectacle of violence, but often strategically forgot the community's approval of lynching—a practice "owned by all the town / though never claimed by us within my hearing," as Allen Tate writes in "The Swimmers"—to preserve pastoral memories of Southern life (Tate 1977, 135). The narrative invisibility of lynching in Faulkner's "Dry September" and, eventually, "Pantaloon in Black," simultaneously preserves and dismantles the collectivity of the act, refusing to show it so that perpetrators of that violence could be at once every citizen and no citizen.

Even before Ralph Ellison's *Invisible Man* (1952), the language of visibility and invisibility typified the discourses around race in America. The hierarchical structure of vision imposed by racial violence evinces that deprivileged subjects do not disappear under the weight of racism. Indeed, invisibility produces its opposite: surveillance of racial others by the dominant culture. Treating the opposition between visibility and invisibility, my fourth chapter, "The Lynched Woman: Kara Walker, Laura Nelson, and the Question of Agency," considers popular and critical responses to two exhibitions—James Allen's *Without Sanctuary: Lynching Photography in America* (2000) and Kara Walker's *My Complement, My Enemy, My Oppressor, My Love* (2007)—as symptomatic of what I call the anxiety of audience, the fear that visual artifacts of racism may be consumed by the "wrong" spectators—ones either committed to white supremacy or overly-invested in their own ability to transcend racism with the act of sympathetic looking. The longstanding association between woman and spectacle activates this anxiety in spectators who gaze at Walker's work, as well as the photograph of Laura Nelson's lynched body in James Allen's collection. Informed by feminist theorizations of the gaze and the politics of pornographic representation, I consider the difficulty of imposing resistant agency as the privileged mode of response to both oppression and spatially-bound spectatorship within exhibition space. Critical deployments of agency often center slavery as the paradigmatic experience of racism, avoiding lynching because scenes of torture provide less fertile ground for locating the resistance of the oppressed.

Moving from my institutional home in Western New York to three lynching sites, my conclusion, "Vacant Lots: Public Memory and the Practice of Forgetting" is at once a travelogue, polemic, and critical essay that examines historical and popular memories of lynching. The tone of this chapter is far more intimate than that of the project from which it is extracted, as it is a memoir that journeys through Greenville, South Carolina, a rapidly-expanding city near the idyllic Blue Ridge mountains where I grew up; Port Jervis, New York, a commuter town on its state's New Jersey and Pennsylvania borders; and Marion, Indiana, where the paradigmatic lynching photograph was taken in 1930 in a spectacle of violence that continues to fuel local debates about memorialization.

In Greenville, I found that the roads that once housed the Southern Provisions Company—a slaughterhouse where the mutilated body of accused murderer Willie Earle was found—have been literally trimmed to make them more remote, cutting off their connection to the Saluda River, the still-functioning railroad, and the junction with Interstate 85. At this site, development is the intimate companion of forgetting, foreclosing lynching's publicness in favor of rural remoteness, whereas Port Jervis exhibits the exceptionalist tendencies of monument cultures, with public space dominated by memories of settlement and war, yet devoid of memory of the lynching of Robert Jackson Lewis in 1892. In Marion, imagined national innocence is belied by living memory of the town's Depression-Era lynching, which its citizens have attempted to forget by repeatedly defeating efforts to place even a plaque on the lawn where it took place (Carr 2006, 457–58). Analyzing public memory and culture through the lens of post-9/11 spectacles of national sentiment, I claim my project's literary and cultural archive as a counterpublic sphere and a counter memorial—occluded by the entrenched desire to locate lynching's violence in states of exception, far from the idealized locations of the American homeland.

Throughout these chapters, but most especially in this introduction and the travelogue that serves as a conclusion, I unabashedly address my position as a scholar, seizing the first-person pronoun with a grip that will prompt moments of pause in readers accustomed to a certain studied objectivity in academic writing, despite the decades of critical theory that have revealed the impossibility and even undesirability of such disembodiment. Others are likely to find this move shocking in a *first* book, since academics are often said to earn the first-person by first proving that they can write without it. But the style and language of this text are not simply rhetorical fireworks; they emerge from a feminist epistemology that guides me even when I write about the most hegemonic male authors, the most pernicious faces of patriarchy. During the final revisions of this book, the remarkable students in my seminars in Women's Studies at William Smith College introduced me to Mary Daly, who proposed that the feminist scholar should ecstatically "commit the crime of Methodicide, since the Methodolatry of patriarchal disciplines kills creative thought" (Daly 1990, 23). In Daly's work, I found—at the risk of sounding essentialist—a long-lost maternal influence for my truculence in response to both academic and personal discipline. Buttressed by Daly's requirement for "couraging" (Ibid., 24) and Patricia Hill Collins's demand for an "ethic of personal accountability" as a dimension of black feminist epistemology (Collins 2000, 265), I opted not to become a *one*, an *us*, or a *this author*, choosing against an unmarked authorial identity that would have maintained white privilege and conferred male privilege despite my desire to eradicate both. Indeed, in a book that argues for the enthronement of singular personhood as politically retrogressive, I paradoxically seize the *I* to remove myself from the staid company of experts, and to reveal the dimensions of white privilege that enable my modest treason against it: I know what racists say when they think themselves in a safe space. Herein, I reveal their secrets and my own.

CHAPTER ONE

"America is Mississippi Now"

The Portable South and the Exile of Richard Wright

Orientations

When I see Southern landscape from an airplane, my eyes follow the winding snake of Atlanta to my mountain home across the state border in Seneca, South Carolina; perhaps I feel more at home with the distance. When I hear that weekend sailors have of late spotted graves and flooded churches through the cerulean waters of manmade upcountry lakes, I swim in my own fear. I remember that those miles of water covering towns and rivers landed my county its starring role as a rural hellscape in *Deliverance* (John Boorman, 1971). From the waters of these lakes, the South smells as green and slick as driftwood. From the coast of South Carolina, it reeks of paper mills and swamp decay. When my dog's ruff is stained red by its clay, I fear, like James Baldwin, that blood dyed the Southern soil. The map is touched by more than memory, yet I cannot escape its simulation of place. I am obsessed with finding the region's borders and delineating its character to mark what makes me alien to it.

The most beautiful names I know mark terrifying places: Dahlonega, Demorest, Honea Path, and Pascagoula lynched men. There are landscapes so lovely that names don't matter; the foot of Canal Street, near where downtown New Orleans becomes Vieux Carre, was once the site of the White League monument, marking the slaughter of freedmen by former Confederates in 1874. The Lynches River—an idyllic site in the Carolina Lowcountry—is rumored to be carpeted with human bones instead of dirt. The map in my mind is folded like an origami dove, but the place itself is a hawk.

If I can find the South at all, I must first acknowledge that it does not exist. Once I might have believed that for the four years between Fort

Sumter and Appomattox, its borders were solid, but now I know otherwise. Southerners may remember the Civil War as a battle over states' rights, but federalism was the Confederacy's occasional prerogative, as race-progressive dissenters in the Free State of Jones found when they seceded from Mississippi (Bynum 2002, 113).[1] Unionist and anti-slavery stalwarts held much of Alabama, Florida, North Carolina, Tennessee, Texas, and Missouri and were occupied by the Confederacy as retribution for exercising their "states' rights." Every Southern state with the exception of South Carolina sent soldiers to the Union as well as the Confederacy (Loewen 1995, 190).

The contestation of the borders of the South and the memory of it as monolithically Confederate reveal the nation's significant investments in the region's opacity, an obsession mirrored in the region's attempt to define itself. On countless occasions, I have heard Southerners debate if Virginia, Maryland, Florida, Texas, and Kentucky are sufficiently Southern places. I have heard the Midwest called "the Northern South." I have heard it suggested that Maine is just Arkansas with whitewash and clapboard, that Pennsylvania is Philadelphia in the East, Pittsburgh in the West, and Alabama in between, and that American geographies exempting New York and Los Angeles are undifferentiated "flyover country." Any beauty reminds me of home; as disorienting and alien as I found the mist and fogs around Irish ruins, they reminded me of nothing so much as the Blue Ridge Mountains' violet horizon. Though I would never dispense with it, I admit that the South is itself a metaphor.

Metaphors—no more imagined or constructed than national and regional borders—depend upon perspective, as Jon Smith and Deborah Cohn maintain:

> Virginians . . . tend . . . to draw the line . . . around Warrenton. South of that line, including Charlottesville, is "the South"; north of it are simply deregionalized suburbs of the nation's capital. Mississippians, by contrast, tend to draw their line . . . somewhere across the Carolinas, thereby demonstrating something of the arbitrariness of the whole enterprise. (Smith and Cohn 2004, 11)

If the South is "dangerous territory" or the id of the nation, then its own desires for differentiation and border certainty are shared by the nation, whose tendency is to define and disavow its regional Other (Ladd 1996, xii). In "Where is Southern Literature? The Practice of Place in a Postsouthern Age," Scott Romine locates six criteria by which the South has been defined: geography, economy, ideology, culture, history, and orientation (Romine 2002,

28). While all of these criteria are relevant to my larger project, the chapter that follows emphasizes ideology and orientation over the rest. Both geography and culture posture as locatable and, thus, seem far too static to illuminate migratory "moments" of the South as represented in Ida B. Wells-Barnett's fin de siècle anti-lynching project and contemporary red state/blue state articulations of the heartland.

Stories of migration from the South—whether rhetorically apparent or not—are attempts to redefine Southern orientation, to treat it as neither legacy nor obstacle, but an ambivalent inheritance. That ambivalence is not always accepted within definitional debates of the South, where, as Romine suggests, "historical exclusion . . . from the category 'southern' " has impinged on African-American self-identification (Romine 2002, 28). Similarly, Nell Irvin Painter defines *Southern* as a racial marker. "*The South* meant white people," she writes, "and *the Negro* meant black people" regardless of regional affiliation and location (Jones 2002, 122). As recently as 1982, Richard H. King's *Southern Renaissance*, which treated 1930–1955—roughly the years of Richard Wright's literary output—excluded the Mississippian with a prefatory caveat. "This study is not intended as a complete intellectual (or literary) history of the Southern Renaissance," King writes. "Black writers are not taken up because for them the Southern family romance was hardly problematic. It could be and was rejected out of hand. The great theme was the attempt . . . to escape the white South which has historically oppressed their people" (King 1980, 7–8). Whatever King's motivation, he does not investigate why other renaissances—whether American or *quattrocentro*—have excluded the same raced and gendered others that he is reluctant to treat. It is telling that King's text is closely contemporary with Jane Tompkins's *Sensational Designs: The Cultural Work of American Fiction* (1986) and Donald Pease and Walter Benn Michaels's *The American Renaissance Reconsidered* (1989), both of which made significant space for deprivileged authors within the canon; King seems unswayed by the spirit of the times.

Certainly King's assertion sounds recherché, but the pages of major journals and edited collections have featured apologias on his behalf in the last decade. In defense of King, Fred Hobson, the dean of Southern letters and author of the canonical *Tell About the South: The Southern Rage to Explain* (1998), asserted that "Southern blacks were incorporated into the canon far too slowly, although for reasons . . . more complicated than simply white racism" (Hobson 1996, 74). Hobson goes on to suggest African-American Southern writers did not fit well into categories advocated for and created by identity politics, because the Southern Renaissance and Harlem Renaissance were kept separate by professionalization in both sub-disciplines of literary studies. The omission of black writers from King's models and his own, he argues, was not "a judgment of literary or personal worth" but occurred because "black writers seemed to fall into a different category of American literature" (Ibid., 81). The categories in question, drawn from Hobson's own *Tell About the South*, describe two Southern tendencies, which he calls "parties"—the party of "remembrance and defense" embodied by William Alexander Percy and the party of "shame and guilt" with which Faulkner has been associated. Black Southerners were "at the *center* of that guilt" so could express neither ambivalence to the violence of racism nor celebration of class and race-based hegemony (Hobson 1998, 81–82).

Ten years after Hobson, Martyn Bone staked out a similarly defensive position about King's omissions. Riffing on Lillian Smith's nomenclature of the South's "race-sex-sin spiral" (Smith 1941, 121) Bone entitled his essay "New Southern Studies and the Race-Sex Gender Spiral." In this favorable review of Tara McPherson's *Reconstructing Dixie: Race, Gender, and Nostalgia in the Imagined South* (2003), he equates McPherson's interdisciplinarity with her ability to "move between and *beyond* the race-gender axis" ultimately equating analytic foci on race and gender with academic orthodoxy (emphasis mine, Bone 2006, 119). While Smith's "spiral" refers to the intersectional relationships between racism, sexism, and homophobia, Bone's referent remains unexplored, leaving the reader with a persistent image of a downward spiral. This sense is underscored by his defense of King, who he pities as a "whipping boy for feminist scholars" (Ibid., 124). Even by the early 1980s, it was no longer appropriate to suggest that ethnic minorities and women did not belong in the literary canon, so apologists performed acrobatic critical leaps of exclusion to defend the white and male particularities of Southern Studies. As the years have passed, motivated by an impulse about which I dare not speculate, these leaps have become more contortionist.

To suggest, as Bone and Hobson do, that an inclusive Southern canon was either justifiably delayed or currently recherché, reads Southern culture as ultimately shaped by privileged subjects whose racial ambivalence is made the chief object of study. That occlusion "flatten[s] out black," as Hortense J. Spillers claimed of orthodox psychoanalysis, "into the same thing despite time, weather, geography, and the entire range of complicating factors that go into the fashioning of persons," by imagining that the South holds no ambivalence—only simple hierarchies and structures of domination—for African-American writers (Spillers 1996, 714). Racism supersedes the neuroses-inducing questions of family and culture, creating an imagined black subjectivity unhindered by complexity.

These dismissals of regional interests as simply matters of escape are poor treatments of a migratory writer like Richard Wright, as well as the orientational Southernness that migration preserved in the flight north to other parts of the same nation. As such, I restore Wright to the Southern context, not because of an accident of birth, but because of his shaping of and participation in contemporary rhetorics of the South as a site of lynch law and racism. Though my Southern analysands are metaphoric, each metaphor illuminates a disparate tendency of the South as regional, national, and international. In contemporary liberal punditry, the South stands in for political corruption and pathology, while academic discourses conceive of the region as post-national diasporic space. Richard Wright's "Southern Night" in *Black Boy* (1945) and *American Hunger* (2003) is the nation from which he sprang but cannot escape; his dual migrations from the South and then the nation bespeak the inadequacy of locating his "night" in the South alone. These moments are part of the larger story of how *Southern* racism occludes *American* racism—by distancing the South from America as a post-national space, constructing it as a stand-in for the American nightmare of racism, or quarantining violence within its porous borders.

As Tara McPherson argues in *Reconstructing Dixie*, the occlusion of American racism is achieved by "lenticular logic" which she defines as a "schema by which histories or images that are actually copresent get presented (structurally, ideologically) so that only one of these images can be seen at a time" (McPherson 2003, 7). Racially, this lenticular vision elides connections between black and white people, allowing "whiteness to float free from blackness" and denying long-standing cultural, social, and reproductive connections. Though a term like *segregation* is historically accurate, it cannot tell the whole story, since there was an integrated private sphere in which black domestics reared white children and people of different races had sexual relationships. The public sphere of separation in schools, shops, and public transportation provides a lenticular vision of its own—whiteness without blackness, blackness without whiteness—a vision that private life could not sustain.

Though lenticular logics of vision have been the guiding modes by which the South has constituted race, America suffers from its own lenticular vision with regards to the South. The commodification of Southern culture through PBS documentaries, the marketing of Scarlett O'Hara, and plantation tours in Natchez and New Orleans have enabled white Americans to "connect imaginatively to Old South traditions of grandeur and elegance" in a "lost world of white dominance and beauty . . . [un]complicated by race or racism" (Ibid., 253). Outside of this culturally approved game of dress up, Americans are less eager to claim Southernness; in fact, the discourse of American exceptionalism requires a lenticular displacement of the region. "The South can function as a demonized other, as the mythic and convenient repository of racism and our racist past," McPherson argues, "conveniently serving to absolve the rest of the nation from accountability or complicity" (Ibid.). The displacement of lynching as a Southern crime rather than a national one is a claim that easily accommodates an American exceptionalism: if national civil religion is conceived with the sense that this country is considerably more moral than others, then the discursive antidote to racist poison is to siphon it to one regional appendage, to amputate that appendage in an attempt to foreclose the potential of collectivity, and to ignore the seamlessness of the national body.

Southern Strategies

The nearness of the South—its presence both incorporated and disavowed with a nearly-Freudian melancholia—necessitates disavowal that has, in the age of the red-state/blue-state dichotomy, posited the problem of the South as a political one. As Riche Richardson writes in Black Masculinity in the United States South (2007), the problem is far more national than local. "Pathological [and] alienated" Southern bodies and psyches translate into bad politics within the national discourse (Richardson 2007, 9).[2] These pathologies have found a willing audience in contemporary American, which seems only too enthusiastic to treat the South's locality as though American coasts have no region, as surely as men have no gender and whites have no race. The marked Southern body is constantly on display for these appetites. Whenever CNN finds an Atlanta street on which to crop off the heads of passersby to focus on their famous girth, Southerners raised on a diet of wilt salad, cheese grits, and fried chicken are inescapably uncomfortably implicated.

The diseased body of the obesity crisis—a disproportionately Southern pathology—translates into the slow-spreading metaphoric political cancer on the national body, perpetuated in the ubiquitous email perpetuated in the website "Fuck the South," which enthusiastically blamed the South for

George W. Bush's reelection in 2004. "Take your liberal-bashing, federal-tax-leaching, confederate-flag-waving, holier-than-thou, hypocritical bullshit and shove it up your ass," writes the anonymous author to the fictive you of the representative Southerner. Who is addressed by the author's second person? Whatever the Southern location, I wager the "you" is white, since African-Americans both North and South are the Democratic Party's most reliable voting block, with 88 percent of self-identified black voters casting ballots for John Kerry in 2004 (Lopez 5).[3] The absence of the South's African-American identity within these contemporary configurations of the region reinforces white supremacist notions that have, in Riche Richardson's words, "typically constituted [African-Americans] as invisible, expendable, and excluded" (Richardson 2007, 127).

The singular, archetypal "you" attacked on the "Fuck the South" website is a chimera, as the South is not monolithically Republican, white, or Christian. The region contains states with near parity—forty-sixty and thirty-seventy splits—between whites and African-Americans in Mississippi, South Carolina, and Louisiana. In addition, the whitest states—Maine, Vermont, New Hampshire, West Virginia, and Iowa—are Northern and Western, while the least white—Louisiana, Georgia, Maryland, California, Mississippi, District of Columbia, and Hawaii—are nearly all Southern. As for the far-Western states, they are not exempt from the potential of being folded into the South. Recounting the affirmative action and immigration debates of the late millennium in *The Possessive Investment in Whiteness* (1998), George Lipsitz referred to California as the "Mississippi of the 1990s" (Lipsitz 1998, 211). Even the traditional Confederacy is not a geographical monolith; it has often been said that there is not one South, but three: up South, down South, and out South, with significant demographic shifts between them. The Prentice Hall anthology *The South in Perspective* (2001) partially abides by this logic, separating Southern literature into Upper South and Lower South categories. Placing Richard Wright in the category of Lower South baffles me—as it evokes moonlight and wisteria rather than the mountains of Upper South or the frontier of "Out South"—but is evidence that the South itself is open to constant revision and interpretation.

The histories of the Democratic Party's losing seasons in 2000 and 2004 will, if they are to be written in punditry's broad strokes, nonetheless affirm the "Solid South," shifting the moniker from Reconstruction's Democratic Party to contemporary Republicans. In *Welcome to the Homeland: A Journey to the Rural Heart of America's Conservative Revolution* (2006), Brian Mann contests the logic of the color-coded map:

> There's only one problem with this split-screen version of America's cultural landscape. It's utter fiction. . . . Examine more accurate maps that break down the country's voting patterns by actual distribution and you find that those tidy ideological provinces dissolve. . . . This model . . . disguises what has become a clear political and cultural divide in America, delineated not by state or region but by the boundary between our progressive cities and inner suburbs and the conservative rural culture that sprawls beyond the urban beltway. (Mann 2006, 64)

A travelogue through the homeland that Mann delineates would take the traveler from the traditional South to places that were certainly slave states (Arizona, New Mexico), solidly Abolitionist and ostensibly blue (central and western New York), as well as those that were Unionist strongholds (Kansas) and one state that was created by the debates over slavery (West Virginia). Population density and proximity to urban centers, rather than geographical boundedness or nineteenth century political affiliations, were the foremost indications of voting patterns in the past three elections. In cartograms organized by party affiliation, population, and uniformity in the popular vote, the South itself nearly disappears, as Northeastern population centers swell the map to the point of regional obsolescence.[4]

It is quite clear that population centers do not determine the results of presidential elections, since rural, empty states have proportionally more electoral votes that consistently deliver elections to Republicans. Nonetheless, the fall-out from Bush's two victories produced a burdened South, as evinced by journalistic companions to the rhetorical excess of "Fuck the South," like Thomas F. Schaller's *Whistling Past Dixie: How Democrats Can Win Without the South* (2006) and Steve Jarding and Dave Saunders's *Foxes in the Henhouse: How the Republicans Stole the South and the Heartland and What the Democrats Must Do to Run 'Em Out* (2007). The deployment of the South to signify Republicanness and conservatism is inaccurate, but common; indeed, Barack Obama would likely have been defeated in 2008 if he took Schaller's advice and abandoned North Carolina and Virginia to Republican hegemony. Nonetheless, pundits who quantify Southern politics seem always to be referencing Lenny Bruce. Almost half of a century ago, the comedian joked that if you are from a city, you are Jewish, even if you are Catholic, but you are equally and intractably goyish if you live in Montana. Perhaps his joke can be updated for the new age of blue cities and red exurbs. If you live in Atlanta, you are liberal and Northern even if you are Southern, but if you live in Crawford, Texas, you are conservative and Southern even if, like George Bush, you are from Connecticut.

Just as Obama's victory opened up a fracture in the South's solidity, quantitative sociological analysis evinces the increasing vacancy of Southern self-identification, as the label wanders outside of geographic boundaries into political ones. Larry J. Griffin and Ashley B. Thompson's "Enough About the Disappearing South, What About the Disappearing Southerner?" (2003) historicizes the tendency to assign whiteness, Protestantism, conservatism, and other political normatives to the region. Though Thompson and Griffin argue that the "Jim Crow, insular, economically impoverished, politically retrograde" South of the 1950s and 1960s is dead, their archive attests to the still-present political litmus test for Southern citizenship (Griffin and Thompson 2003, 51). In 1971, a poll of over a thousand white and black North Carolinians produced a definite racial split in Southern self-identification. While 82 percent of whites identified as Southern, 73 percent of African-Americans did the same, suggesting that the racist public sphere created by the backlash against civil rights diminished black Southerners' willingness to self-identify as citizens of the region (Ibid., 53). The Southern Focus Poll's answers from 1991 to 2001 evince a broader unwillingness to identify with the South, with the largest proportion of disaffection among ethnic minorities, the young (ages seventeen to thirty-four), current college students, non-Christians, Catholics, Democrats, liberals, and independents. The smallest declines, on the other hand, were among wealthy college graduates who identified as conservative or Republican and attended a Protestant Church. The spread of numbers is significant, though decreases are constant; while Southern self-identification among Hispanics declined by almost 20 percent in a time when the Hispanic population of the American South increased by a quarter, it declined merely 0.1 percent among Republicans and 0.4 percent among conservatives (Ibid., 55–56).

After Benedict Anderson's *Imagined Communities* (1991), it is difficult to read these numbers without locating the subject of the forced-choice questionnaire in relationship to the collective invoked by its language. One wonders what these numbers would have looked like if the participants had been asked "who do you consider Southern?" in addition to "do you consider yourself Southern?" Would conservative white Protestants have included only members of their religious and ethnic communities, rejecting minorities as outside the tie of Southern community formation? Perhaps the rhetoric of the 2000 and 2004 election cycles policed the borders of the South, discursively ejecting nonwhites and liberals who are no longer represented in the clean sweep that the all-or-nothing dispensation of electoral votes suggests. The tenuousness of these communities and borders underscores the key terms of Anderson's theorization of the nation as "an imagined political community . . . imagined as both inherently limited and sovereign" (Anderson 1991, 6). Responding to Anderson in the context of Southern identity, Richard Gray argues that the singularity of the term *community* must be broadened to define the South as "an imagined community made up of a multiplicity of communities, similarly imagined" that are linked not by proximity, culture, or temporal continuity but by the "act of imagination" that delineates a "place in the world with the aid of talk and ceremony, language and communal ritual" (Gray 2002, xxiii). This multiplicity is diminished when the sovereignty of the South's imagined community is hegemonically located within neo-Confederate yearnings for freedom from "the imperial North," a yearning most keenly expressed in the desire to locate and stabilize Southern borders (Williamson 1980, 78). The nation no longer stands in for region within the New Southern studies—but the old South certainly constructed a sovereign, limited South, perhaps in accordance with pre-Civil War conceptions of state- and nation-hood expressed by Thomas Jefferson's longing for his "country" of Virginia while he served in the White House. The characters in Thomas Nelson Page's *Red Rock* (1898) similarly refer to the South as their county, section, and country; nonetheless, Walter Benn Michaels's reading of Page's plantation romance as anti-imperialist suggests that these terms are not national, that the text "avoid[s] the perils of empire by avoiding the perils of nationhood first" (Benn Michaels 1995, 17).

Advocates of the "new" Southern studies—which provide an occasion for comparison between the American South and the global South—problematize the nation in accordance with Walter Benn Michaels's paradigm: post-colonialism and post-nationalism. The Zizekian principle of nation formation as a dialectical process by which the good nation defines itself against the bad has become a standard citation in the New Southern studies (Baker and Nelson 2001, 235; Kreyling 2005, 10; Yaeger 2000, 229). "Eastern Europe functions for the West as its Ego-Ideal: the point from which the West sees itself in a likeable, idealized form, as worthy of love," Slavoj Zizek wrote at the end of the Cold War. Replace "East" with "South" and "West" with "North," the new pioneers of Southern studies assert, and you have the constitutive national crisis of the American Civil War's triumph over Southernness. "As a nation, we are always already in 'The South,'" write Houston A. Baker and Dana D. Nelson, ". . . it is unequivocally and intricately lodged in us, a first principle of our being in the world" (Baker and Nelson 2001, 20). Regardless of their deployment of Zizek, Baker and Nelson's first principle suggests not the good nation/bad nation trope, but the pervasive, inescapable trace of the South that the migrant carries with her despite fervent disavowal. Similarly, the migrant brings the South with her from Memphis to Chicago, from Atlanta to Harlem.

In postcolonial theory, Trinh T. Min-ha's recognition of "the existence of a Third World in the First World, and vice versa" is repeated almost as a truism (Min-ha 1992, 201). Within discourses of American exceptionalism, the disavowed other is the Southern Third, clenched tightly within imagined borders, behind a chained and locked gate to achieve the illusion that America is safe from the plagues of racism, poverty, corrupt government—and, with rates of infection skyrocketing in the urban South, HIV disease. A refusal to accommodate the rhetoric of a problem region is not novel, nor invented by academic Southern studies; Malcolm X curtailed that logic at the height of the Civil Rights Movement in 1963, when he told a group of activists to "Stop talking about the South. As long as you are South of the Canadian border, you are South" (X n.d.). The sentiment has been used more recently to suggest that racism has circulated, spreading uncontrollably throughout the American body. In his meditation on the state of the South, Jack Butler writes "America is Mississippi now. You don't think it is? You wrong" (Butler 1996, 37).

An extension of postcolonial theoretical language to the South opens a definitional gap into which a number of older ideologies, both pernicious and apologist, can shift. The chief proponent of this school—Deborah Cohn and Jon Smith's bravura statement *Look Away! The U.S. South in New World Studies* (2003)—takes its critical warrants from Southern apologists like Allen Tate and C. Vann Woodward, leaving the reader with a troubling sense of moral equivalency between the post-national South and the Confederacy. Tate's assertion that "not even literary nationalism could abort a genuine national literature when it is ready to appear; when, in fact, we become a nation," is quoted early in their introduction, suggesting sympathy for Southern nationalisms (Tate 1968, 536; Smith and Cohn 2004, 1). Woodward's apologist claim that the South "had undergone an experience that it could share with no other part of America—though it is shared by nearly all the peoples of Europe and Asia—the experience of military defeat, occupation, and reconstruction" models both antebellum romanticism and global borderlessness (Woodward 1993, 190). Cohn and Smith simultaneously define it as "exclusionary and exceptionalist myth" and a "corrective to the provincial hubris of the imperial United States" (Smith and Cohn 2004, 1). The suggestion that they can fuel their argument with the second half of that construction while discarding the first is one that I greet with skepticism.

The ideology of the Confederate nostalgist—who I would distinguish from the more politely restrained Southern apologist—is perhaps best represented in Allan Gurganus's novel *The Oldest Living Confederate Widow Tells All* (1989), in which the narrator finds her husband teaching their children an altered version of Innes Randolph's 1914 song "A Old [sic] Rebel." The aging veteran, dressed in a mock-up of his Confederate uniform with starched gray broadcloth and gold brocade he never would have seen under scarcity conditions on the frontlines, performs the song for a reporter from a glossy Northern magazine based, presumably, on *Life*:

> I hates the Constitution this Great Republic, too.
> I hates the Freedman's Buro, in uniforms of blue.
> I hates that nasty eagle, with all his brags and fuss.
> The lyin' thievin' Yankees, I hates 'em wuss and wuss.
>
> Three hundred thousand Yankees is stiff in Southern dust.
> We GOT three hundred thousand before they conquered us.
> They died of Southern fever and Southern steel and shot.
> I wish they was three million instead of what we got. (545)

Though the song is of more recent invention than the war itself, the historical core rests in the portrait of the angry rebel who sees himself as a guerilla fighter and federal authorities as persistent occupiers of the fallen South. More recently, the song appeared in the film The Assassination of Jesse James by the Coward Robert Ford (2007), providing a backdrop to James's theft of the Glendale Train, a crime he committed with the help of other embittered Missouri "pukes"—white working-class veterans who had owned no slaves, but opposed the end of slavery. While the "old rebel" of the song acknowledges defeat—jettisoning the stereotype of the Southern apologist who refuses to personally surrender, as his former army and government did at Appomattox—he casts it as victory. His meager score is subordinate to his grander desires for total annihilation; in order to save his conscience, he casts this bloodthirsty wish as victimhood.

Lest the reader mistake this doggerel for a tendency long vanquished in Southern culture, note the similarities between Gurganus's historical fiction and Mississippian T. R. Hummer's autobiographical poem "The Real":

> The winter John Kennedy died
> Some of my classmates cheered.
> I didn't, but I didn't know
> If it was right to grieve.
> That's a hard thing to admit.
> But I was confused. Those were confusing times.
> The South had spent a century
>
> Perfecting the purity of hate.
> It was them or us, we said.
> We hated the North, communists, Russians,
> Catholics, Negroes, liberals, and atheists. (Smith 1996, 153)

Recalling the years surrounding the "Battle of Oxford," which raged in response to the integration of the University of Mississippi and is often remembered by Confederate nostalgists as the last battle of the Civil War, Hummer's poem renders the terrors of childhood in the Confederacy—a nation, it seems, that still governed twentieth-century Southerners with exclusionary models of community and citizenship (Doyle 2001, 56).

Running parallel but proximate to the history of the United States—as the film Ken Burns-inspired mockumentary *CSA: Confederate States of America* (Willmott 2004) illuminates—the Confederate ur-nation unendingly celebrates its suffering. Even in Willmott's alternative history in which the Confederacy won the Civil War, the nation demands recompense for its suffering, suing Canada in international courts to pay former slave owners reparations for slaves who fled North. Idealized victimhood is celebrated within the Southern realpolitik, but not only on the political right; Southern partisans benefit from the lazy axiom that "one man's freedom is another man's freedom fighter." Though such relativism has often been associated with the political left, Southern partisans purvey it liberally. In 1994, the Virginia state legislature voted to name Martin Luther King, Jr. Day "Lee-Jackson-King Day" because Stonewall Jackson and Robert E. Lee were also "defenders of causes" (Horowitz 2001, 41). Appropriating the language of civil rights without distinction regarding cause or commitment, Southern partisans refer to neo-Confederate sympathy as a "niche of the civil rights movement" (Ibid., 249).

Thus, naming Southern whites "postcolonial" provides that population with precisely the sense of victimization that shores up the most pernicious myths of the Civil War. Allen Bragdon's 1976 survey of college freshmen revealed that a majority believed that Reconstruction led to corruption "among the entrenched carpetbagger governors and their allies in the black dominated legislatures of defeated states" (Bragdon 1987, 129–40). During his Guggenheim-funded survey of American high school textbooks in the 1990s, sociologist James Loewen found that the "Confederate Myth of Reconstruction"—the belief that former slaves were integrated into the Union at the expense of Southern whites—was still not refuted. According to the most-popular textbook in American history classrooms, Reconstruction ended because of a failure of citizenship by both African-Americans and their Northern allies; "northerners grew weary of the problems of black Southerners and less willing to help them learn their new roles as citizens," they assert (Loewen 1995, 160). These myths—transferred from Thomas Nast's Reconstruction-era caricatures of black legislators to D.W. Griffith's *Birth of a Nation* (1914) to the general populace—celebrate the victimization of the defeated, occupied South.

The myth persists not only in the South, but also outside of it, wherever federal authority is seen as violent imposition. As Thomas Frank argues in *What's the Matter with Kansas?* (2004), the political right must declare its oppression at the hands of "profound, all-corrupting liberal cultural influence," since loss of privilege and nostalgia are "absolute ontological necessit[ies]" for conservatism (Frank 2004, 136). Those impulses rule in Tony Horwitz's interviews with neo-Confederates in the 1990s; he found them touting victimhood as the connective tissue between the Lost Cause and contemporary politics:

> I asked Tarlton what he knew about his own Civil War forebears.
> "Bunch of poor dirt farmers, like most folks were around here, and like a lot still are," he said. "Didn't own any slaves."
> "Why do you think they fought?"
> "The way I see it," Tarlton said, "they were fighting for their honor as men. They came from stock that was oppressed and they felt oppressed again by the government telling them how to live."
> "Same as today," another man chimed in. "Government's letting niggers run wild." (Horwitz 1998, 35)

Similarly, early Lost Cause advocates engraved Jefferson Davis's statue on Richmond's Monument Avenue with Christ's injunction: "Blessed are they which [sic] are persecuted for righteousness's sake, for theirs is the kingdom of heaven" (Horwitz 1998, 248). Wherever the impulse of reactionary nostalgia has ruled, the "oppressed" have seized on the memory of the defeated Confederacy to justify violence. Domestic terrorist Timothy McVeigh, who hails from Lockport, New York, wore a t-shirt purchased from Southern Partisan when he delivered his fertilizer bomb to the Murrah Federal Building in Oklahoma City. It was emblazoned with the words Sic Semper Tyrannis, John Wilkes Booth's rallying cry upon the assassination of Abraham Lincoln. When news of McVeigh's fashion statement made the newspapers, Southern Partisan sold out of the t-shirt ("Southern Partisan: Setting the Record Straight").

Even if McVeigh's notion of white male victimhood is sensibly avoided, figuring indigenous and African peoples as colonized provides no more comfortable a postcolonial nomenclature for the region, even if it renames the tyrants in question. Certainly much of the South is creolized, with the genealogy of Native Americans persisting in both black and white-identified Southerners, particularly at the sites of former triracial isolates like Louisiana and Florida. That accident of blood lineage shores up Southern claims of authenticity, victimhood, and oppression. Influenced by the axiomatic logic that people of color cannot be racist because racism is a combination of prejudice and power, white Southerners might then divest themselves of white privilege by rhetorically exhuming part-Cherokee grandmothers. That divestiture of white privilege is no less present in a desire to name the South "postcolonial" because of its violence against—rather than amalgamation with—indigenous peoples and African slaves. Such a move is neither novel nor trailblazing, as postcolonial critic Chandra Talpade Mohanty used the term *Third World* to "designate peoples from formerly colonized countries, as well as people of color in the United States . . . [as an] oppositional designation that can be empowering even while it necessitates a continuous questioning" almost twenty years ago (Mohanty 2003, 268). This logic of the postcolonial South locates both genocide and slavery solely in one region—replacing King Phillip's War with the Trail of Tears, Massachusetts's slaves with Georgia's, the Pequod War with the Yemassee, and Wall Street's slave market with Charleston's.

Though a complete history of American racism recalls atrocity on both sides of the Mason-Dixon line—which, incidentally, bisects Pennsylvania—a total memory across regional lines would reveal the poverty of calling the South "postcolonial," as it would be no more explanatory than applying the term to the entire nation. Some regional differentiation is certainly necessary, as there is a wide gap between the nation's stated drive for the preservation of "inalienable rights," and the "Cornerstone of the Confederacy" as defined by Confederate Vice President Alexander Stephens. "Our new government['s] . . . foundations are laid," he wrote, ". . . upon the great truth that the Negro is not equal to the white man, that slavery—subordination to the superior race—is his natural and normal condition" (quoted in Durden 2000, 7–8). Though the American experiment failed people of color, its deeply conflicted relationship to democracy nonetheless maintains the national corrective of amending and revising its constitution toward greater freedom, even if those revisions have not always followed the trajectory of progressive revelation. The distinction between these two nations requires an understanding of the South as multiracial place and Confederate ideology as its uniracial colonizer.

Growing up in Upcountry South Carolina, a region that was, like much of Appalachia during the Civil War, divided in its loyalties, I learned the fictiveness of Civil War legacy groups and witnessed the memory that rested on Stephens's cornerstone (Reid 2001, 871). Confederate flags fly from houses that line the route to Shelton Laurel, North Carolina, the place where native Southern Union sympathizers and their children were slaughtered by the Confederate Army in 1863. Driving from Rochester, New York to Seneca, South Carolina, I am continually saddened by the Confederate battle flags decorating cars in West Virginia, a place that would not exist had it hung those flags in 1861. Reenactors camped for three days every summer from 1998 to 2008 in Pickens County, South Carolina to playact the Battle of Central, turning a "mild skirmish" into a major tourist attraction ("Battle of Central Re-Enactment Canceled"). Theorist Barbara Christian warned of theoretical practices that suggest that "reality does not exist, that everything is relative, and that every text is silent about something" (Christian 1998, 73). Though I find her formation to be a particularly undercooked reading of deconstruction, I deploy it against any reclamative Southern studies that suggests parity between experience, perception, and history without distinction between the truth claims of historians, slave narratives, and Southern partisans. There are truths, some accessible, some not; eschewing them in favor of regional exceptionalism, Southern apologists perpetuate a monstrous deceit. "We are sometimes asked in the name of patriotism," said Frederick Douglass on Memorial Day 1871, ". . . to remember with equal admiration those who struck at the nation's life, and those who struck to save it—those who fought for slavery and those who fought for liberty and justice . . . May my tongue cleave to the roof of my mouth if I forget the differen[ce]" (Douglass, quoted in Blight 2002, 106).

Though scholars aligned with global southern studies strive to occupy the space between apologist and critic, the justifications are often wanting, as evinced in Cohn and Smith's preemptive defense against the charge of nostalgia:

> To characterize even a of Confederate genuinely biracial (and increasingly multiracial) U.S. South as a postcolonial space . . . might be considered a regression to southern apologetics. It is not, if only because . . . postcolonial studies has finally begun to move beyond . . . the simplistic moral dichotomy between 'bad' colonizer and 'good' colonized that fails to differentiate among and within colonized cultures. (Smith and Cohn 2004, 5)

Most critics would agree that simple dichotomies are undesirable, even in teachable moments, but Smith and Cohn's own search for indeterminate middle grounds leads them to a diminished moral position from which to describe African chattel slavery in the New World. When the South is remembered as colonized by both "the African American experience of defeat under slavery" and "white men's surrender at Appomattox," Cohn and Smith are in dangerous territory (Ibid., 5). The use of the term defeat to describe the experience of slavery is denial of its horrors, at worst, and translocation of war and slavery at best. Fork our critical tongues if they elide the difference between a treaty and a bill of sale, mistake the transfer of land for the transfer of human property. Iterations of the South previously treated in this essay argue for its transferability, its graftability onto available regional glyphs. Certainly the South's polysemic text is one that I—like Allen Tate, Cohn and Smith, and Richard King—struggle with, but if our critical practices are grounded in history and informed by the liberationist struggles that have preceded our entry into the discourse, we must distinguish between the fluid South and the nation that offered it false unity. One may journey South to a new place, but the Confederacy is not a desirable destination. Imbricating the South and the Confederacy can have two equally undesirable outcomes—the sanitization of the Confederacy or the blanching of the South.

To clarify this distinction, antiracist Southerners must cede some ground to Confederate nostalgists, insofar as resistance to the interpellative power of a bumper sticker culture that chides them with reminders that "our president is Jefferson Davis" will enable further restrictive political delineations of the term *Southern*. My chief concerns, however, are for the soul of cultural studies as it turns its compound eye to Southern text. Tara McPherson's *Reconstructing Dixie* (2003) treats the newest face of the Southern nostalgist or partisan—the Cyber Confederate. Like the mostly leftist postmodern geographers, Cyber Confederates are alarmed by the erosion of public space and discourse, though their counterpublic spheres are less concerned with inclusion. Groups like Dixie-Net and the Confederate Network "deploy the electronic realms of the Internet to reassert a particular sense of place and identity at the very moment that global capitalism appears as a homogenizing force across the South" (McPherson 2003, 106–107). In his interviews with Tony Horwitz, Heritage Preservation Association president Lee Collins discussed his organization's mission to restore to American public life a "Southern culture . . . that's been bleached from the fabric of America" (Horwitz 1998, 289). Though there is no doubt that such rhetoric is resistant, it is deployed—as theologian Karen Armstrong has argued of religious fundamentalism—to combat modernity, otherness, and difference (*The Battle for God*). I caution against labeling it *counterhegemonic* or *subversive*, when these terms too easily pass as honorariums in cultural studies. Instead, Southern studies should highlight another resistant culture: the memory behind the monuments, the truth beyond the map. In the section that follows, I suggest that Richard Wright authors a counternarrative that both scripts and reads the South, leaving the reader with a sense of the nation as metonym for the South, rather than the South as its own nation. As evinced by Wright's memoir, this nationalization of racial violence—and the transferability of borders of the South—took place even at the moment of migration, when the political value of northward optimism was paramount. Turning to *Black Boy*, I consider the portability of Southern borders in relationship to the practice of lynching.

Sprawling Lands of Suffering

In March 1920, The Crisis, the house journal of the National Association for the Advancement of Colored People, published an illustration by Albert A. Smith called "The Reason." It shows an African-American man, labeled "the Southern Negro," fleeing north away from the spectacle of a lynched body, positing mob violence as the cause of the migration of seven million African-Americans from the South, a region that housed an overwhelming majority of the nation's black population before World War I. I begin with Smith's illustration—which has become iconic in the overlapping magisterium of African-American and Southern Studies—to both affirm and contest the logic of the image. Certainly racial violence was a primary reason for the evacuation of the South by black migrants, but many other factors influenced this practice, a phenomenon so crossracial that historian James N. Gregory calls it "the Southern Diaspora" in acknowledgment of extraordinary rates of white migration (Gregory 2007, 12). The trajectory of Richard Wright as migrant and author evinces something of the futility of fleeing north from the national practice of lynching, as the urban metropolis perpetuated mob violence and other strategies of containment against black migrants that began in the epoch of Ida B. Wells-Barnett's anti-lynching campaigns.

However, Smith's illustration also speaks a great truth: as the migrant looks back toward the lynched body, his face bespeaks his identification with the spectacle of torture. Within Richard Wright's memoir, this identification exceeds the feeling of sympathy and traverses into what psychoanalysis names "introjection"—the practice of psychically and somatically incorporating trauma into one's own subjectivity. Within Wright's *Black Boy*, the narrator's introjection is revealed in a number of scenes I call "practice lynchings"—moments when representations of "real" lynchings are deferred to transform Wright into the perpetrator of violence rather than its victim—killing a kitten, threatening his family's life with fire, beating his brother—and therefore, transforming himself into a burdened and guilty subject who prefers imagined accountability for violence to the admission of radical vulnerability to white supremacy.

These two strains of my argument—the claim for the national character of lynching and Wright's presentation of himself as violence's agent—emerge from the vexed publication history of the memoir, a history that illustrates the Northern publishing industry's desire to present Wright as heroic and triumphant while diminishing national (rather than regional) responsibility for the crime of lynching. The publication of Richard Wright's memoir *Black Boy* (1945) occupies a number of firsts and lasts. It was the rare successful literary memoir by a writer who was not yet forty when he wrote it, with a texture so invented that—sixty years before largely fictional memoirs by James Frey and Herman Rosenblat—its veracity became subject to public debate. Decades before Oprah Winfrey's book club, it was the first African-American memoir to be chosen as a Book-of-the-Month club selection. Though this detail might seem trivial, according to literary critic Jeff Karem, the governing body of the Club had the most influence on how Wright's work was read and received by his first-generation audience. More than his editors or his usual readers, friends, or critics like Ralph Ellison and James Baldwin, the Club shaped public memory of Wright's life, composing a narrative of triumph by excising the half of the book—the section named "The Horror and the Glory"—that details Wright's struggles within the Communist Party after migration to Chicago from Mississippi. One of Harper Publisher's readers argued for the omission of the Communist sequences so that "the story carrie[s] on to the years of Wright's success . . . [so that] his own feeling of hope, his own preservation through adversity" would shape the audience's perceptions of his fame and the success of *Native Son* (Thaddeus 2003, 73).

Indeed, as Jeff Karem writes, "desires for Wright's autobiography to end on a note of 'success' would continue to haunt the manuscript [throughout the editorial process]" (Karem 2001, 699). If, as the voting body of the club and first-generation reviewers suggested, Wright's genius was brought into the light of day by the publication of *Native Son*, arising from the "Southern night" of his upbringing in Mississippi and Arkansas, than it was a few short hours till the dawn of his talent, to steal the memoir's crepuscular metaphors. Eventually, those editors would settle for omission rather than inclusion, so that readers could make "the easy leap from the trip north to bestsellerdom and success" (Thaddeus 2003, 76). Because of editorial shaping that halts Wright's life at his migration north, his subsequent exilic works are absent from the American canon, which has favored his domestic works, *Native Son* and *Black Boy*. Only recently have Wright's exilic works been recovered and read, due in no small part to Cedric Robinson's *Black Marxism*, which contextualizes Richard Wright's European production with the work of exilic theorists like C. L. R. James and W. E. B. DuBois, writers who are shared by postcolonial and African-American studies.

Wright's own nomenclature for the memoir's chapters—restored in the Library of America edition of the memoir—provides an unequal pairing between (Section 1) "Southern Night" and (Section 2) "The Horror and the Glory." Whatever motivation drove him to collaborate with the Book-of-the-Month club's censorious pen, the lopsided pair denies the convenient fiction of dawn in the North to which he migrated. The ideological purpose of the Book-of-the-Month Club's omission is the denial of atrocity; removing Wright's sojourn in Chicago transforms the story from an account of a national tragedy to a local one, filled with Southern rather than American violence. Karem argues that the editorial destruction of 140 pages of *Black Boy* confined it to a "regional narrative of childhood and adolescence," in accordance with the traditional canon of American realism as a collection of regional, local colors and "minor" literatures (Karem 2001, 694). Though Karem is right to illuminate racism's national character and argue that editorial practices limited the memoir's scope, he does not consider the conditions that create continuity between the North and South and, therefore, unsettle the narrative of triumph. The connective tissue is the psychic reshaping of the black subject under racism; it is not accurate to say that the North and South in which Wright lived are racist in precisely the same mode. Wright's own theorization of region and migration, however, suggest that the black subject's experience of Southern racism mediates his "liberation" in the North. Indeed, as Ralph Ellison suggests, "it is not enough merely to reject the white South, but . . . to reject that part of the South which lay within"; this task was one that the editorial trimming of *Black Boy* attempted to accelerate (Ellison 2003, 59).

Consistent with Ellison's sense that it is not "the individual . . . but that upon which his sensibility was nourished" that informs Wright's sense of self, I explore Wright's conception of burdened subjectivity with attention to the inventiveness and fictiveness of his portrayal—a theorization of a narrative self that is not necessarily a one-to-one ratio between author and character (Ibid., 49). By interrogating Wright's simultaneously existentialist and psychoanalytic conceptions of both subjectivity and citizenship, the continuity can be located within the individuated subject who is policed by white lynchers, his own family and community, and most pointedly, his burdened desires. Traditional psychoanalytic readings like Mary McCarthy's first-generation review "Portrait of a Typical Negro?," focus on the pathological individual and can thus be faulted for the tendency to see the autobiography as "irrelevant to the situation of the Negro in the South [since] the author, who was a victim of a classical Freudian family situation, was already firmly established in the mode of hatred and rejection when he discovered he was black" (McCarthy 2003, 44). Implicit in Wright's own formations is the desire to locate that individual—whether or not he is constructed under Freudian paradigms—within a culture of violence demarcated by the text's deployment of lynching as metaphor for self-injury that leaves no space "between the world" and Wright. In his poem "Between the World and Me," Wright's narrator stumbles upon the site of a lynching that, despite the temporal juncture from the crime, freezes him in place and "grips" him to the ground. The body of the dead man "stirred, rattled, lifted, melting themselves / into my bones," transforming the not-quite witness until he announces, fully introjecting the experience of trauma: "Now I am dry bones and my face a stony skull" (Wright 1935, 19). The memoir literalizes this experience through repetitions of traumatic violence by the young Wright, whose attempt at escape—an attempt to blind his eyes against witnessing violence—is figured as migration from the South.

Written evidence of life and experience rests in a reader's hands and memory as a product, not a process. Because of the suspended textual condition of the bound book, *Black Boy* (1945) omits the most tellingly national fact of Wright's migration: he could not stop in Chicago once he left Mississippi. No measure of peace found Wright until he left America. Wright articulated his inability to remain in America in a 1945 letter to George Davis. He expresses a desire to represent a unitary African-American experience, typified by "the Negro" who evolves "starting with his oneness with his African tribe" through both slavery as expressed by "the plantation system" and modernity typified by "his gradual trek to the cities of the nation, both North and South . . . and finally his ability to create a new world for himself in the new land in which he finds himself" (Fabre 1993, 273). Emerging in the final sentence of the passage, the "new land" of expatriation is explicitly distanced from—rather than aligned with—the new land that African captives found at the end of the Middle Passage and, indeed, the one that white European imperatives invented in North and South America. Even before his permanent move to Europe, Wright expresses to Davis his awareness that he could not simply settle in the urban North, because it contained no alternative to the horror that produced him.

The new land must be invented but, in accordance with Wright's Marxian principles, it cannot be created out of thin air. "Men make their own history," Marx writes, "but they do not make it just as they please; they do not make it under circumstances chosen by themselves, but under circumstances directly encountered, given, and transmitted from the past" (Marx 2000, 329). One hundred years before Wright, responding to Louis Napoleon's seizure of power in France, Marx crafted a statement that might have been written about the cultural memory of chattel slavery. But the less-often quoted passage that follows also speaks to the concern that Wright shared with his contemporaries, the fear that African-American culture and resistance could not emerge from the shadow of oppression:

> The tradition of all the dead generations weighs like a nightmare on the brain of the living. And just when they seem engaged in revolutionizing themselves . . . in creating something that has never yet existed, precisely in such periods of revolutionary crisis they anxiously conjure up the spirits of the past. . . . In like manner a beginner who has learnt a new language always translates it back into his mother tongue, but he has assimilated the spirit of the new language and can freely express himself in it only when he finds his way in it without recalling the old and forgets his native tongue in the use of the new. (Ibid., 327)

Much like Marx, his predecessor in both materialism and expatriation, Wright acknowledges the productive enclosure of the modern subject within both individual and social pasts. Those constraints are posited in Wright's Twelve Million Black Voices (1941) as a question of language, affirming Marx's metaphor of learning language anew. "We stole words from the grudging lips of the Lords of the Land," Wright says of African-American slaves, ". . . Though they were the words of the Lords of the Land, they become our words, our language" (Wright 2002, 40). Wright's reflexive "we" in the passage quoted above suggests that the African-American vernacular is a language of secrecy, learned in part by productive forgetting and elastic recombination of "common, simple words" with "new meanings . . . which enable[d] [the oppressed] to speak of revolt in the actual presence" of whites without revealing their purpose. That vernacular bricolage enables Wright's reflexive we in Twelve Million Black Voices, suggesting his psychic continuity with chattel slavery.

Yet, Wright's own Marxian forgetting is rendered in *Black Boy* as the young boy's unending desire for differentiation from his surroundings, a desire that fails in transit and migration. As James Olney argues, the community "attempt[s] to impose numerous identities" on the protagonist "all of which he finds false and all of which he resists furiously" (Onley 1996, 137). Ultimately, Wright regards separation as an impossibility, since he "could never really leave" the culture in which he was made. Despite translocation from early influences, his burdened subjectivity is created by oppressions both lateral (between African-Americans) and hierarchical (between whites and blacks) the possibility of agency in intellectual resistance is a potential he locates only in transit, rather than in "expatriation," figured as the creation of new meaning in an utterly foreign location.[5] Though the originally published text of *Black Boy* isolates the critique of racism to the "Southern Night," it also attempts—counter to Jeff Karem's claim that the text "confine[s]" Wright—to show its author in transit and suspension, traveling from region to region. Narratively, the 1945 text does not end with Wright's bare claim that the South "was the terror from which [he] fled" (Wright 1993, 257). Instead, from the original text, the reader is led to believe that Wright's final meditation on place is chronologically placed *before* he arrives in the North:

> So, in leaving, I was taking a part of the South to transplant in alien soil, to see if it could grow differently, if it could drink of new and cool rains, bend in strange winds, respond to the warmth of other suns, and, perhaps, to bloom . . . And if that miracle ever happened, then I would know that there was yet hope in that southern swamp of despair and violence, that light could emerge even out of the blackest of the southern night. (Wright 1945, 228)

Despite its publication a full decade after Wright's migration, the narrative voice grammatically locates this longing before arrival in the North, using the future tense to suggest that the potential liberation of the North is, as yet, an unknown variable. This tactic simultaneously amends the text to meet readers' demands and undermines them. The hope of the North might lie ahead, but as yet, nothing is known.

Within Wright's memoir, the pangs of geography evacuate the space contained by the borders of the South, locating trauma psychically rather than writing it on the landscape, as in the displacement of Southern sunshine into chilly Chicago. For a text with a regional marker in its name, "Southern Night" is shockingly bereft of location. As a reader, I can never see outside of Wright's psychic landscape; no description quite meets the ocularity and sonic texture of Bigger Thomas fleeing through the ghetto, caged by the strobe lights and megaphones of a culture of racist surveillance in *Native Son*. Aside from the terrifying description of Uncle Hoskins leading young Richard into the Mississippi River, most of the landscape in the memoir emerges as anti-narrative. Perhaps it is not a coincidence that Wright's most visual rendering is of an event that he borrowed from Ralph Ellison's childhood, rather than recalled from his own; he seems to have no visual sense of his own traumas, and allows his to eye to reside more comfortably in fictions and secondhand accounts of violence (Adams 2003, 176). When Wright describes the South, it is limited to very lyrical brief sections that resist narrative acceleration, as in his early memories of "sweet magnolias . . . [and] the feeling of impersonal plenty" evoked by the sight of cotton bolls falling from the stalk (Ibid., 45). These brief sections suggest, through narrative aporia, environmental stasis of the Southern landscape removed from its history.

Despite the beauty of the Delta from which he fled, it is only geographically in Chicago and discursively in "The Horror and the Glory," the suppressed section of his memoir, that it is able for Wright to find the narrative "land" that he had been missing in Memphis, Mississippi, and Arkansas:

> A dim notion of what life meant to a Negro in American was coming to consciousness in me, not in terms of external events, lynchings, Jim Crowism, and the endless brutalities, but in terms of crossed-up feeling, of psyche [sic] pain. I sensed that Negro life as a sprawling land of unconscious suffering, and there were but few Negroes who knew the meaning of their lives, who could tell their story. (Wright 1993, 267)

One could reasonably contest Wright's troubling contempt for other African-Americans, his reversion to the earlier, controversial claim—one that was assailed by W. E. B. DuBois in a first-generation review—of the "absence of real kindness in Negroes . . . how lacking in genuine passion we were, how void of great hope, how timid our joy, how bare our traditions . . . and how shallow even was our despair" (Wright 1993, 37). DuBois, perhaps preferring a more respectable face for black resistance or simply resisting Wright's totalizing rhetoric, denies that a boy "born on a plantation, living in Elaine, Arkansas, and the slums of Memphis" can "know . . . the whole Negro race" (DuBois 2003, 34). This abnegation of a resistant self—so troubling to DuBois—provides a compelling thesis for Wright's memoir: in the absence of national citizenship and regional belonging, the African-American subject is a burdened citizen of an interior native land, policed by mechanisms of self-injury learned from racist violence.

Even the language of state authority takes on a metaphoric texture when Wright, newly-arrived in Chicago, meditates on the potential for African-American citizenship in the suppressed text of his memoir; he muses about distance from Mississippi, but with proximity to America. The passage, quoted below at length, plays constantly with the dual meanings of *state*; it is both the citizen's condition and the imposition that power places on the land and, thus, on the individual:

> From the Negroes' ultimate reactions to their trapped state a lesson can be learned about America's future. Negroes are told in a language they cannot possibly understand that their native land is not their own; and when they . . . try to assert a claim to their birthright, whites retaliate with terror, never pausing to consider the consequences should Negroes give up completely. They never dream that they would face a situation far more terrifying if they were confronted by Negroes who made no claims at all than by those who are buoyed by social aggressiveness. . . . No man can possibly be individually guilty of treason . . . an insurgent act is but a man's desperate answer to those who twist his environment so that he cannot fully share the spirit of his native land. Treason is a crime of the state. (Wright 1993, 302)

The trapped state is not simply the land within artificial lines of demarcation—borders and boundaries discussed in other chapters of this book as real-but-porous places—but also the alterity imposed on African-Americans who are simultaneously seen as autocthonous agrarians because of slave labor's attachment to the land, but distant aliens because of the historical denial of the privileges of birthright citizenship.

Because of affective investments in the land by the black citizen, Wright argues, the state is sustained. Though whites violently squash black resistance, Wright suggests that an abdication of citizenship on the part of African-Americans would result in a far more devastating consequence for white supremacy: the refusal to accept the law that offers the privileged subject total protection and the subaltern none. Thus, the struggle for civil rights is read as a quite conservative gesture (and one marginally protected by existing power structures), since it collaborates with the myth of the American Dream even as protestors declaim it; in his own Marxian formations, Wright might call this "false consciousness." His refusal of the conventional delineations of civil rights defines treason as the state's betrayal of the individual, and the ontology of black citizenship as perpetual treason. That statelessness or exile reads as a burdened subjectivity, where the individual must self-govern in response to both brutality and liberation. The state does not disappear because of violations of trust and belonging; it migrates within.

This textual sense of unrelenting self-governance is underscored by Wright's modes of narrating the violence of lynching. Though Wright affirms lynching as an everyday horror of life in the South, the lynching of Uncle Hoskins is neither witnessed nor described by the text. The omission literalizes one of the mechanisms of racial violence: the disappearance of the singular subject or wholesale clearance of community that defines black citizenship as an embodied national absence—or regional absence, considering widespread migration out of the South in Wright's lifetime. At the same time, readers witness a number of "practice lynchings," moments when young Wright exercises—but cannot exorcise—his own violence against family and community. In the most famous of these moments, the kitten shared by young Richard and his brother cries and meows in the presence of his father, who says "kill that damn thing!" Seeking revenge on the father he hates, Wright opts for a "literal acceptance of his word" which he enacts by making a noose and hanging the kitten from a nail in the wall (Wright 1945, 10–11). With explosive anger, Wright's mother demands that he identify with the kitten, imagine himself being hanged, and pray that the universe did not right itself by "snatch[ing] the breath of life from [him]" (Ibid., 14). This demand, combined with his guilt that his family "had . . . not fought back" against the men who lynched his uncle, and the existence of men who could "violate [his] life at will" provoke both fear and agentic violence from the narrator. Wright spares his reader none of this violence. When the memoir begins, one of these acts is already underway; at four-years-old, the author is lighting his mother's house on fire.

During the fire, Wright's narration suggests that lynching is embedded in interior psychic space; violence is rendered as a self-inflicted wound. "The fire soared to the ceiling and I trembled with fright," Wright recalls. "I was terrified; I wanted to scream but was afraid. . . . Smoke was choking me and the fire was licking at my face, making me gasp. . . . I had done something wrong, something which I could not hide or deny" (Ibid., 4–5). The scene portrays the lynched man, his body caged by fire; he is utterly alone, watching the fire destroy above and around him, waiting for it to destroy him as well. The child replaces the burned man, describing a common method of extermination that afflicted two of his era's most famous lynched men: Sam Hose (Newnan, Georgia, 1903) and Jessie Washington (Waco, Texas, 1916).[6] Though the narrator is trapped in an enflamed psychic space, he realizes that his action can impinge on the bodies of others as well as his own. Wright's perspective switches so that he is not only lynched, but also a witness to a lynching. "I saw the image of my grandmother lying helplessly upon her bed and there were yellow flames in her black hair," Wright writes, "Was my mother afire? Would my brother burn? Perhaps everybody in the house would burn!" (Ibid., 5). Though his own life was vulnerable to state and community violence, Wright regards himself as ultimately responsible for that vulnerability, thereby transferring power from the lynch mob to the black subject capable of punishment and violation on their behalf. Power, within Wright's conception of American racism, is available to African-Americans only in lateral oppression, rather than through an "essentialism that may have some strategic or interventionary value" (Fuss 1989, 20). As such, Wright is ambivalent toward family structures, even the matrilineal one in which he was raised. "Having accepted . . . the terms of racism," Elizabeth J. Ciner writes of Wright's representation of kinship, "family members become accomplices of and agents for the State" (Ciner 2006, 126). In the fire sequence of *Black Boy*, family is not just an agent of the state, but an agent of the lynch mob, the state-within-a-state. More troublingly for young Wright, whose narrative underscores his exceptional status in an intra-racial community, vulnerability to racist violence is posited as a form of self-injury.

Within these textual moments—all approved by Wright's publishers and the Book-of-the-Month Club—it is understandable that the author would have believed, as a young man, if not an adult, that the South was the seat of oppression best left without the nostalgia of Lot's wife gazing backwards at Sodom or Smith's migrant gazing backwards at the lynched man. But in Chicago, Wright learns the impossibility of freedom, articulated in his redefinitions of state and subject. Recalling his Memphis acquaintance Shorty who had "offered himself to be kicked by the white men," Wright acknowledges that "a kick was better than uncertainty" (Wright 1993, 265). Though he refused to "submit" while he lived in the South, the city of Chicago enforces the necessity of submission and provides grounds from which to sympathize with Shorty (Ibid., 266). Receiving a kick upon arrival in the North might, in Wright's words, make the African-American "feel at home" but it is not the South that provides that home; it is the interior space of subjection chartered by white racism, which provokes forms of intra-racial as well as interracial violence.

Three decades ago, Fred Hobson's *Tell About the South: The Southern Rage to Explain* (1983), delineated two perspectives from which Southerners write about the region they left behind. His two "parties"—the party of remembrance and defense and the party of shame and guilt—maintain their power within Southern Studies, as methods of organizing a canon as reliable as the *Out South*, *Up South*, and *Down South* distinctions, terms that many use to distinguish between the Southern frontier of the Mississippi hill country, Texas, and Arkansas (out); the mountains of Georgia, Kentucky, and the Carolinas (up); and the splendor and slumber of cities like Savannah, New Orleans, and Charleston (down). Revising his paradigms in 1998, Hobson wrote that Black Southerners were "at the *center* of that guilt" so could be of neither party, since they could not express ambivalence to racism or celebration of its hegemony (Hobson 1996, 81–82). Even if it were the case, as Fred Hobson argues, that the Southern canon is shaped by these ambivalences, then Wright's articulation does not unsettle the critical schema unless one imagines race as trumping all categories, impulses, and tendencies. The experience of racist oppression does not fill Wright with certainty about leaving the South behind; indeed, as he leaves it, he posits its oppression as provoking hunger for justice—a hunger that was ultimately unsated in Chicago, a hunger that he pursued in Paris and Africa until he died in 1960. Hobson might ask of Southern writers: remembrance and defense or shame and guilt? Wright answers the question with a question: *why not both?*

CHAPTER TWO

Beneath the Skin

George Schuyler and the Fantasy of Race

After the Flame

Rendered in vivid color language by a writer who aspired to be post-racial and post-black, Jean Toomer's "Portrait in Georgia" posits the flame of lynching as the consummating fire of sexual desire. The romantic description of the "white" woman—at once standing across a chasm and in intimate distance from a lyric poem's exegesis on the beauty of the beloved—suggests that the oppressive forces of racial differentiation structure the ability to look. The narrator can neither see beauty nor fantasize about touching it outside of the consequences of the racialized gaze; violent regulation simultaneously creates the desire to look and hinders the ability to touch:

> Hair—braided chestnut,
> Coiled like a lyncher's rope,
> Eyes—fagots,
> Lips—old scars, or the first red blisters,
> Breath—the last sweet scent of cane,
> And her slim body, white as the ash
> Of black flesh after flame. (27)

The woman's hair and eyes are the common weapons of lynching—fire and the noose—while her lips and body are lacerations and embers, the afterimage of that violence. The "after" of the final line is, as Jack Murnighan, editor of The Naughty Bits, an anthology of sex scenes in literature, has said, a one-word sex scene, the most common in the canon, just as "fade to black" is the most common sex scene in all of cinema (Murnighan 2001, 2). In

"Portrait in Georgia," the more intimate the corporeal appendage, the closer the poem comes to actuating violence; ultimately, it concludes by racially categorizing the woman. The placement of that word—white—is notably scrambled. Brown and red chronologically precede the lynching, but whiteness is created in its aftermath; the rituals of mob violence create and naturalize racial categories. As Walter Benn Michaels writes, "black flesh is burned in order to make a white body. What begins as a narrative of the attempt to preserve racial difference turns out to be a narrative of the origins of racial difference" (Benn Michaels 1995, 62).

Dwelling in and contesting the language of difference, the poem's five descriptions begin with the most immediately visual. Hair and eyes, gazed at from a distance, pose a limited threat of taboo crossing. They are, as Shakespeare's sonnet cycle attests, the organs of fantasy. Coloring both the poet's dreams and the racist's fixations, the eyes and hair are obsessively categorized; their color is so immediately visible and quantifiable that the presumptive absence of difference provokes the sense, in the language of racism, that all people of color look alike. As the poem progresses, the voice moves across the flesh to the interior space of the penetrable body: the consuming open mouth of kissing and oral sex, the panting breath that emerges from it in the moment of orgasm, and the pallor of nudity too often covered by clothing. Grafted onto the objective correlative of the woman's body are two timelines—the progressive narrative of sexual fulfillment and the escalating sequence of bodily violations—that correspond to fantasy and reality. When these chronologies touch, the reader is left with the flesh: transformed by desire in one narrative and violence in the other, resulting in an uncomfortable parallel between the two.

This lyric theorization of fantasy removes the potential for resistance to the ritual scripts of mob violence within its psychic gates. Using Toomer's poem as a departure point, I explore the character of fantasy under white supremacy through the archive of psychoanalysis and racial science, as well as George Schuyler's *Black No More*—a 1931 novel of literal race-crossing—in which America is transformed from a nation of color variation to monolithic whiteness by a machine that uses electrical currents to strip away racial difference. Schuyler, at once an anti-essentialist racial theorist and ardent political conservative, was a dedicated anti-Communist, John Bircher, enemy of the Civil Rights Movement, and supporter of Richard Nixon. Indeed, Schuyler has "been identified as perhaps the most politically conservative black man in American history" whose theorization of race reveals symmetry between radical constructivism and conservative "color-blindness" (Tucker 1997, 138).

Though a more complete account of Schuyler's absence from the canon would treat his long career, which includes an oeuvre with a page length exceeding that of Charles Dickens's, I focus on an under-explored motif in an under-theorized novel, *Black No More* (Williams 1993, xi). Within the universe of the novel, racial fantasy is an entry to, rather than departure from, racial violence. From protagonist Max's initial desire for the metaphoric race crossing of miscegenation to his visit to Black No More Enterprises to literally cross, to the final scenes of the lynching of putative whites in blackface, the novel suggests that no utopia awaits the race traitor. Even in a world of universally "pork-colored skin," traversing racial boundaries ensures violent recrimination. In the actuation of violence, the limits of fantasy as a genre and space of subversion are revealed: desires for both sexual consummation and political reconciliation are subsumed by the flames of lynching. Under white supremacy, there is no private space, not even our headspace. There is nothing more real than fantasy; "nothing more public than privacy" (Berlant and Warner 2005, 187).

Within the novel and the realpolitik of Schuyler's America the most commodified, violable form of privacy was fantasy, a psychic phenomenon that psychoanalysts since Freud have linked to the construction of race. In *The Interpretation of Dreams*, his most extended treatment of the unconscious processes of wish-fulfillment, Freud posits the psychic phenomenon of fantasy as a place of passing and transformation, of visual sameness and interior differentiation:

> On the one hand, [phantasies] are highly organized, free from self-contradiction, have made use of every acquisition of the [conscious] system and would hardly be distinguished in our judgment from the formations of that system. On the other hand they are unconscious and are incapable of becoming conscious. Thus *qualitatively* they belong to the [preconscious] system, but *factually* to the [unconscious]. We may compare them with individuals of mixed race who, taken all round, resemble white men, but who betray their colored descent by some striking feature or other, and on that account are excluded from society and enjoy none of the privileges of white people. (Freud 1957, 191)

The vacillation between conscious and unconscious processes that characterizes fantasy's psychoanalytic category reveals the tension between what is seen and unseen. Like the striking feature—either physical or psychic—that reveals race, the fantastic shift from conscious to unconscious hinders the subject's ability to "pass," forcibly placing him or her in one definitive category, and marking what was once (safely) under erasure. Freud's lapse into racializing discourse suggests a troubling essentialism. Race, even when invisible, is vestigial and ready to be revealed without intention or will.

To engage with Freud's analogy, it seems that—like the child of two ostensibly white people who "reverts to form" and is born with dermal markers of another racial group—hidden racial identity stands at the threshold of revelation, teasing the passing subject with the possibility of exposure. The return of the repressed, Freud suggests, reveals the essence of the subject as something unseen yet accessible, hidden but foundational. Yet, just as Freud's famous injunction that "biology is destiny" can be read as *either* an essentialist or constructivist claim, depending upon whether or not the reader places faith in the possibility of an objectively biological account of sex and gender, this formulation can be shifted, too. For, if the organs of sensation reveal a fictive, shifting race that can be overturned with the revelation of the "striking feature" of essence, than no acquisition of racial identity is trustworthy.

Yet, the theorization of race that elucidates Freud's claim is an analogy for rather than definition of fantasy. Fantasy—most closely aligned with the "striking feature" of Freud's analogy—stands at the threshold between conscious and unconscious, between perception and actuality. Though located in the unconscious spaces of human perception, race can pass into the conscious world against the subject's will, resulting in both pleasure and regulation. Like race itself, fantasy is a thought construct with material consequences, residing in the interstices between the real and phantasmatic—between oppression and the pernicious ideology that underpins it. It is precisely in these liminal spaces—between the conscious and the unconscious, between hiding and display—that race resides in George Schuyler's *Black No More*. Within Schuyler's not-so-alternate universe—which I call the "Schuyler-verse"—every standard by which race can be assessed is deemed inadequate. Both facial features and dialects are dismissed by *Black No More* inventor Junius Crookman, who locates the broad lips and nose of the minstrel phenotype in "so-called Caucasian" cultures of the Mediterranean and Ireland and argues for the "darky dialect" as a marker of class, not race (Schuyler 1999, 14–15). The violent necessities of white supremacy, responding to the instability of race, locate it by tearing into the interior of black bodies in search of essence, hoping to mark the Freudian seen and unseen as fixed, biological imprints.

The "Science" in Science Fiction

Since the closely contemporary events of Octavia Butler's 1995 MacArthur Genius Grant and the publication of Sheree Thomas's *Dark Matter: A Collection of Speculative Fiction From the African Diaspora* (2000), interest in fantasy and science fiction by writers of color has grown. It is in this milieu that George Schuyler was rediscovered and that his work has been critiqued. Though other readings of Schuyler—particularly essays by Stacy Morgan and Jane Kuenz—have treated his relationship with science, I stake a different position by connecting the languages of science and psychoanalysis within the novel. Moreover, I am less compelled by the ethnological language of citizenship that Kuenz locates as a fundamental part of racial science (cf. arguments by eugenicists Lothrop Stoddard and Madison Grant that democracy was impossible for people of color, but part of a racial patrimony for whites) or the reproductive regulation described by Morgan than I am by science's quest for racial essence beyond the haptic layer of color and pigment (Kuenz 1997, 180; Morgan 1999). Indeed, my reading of Schuyler locates the quest for racial essence within the violent penetrations of the body associated with lynching rituals. Focusing on fantasies of racial difference and their relationship to scientific discourses of race, I draw primarily on the conversation between Jeffrey A. Tucker's "Can Science Succeed Where the Civil War Failed? George S. Schuyler and Race" (1997) and Sharon DeGraw's *The Subject of Race in American Science Fiction* (2007) to consider definitions of both science and rationality. These two studies offer radically oppositional frameworks in which to locate Schuyler's investments in scientific empiricism and racial essentialism.

Writing at the moment of black conservatism's resurgence with the fame of writers Thomas Sowell and Shelby Steele, as well as the political successes of Supreme Court Justice Clarence Thomas and 1996 Republican primary candidate Alan Keyes, Jeffrey Tucker locates Schuyler's constructivist critique within his conservative political praxis—which called, much like late-1990s backlash conservatism, for a color-blind or color-neutral society. The assertion that race is a "socially constructed illusion," Tucker writes, was used to "critique black race leaders as often as white supremacists"; indeed, this rhetorical gesture is typical of conservative arguments against civil rights which have, since the nineteenth century, posited parity between racist violence and "liberal" but regulatory antiracist paternalism (Tucker 1997, 137). The idealized color blindness of Schuyler's critique provides him with the language of conservative reversal: the Klan is paired with the NAACP, while racist ethnologists are seen as trafficking in the same historical fictions as Garveyite celebrations of Africa.

Rather than placing Schuyler in conversation with either contemporary politics or late millennial backlash conservatism, DeGraw responds to Tucker's political genealogy with accusations of bias, presentism, misreading, and recherché Afrocentrism (DeGraw 2007, 76). Preferring to place Schuyler in conversation with contemporaries that she reads as radical constructivists, like W. E. B. DuBois, Franz Boas, and Franz Fanon, she celebrates Schuyler as a "generic and rhetorical pioneer" of science fiction who imagined race as both a "vehicle for individual expression" and a "cultural construction" (Ibid., 102–104). Placing Schuyler in the company of Boas (whose profession he loathed), DuBois (whose politics he hated), and Fanon (whose national liberationist project he shared as a young socialist, but rejected as a conservative), requires a significant recalibration of Schuyler's claims to align them with the contemporary paradigm of racial constructivism.[1] DeGraw's representations of Schuyler's positions suffer from a determined refusal to place him within a conservative political genealogy whose contemporary ramifications are unpalatable. Intent on finding what is subversive about Schuyler's work, she elides much that is reactionary.

I differ from both Tucker and DeGraw in the tendency to call Schuyler a constructivist. Though many "ists"—journalist, satirist, individualist—should punctuate any treatment of George Schuyler, constructivist is simply not one of them. In order to align with the paradigms of a culturally-based racial lineage, Schuyler would have had to believe that an African-American culture existed at all. As his often-anthologized essay "The Negro-Art Hokum" evinces, he believed black culture to be a phantasm:

> True, from dark-skinned sources have come those slave songs based on Protestant hymns and Biblical texts known as the spirituals, work songs, and secular songs of sorrow and tough luck known as the blues, that outgrowth of rag-time known as jazz (in the development of which whites have assisted), and the Charleston, an eccentric dance invented by the gamins around the public marketplace in Charleston, S.C. No one can or does deny this. But these are contributions of a caste in a certain section of the country. They are foreign to Northern Negroes, West Indian Negroes, and African Negroes. They are no more expressive or characteristic of the Negro race than the music

and dancing of the Appalachian highlanders or the Dalmatian peasantry are expressive or characteristic of the Caucasian race. (Schuyler 1995, 310)

Locating authentic black art in the "numerous black nations of Africa" and uniquely African-American music and dancing in Southern culture, Schuyler "declares the primacy of nation over race in determining black American cultural identity" while "uncritically posit[ing] nationality as the defining matrix of identity" (Ferguson 2005, 184: Morgan 1999, 334). Even in this formation, culture is not entirely quantifiable to particular land masses or borders; the history of slavery plays a foundational role in determining cultural forms. Emerging from the work songs of slavery and styles of worship derived from plantation syncretism, the African-American musical tradition is, according to Schuyler, one he can neither own nor appropriate, because he theorizes culture as "shaped by experience and historical conditions rather than organic or spiritual 'racial' inheritance" (Hutchinson 1995, 70).

Raised in Providence, Rhode Island and Syracuse, New York by a family that boasted of its long lineage as free people of color, Schuyler foreclosed identification with cultural forms that sprung from the history and geographies of the plantation experience (Schuyler 1966, 3–4). He wrote of the sole Southern connection of his childhood—his stepfather, who migrated from Georgia to central New York—with disgust at a stocky body, light skin, and glass eye to which Schuyler's own dark skin and able body presumably provided an opposite (Ferguson 2005, 10). Leaving central New York for the city, he did not identify with the alternative forms of black culture found in Harlem. Emerging from neither the South nor the city, Schuyler superimposed the borders of black culture onto the geographical borders into which African-Americans have been segregated, offering constructivism unevenly paired with a discomfiting sense of oppression as an optional condition for the oppressed.

The migrations of his youth from Providence, Rhode Island to Syracuse, New York, and finally New York City—locations he touted as "formative"—were not his only abodes. Though he wrote of his military service (1917–1918) often and identified himself as a patriot, his relationship to the nation was not uncomplicated. While in the military, he encountered a Greek immigrant bootblack who refused to "shine a 'nigger's' shoes." Deciding that he would be a "son-of-a-bitch" if he "serve[d] this goddamn country any longer," Schuyler deserted. A crosscountry trek took him from Des Moines, Iowa to Chicago and finally, to San Diego, where he turned himself over to the authorities. He was sentenced to five years' imprisonment on Governor's Island, New York. Though he never wrote about this incident and kept the secret through his long public life, we should add prison to the list of locations that formed his political consciousness and, perhaps, the anger that characterizes his early writings (Ibid., 12–13). Perhaps the reticence to reveal the secret emerges from both his politics and what Ann Rayson reads as Schuyler's aesthetic and political refusal to engage in the "confessional" genres of contemporaneous black protest literature (Rayson 1978, 102–106).

In his background and schema, if not his claims, we might align him with W. E. B. DuBois, the scion of free black people from Great Barrington, Massachusetts, whose formative intellectual experiences took place in Berlin. Responding to his own spatial isolation from the iconic locations of black culture, DuBois's "double consciousness" distinguishes between the oppositional impulses of race and nation that govern black subjectivity. DuBois wrote, "One ever feel his two-ness—an American, a Negro—two souls, two thoughts, two unreconciled strivings; two warring ideals in one dark body" (DuBois 1999, 11). For DuBois, this two-ness gave African-Americans the curse and gift of double consciousness; Schuyler resolved the conflict by choosing to no longer name race, the barrier to seamless, privileged citizenship in a herrenvolk democracy, as second sight.[2]

Without culture as a receptacle in which to place concerns, cohesion, and conditions emerging from what he calls "color" rather than race, it might seem that Schuyler is adrift in modern theoretical debates about race, but I would suggest that he has one—if only one—descendant. If Schuyler has a contemporary intellectual heir, it is literary critic Walter Benn Michaels, who believes that race is not culture or heritage, but a *mistake* that is fraught with devastating political consequences. To align race with culture, Benn Michaels has argued, is to perpetuate that error by asserting that culture can be located in bodies whose affinities—jazz or Mozart, Emerson or Douglass—are assumed based on biologically-determined phenotypes. Such a claim does not ignore the legacy of race as an organizing structure in American culture:

> We might think that the reality of race consists in the fact that we live in a world that is still organized along racial lines. And the point of our new knowledge—the knowledge that there are no biological races—would be to undo the consequences of our old ignorance, to produce a world in which race was *not* a compelling reality. (Benn Michaels 1997, 131)

Decades before Benn Michaels, Schuyler confidently asserted that race is a "superstition," bound in culture only insofar as culture perpetuates a falsehood, one that, once disproven, will create a society where the only "color line" is a perceptual assessment of people's varying skin colors (Schuyler 1966, 352). But this is not to say that either Benn Michaels or Schuyler doubt that racism exists; to believe that race is a logical error and pernicious political mistake in fact requires the violence of racism to draw its polemical force. In making this claim, I fundamentally agree with Jeffrey A. Tucker's definition of racism as "more than just the imposition of unfair difference" because prejudice includes the "unfair disregard of constitutive differences" (Tucker 1997, 148). The differences are located in the linkage between those two definitions, as a critic of civil rights might refuse to acknowledge the constitutive difference imposed by unfairness itself—arguing, as have many opponents of affirmative action, that people of color no longer face racism, but instead wield hegemonic power within the economic sphere.

In her own polemic, DeGraw differs not only in the contexts in which she places Schuyler, but also in her assessments of his relationship to science. For Tucker, the assertion that race is a fiction fails to adequately consider the lived experiences of people of color because of its fixation on "rational, scientific, and supposedly nonpartisan objectivity" in lieu of black subjectivities and lifeways (Ibid., 137). DeGraw, on the other hand, claims that, while Schuyler believed in the progressive trinity of rationality, technology, and progress, he regarded science as ample ground for satire and critique, as demonstrated in the connections between "science and capitalism [as well as] science and social norms" that are vividly drawn in *Black No More* (DeGraw 2007, 86). Though DeGraw consistently places herself in opposition to Tucker, these are not claims that I see as mutually exclusive; indeed, American racial science is nothing if not *bad* science. A rationalist of Schuyler's temperament could look at its findings and yearn for both the scientific method and the satirist's pen.

Modern as he was, Schuyler differentiated between science and reason. Reason and rhetoric, the only tools he believed could be used to overturn the fiction of race, were ones he deployed against racial science.[3] Punning on the relationship of racial science to the science fiction genre, Gregory Rutledge argues that "the advent of and devotion to science . . . ha[d] been used, as a *science fiction* . . . to justify slavery and the inferiority of Blacks" (Rutledge 2001, 241). Aligning science with the Jeffersonian legacy of racial categorization in eugenics and ethnology, Schuyler connects the pseudoscientific rhetoric of arguing for race's hidden essence to the vicious practice of lynching. Both the quest for racial origins and the violence that quest necessitates require grounding in another modernist discourse: the psychoanalytic conception of fantasy. Lynching and the ideology that underpinned it draw their violence from fantasies of difference that haunt the dreams of black protagonist Max Disher and the waking hours of the novel's most vicious racists. Locating his first lynching in Max Disher's private dreamscape and his second in the public space of Happy Hill, Mississippi, Schuyler evinces the transversability of the private space of a subject impinged upon by racism. Just as the body could be penetrated by racial violence, so too could the mind be invaded by white supremacy. The dream theaters of real lynching victims—those located outside of Schuyler's narrative—were similarly permeable.

Dream Theaters

In October 1900, Melby Dotson boarded a train heading from West Baton Rouge Parish to New Orleans. He fell asleep, but the interior space of his dream was not a peaceful place. Three months earlier, Robert Charles had been killed by the New Orleans police after shooting two officers, then fleeing for a three-day spree of violence in which he shot twenty-eight more people (Gussow 2002). The panic over Charles's crimes led to his near-legendary status as the "bad nigger" and martyr of New Orleans (Hair 1976, xiv), as well as the cultural memory of the insurrectionary black radical in African-American popular texts like Mamie Smith's "Crazy Blues," N.W.A.'s "Fuck Tha Police," and, of course, Ice T and Body Count's "Cop Killer" (Gussow 2002, 162).

Since the death of Robert Charles in New Orleans, Melby Dotson had been plagued by "alcoholic nightmares that he was being lynched" (Hair 1976, 184–85). He dreamed that a mob surrounded him, tearing at his clothes and beating him. To smother his cries that he was innocent of a crime his dream space did not reveal, the imagined mob tightened a noose around his neck (Dray 2002, 17). Passing Dotson's restless body, still located in the exterior space of the train, the white Pullman porter demanded that, for the comfort of other passengers, he stop weeping. Springing from the interior world to the exterior, Dotson awoke and, believing the porter to be one of the dreamed-of mob, drew his revolver and fired. Dotson was held for a day in jail at Port Allen, Louisiana where, after another presumably restless sleep, he was dragged from his cell by a lynch mob and hanged from a telegraph pole, revealing the permeability of his psyche. Just as people of color had no rights a white man need respect, they had no impulses that Jim Crow America would not regulate. Resistance, desire, fear: all were harnessed as fuel for lynching's fire.

Seven years after Dotson's dream came true, a young woman felt her body encroached upon, in a dream drawn in vivid black and white. *The Atlanta Constitution* wrote on September 6, 1906:

> Crazed with a frenzy of fright at the dream that a negro was trying to kill her, Miss Annie Morgan was overcome with an attack of heart trouble and died within a few minutes. Crying out in her fright, Miss Morgan ran out of her room shouting, "A big negro is standing over my bed trying to kill me with a knife," then she sank to the floor, unconscious. (Dray 2002, 164)

The headline above the story read, "Negro, Seen in a Dream, Causes Death of Girl." Despite the evident fictions at play both in her dream and the account of it, Atlanta citizens could not hazard the risk of politically empowered African-Americans haunting the dreams of white Southern women; sixteen days later, after an incendiary political address by Populist Williams Jennings Bryan, a white mob tore through the city, attempting to clear it of its large African-American population. Thirty black men were murdered, hundreds were injured, and thousands fled the inhospitable city.[4] Though the racial clearance was unsuccessful in Atlanta, over the next ten years, six bordering North Georgia counties—Forsyth, Towns, Union, Dawson, Fannin, and Gilmer—became "sundown" or all-white communities (Loewen 2006, 178).

If I can speak of two fin de siècle newspaper stories in the language of literary analysis, these two dreams—Dotson's and Morgan's—constitute, if not a trope, than at least a tendency of white supremacy to police the interior space of marginal subjects—both racially marked subjects like Dotson and sexually guarded ones like Morgan—for fear of retributive violence against white supremacy and interracial sexual desire. As Dora Apel argues, these two contested spaces—the black man's libido and the white woman's body—are intimately linked. Lynchings "predicated on the threat of [black male] sexuality" often had, as either accusers or scapegoats, hysterically fearful or irredeemably lustful white women:

> The hysteria of the white woman is the implicit counterpart to the danger of the hypersexed black male. . . . The black male's

proximity to the white woman becomes an assault, not on her person but on her senses, causing irresistible feelings of panic, frenzy, and fear. . . . Thus the position of the white male as protector and defender of the helpless white woman is legitimated. According to racialized sexual codes, the white woman's hysterical body is integrated back into the social body while the hypersexed black body is scourged and destroyed as inimical to the social body. At stake is the silence about and denial of interracial desire and sexuality, especially between black men and white women. (Apel and Smith 2007, 57)

Following this logic, one might read the racialized violence of the Atlanta riot as not just a message to African-Americans about political agitation and ambition, but also to white women about the cost of citizenship. Indeed, in a time when even privileged white women had incomplete access to the public sphere and democratic citizenship, the spectacle of riots and lynchings—which promised protection of their virtue—had the power to both produce and constrain white women's encroachments into public space as well as their free and desirous sexual object choice. Thus, they were incomplete lynch mob citizens: present and absent, integrated and apart.

The Psychic Investment in Whiteness

The limits of psychoanalysis as a method of inquiry into racial oppression have been revealed by critics like Hortense Spillers and Jacquelyn Goldsby, whose masterful *Spectacular Secrets: Lynching in American Life and Culture*, overturns the assignation of the primitive, a privileged term of psychoanalysis, in explorations of racial violence. She replaces primitivism with modernity and technology, since these conditions were ones to which lynch mobs aspired when they used electric lights, stereoscopes, nascent audiovisual techniques, and transportation technologies to both enact and record lynching. Even when psychoanalysis has touched on social issues—as in Joel Kovel's *White Racism: A Psychohistory*—it has often tread dangerously close to the broad sweeps of pseudoscience. Consider Kovel's examination of the relationship between primal fear and colonizing, enslaving racism:

> People of all cultures have always been afraid of darkness. Children certainly are, and doubtless they have been since Paleolithic

times. What has distinguished the West from other cultures is that these elementary issues, without losing their infantile core, have taken on a fantastic elaboration: They have been employed systematically and organically in the generation of *power*. (Kovel 1984, 95)

The racism of Kovel's claim emerges in the association of dermal variation with the threatening, primal darkness outside the openings of Paleolithic caves. Though it posits itself as an attack on racism, its naturalization of prejudice functions as its defense, since naturalness is so often the "gold standard" of political discourse (Laqueur 1990, 155). Few contemporary psychoanalysts would make Kovel's cognitive leap; yet, the contemporary dogma of evolutionary psychology that posits human behaviors as eternally emerging from evolutionary sources does little credit to the complexity of motive, intention, and desire. The evolutionary psychological turn—though not so far removed from the invented narratives of Paleolithic caves or Freud's primitive horde in *Totem and Taboo*—yearns to reduce the complexity of human emotion and responds to the invisibility of intention within the psychoanalytic paradigm by making the unknowable visible.

Rather than acknowledge the difficulty of knowing what drives human emotion, evolutionary psychologists reduce it to the simplest possibilities: reproductive desire, primal fear. If, as evolutionary psychologists Leda Cosmides and John Tooby argue, "our modern skulls house a Stone Age mind," than social conditions like sexual and racial violence—as well as logics of alterity—become part of the gold standard of human behavior valorized and rationalized by conceptions of the natural (Cosmides and Tooby 1997). Indeed, one might productively practice such a rationalization with regards to race: differences in pigmentation evolved to mark and separate strangers to protect the racially monolithic primitive horde against resource-poaching by other nomadic groups. Aversive racism is, thus, an evolutionary adaptation. Is this claim persuasive? Perhaps. Is it intellectually sound? Emphatically not.

In the early part of the twentieth century, the progenitors of contemporary evolutionary psychologists attempted to explain what they saw as the innate desire of African-Americans to desire white woman and of white men to police that desire, in evolutionary terms, arguing that "the lower races . . . experience an unusual . . . sexual desire for members of the higher races because they dimly and instinctively realize that the improvement of their own race" results from breeding upward on the hierarchical ladder of race (Gossett 1997, 166). Or, in the words of Social Darwinist Lester F. Ward, who provided an evolutionary explanation of lynching in the 1930s:

> Although the enraged citizens who pursue, capture, and 'lynch' the offender do not know any more than their victim that they are impelled to do so by the biological law of race preservation, still it is this unconscious imperative, far more than the supposed sense of outraged decency, that impels them to the performance of a much greater and more savage 'crime' than the poor wretch has committed. (Ward, quoted in Gossett 1997, 166)

Though Ward's sentiments—another putative critique of racism that rhetorically gestures toward its inherent nature—might seem alien to contemporary evolutionary psychologists, the "just-so stories" they provide in lieu of scientific evidence are not so unlike his. When confronted with their justifications of discourses of alterity that have rationalized inequality and violence, Leda Cosmides and John Tooby simply bemoan "political correctness," the bogeyman of the political right that serves as a bulwark for reactionary logics against critique (Cosmides and Tooby 1997).

If these attempts to locate the origins of racism and racial violence have any intellectual tradition in American culture, they begin with the attempts to find an origin of race itself. Not content with the apparent ocular differences in skin color—perhaps because variations in skin color are so evidently ordinal, rather than typological—writers since Thomas Jefferson have attempted to find racial difference *beneath* the skin.

> Besides those of color, figure, and hair, there are other physical distinctions proving a difference of race. They have less hair on the face and body. They secrete less by the kidneys, and more by the glands of the skin, which gives them a very strong and disagreeable odor. This greater degree of transpiration renders them more tolerant of heat, and less so of cold, than the whites. (Jefferson 2002, 176)

Jefferson's catalog vacillates between the apparent and the hidden: from color to hair to kidneys to skin to glands to odor to feeling, bridging the distance between what he can see (skin) and what only the anatomist could (the kidneys) as well as what he could attest to (odor) and what only the slave could (tolerance of temperature). These vacillations are consistent with the ocular problematic of slavery. As Jefferson, the father of mixed-race slaves, knew, the intimate oppression of slavery made it difficult to "ascertain 'true' racial identity by eye alone" as biracial and triracial generations were made in plantation breeding camps (Smith 2006, 5). In the absence of table and predictable skin color, historian Mark M. Smith argues, a racist society found increasingly invisible means of locating race, whether by linking color difference to exposure to leprosy in Africa as physician Benjamin Rush did, or to the alleged presence of more nerve synapses and harder bones in Africans as argued by physician and Confederate statesman, Samuel Cartwright, or acts of separate divine creation posited by ethnologists, Samuel George Morton and Josiah Nott.

Quite apart from these pseudoscientific luminaries, white slaveowners had intimate contact with black slaves, whose difference they located apart from color—naming odor, haptic texture and toughness, and sensual acuity as aspects of racial difference. Mistaking difference for essence, they argued for alterity, a condition that was created in and punished by the regulatory violence of lynching after Reconstruction. By the heyday of lynching, whites with aspirations to scientific empiricism and an interest in testing the depths of racial difference had skin to flay, bones to collect, and pain to observe. The essence of difference was established not just by mob citizenship, but also in the increasingly unrecognizable flesh and bone of the mutilated, lynched body. Lynchings and the photographic artifacts that emerged from their spectacles "do . . . ideological labor by representing white people to themselves as whole, living . . . bodies, constituted as such by their opposition to dismembered, dead, black . . . bodies" Jones 1995, 132). Chasing the fantasy of essence, white hands tore into black bodies to expose their difference, a scene of violence with which George Schuyler concludes *Black No More*.

Unlike the planters of antebellum America or the eugenicists of Reconstruction, white supremacists of the Schuylerverse admit race's ontological slipperiness, though they do so with fear in their hearts. "Day by day," argues the fictional *Tallahassee Announcer*, "we see the color line which we have so laboriously established being rapidly destroyed. . . . Will the proud white men of the Southland so forget their traditions as to remain idle while this devilish work is going on" (Schuyler 1999, 32)? Racial partisans, though arguing for the necessity of segregation, acknowledge that the line is an arbitrary one, smitheried into being by centuries of caste-based separation, Jim Crow legislation, and racist agitation. Consequently, race is imagined as the product of labor that *produces*, rather than *requires*, belief in difference.

Racist ideology shares space with the public sphere, enfolding it like rings of concentric circles.

In the first chapter of *Black No More*, the sexual fantasies of protagonist Max Disher reveal the permeability of public and private space, the eroded boundary between the body and the state. Though the setting—a raucous Harlem nightclub—is one thousand miles away from Toomer's pastoral "Portrait in Georgia," Schuyler's language demonstrates a similar fixation on color. Max Disher is "smooth coffee-brown," but also "damnably blue"—a phrase I read as playful idiom for too dark in complexion—because his "yallah" girlfriend has left him among "the crowds of white and black folk" (Ibid., 5). With Bunny Brown, his friend and former comrade-in-arms from the European front of World War I, Max watches "a black-faced comedian . . . three chocolate . . . dancers . . . and an octette of . . . mulatto chorines" onstage at the Honky Tonk Club (Ibid., 7). They watch as a prismatic continuum of "black" skin evinces Schuyler's claim—as articulated in his 1926 essay "The Negro-Art Hokum"—that black is not a stable category, but a fiction imposed upon a broad spectrum of both color and opinion.

In the black counterpublic sphere of Harlem, the "subordinate status" of the location "form[s] and transform[s]" perceptual racial identity, bringing under contestation the race of Helen Givens, whose appearance in the nightclub interrupts Max's reverie (Warner 2005, 121).[5] Helen, "tall, slim titian-haired girl who had seemingly stepped from heaven or the front cover of a magazine," enters the club with a group of friends and immediately inflames Max's desire (Schuyler 1999, 5). Her hair, a mixture of both red and blonde, is an allegedly stable, biological signifier of whiteness that fails, since her race cannot be visually determined at a distance. Max and Bunny ardently debate whether she is a "cracker" or a "high yallah;" she is placed reliably into the former category only when she rejects Max's request to dance with the horrified interjection: "I never dance with niggers!" Returning to Bunny's side, Max now *knows* she is a "cracker"; the force of her rejection is the best evidence because it shores up the boundary between the races. The fiction of race emerges not in biology or ocularity, but in regulations of interracial intimacy. The hazard of fluid sexual boundaries between racial categories is revealed only when Max returns home, falls asleep, and dreams of Helen:

> Dreamed of dancing with her, dining with her, motoring with her, sitting beside her on a golden throne while millions of manacled

white slaves prostrated themselves before him. Then there was a nightmare of grim, gray men with shotguns, baying hounds, and a heap of gasoline-soaked faggots and a screeching, fanatical mob.

  He awoke covered with perspiration. His telephone was ringing and the late morning sunshine was streaming in his room. He leaped from bed and lifted the receiver. (Schuyler 1999, 9)

Just as Melby Dotson's nightmare of the mob preceded his lynching, Max's dream is interrupted by the imposition of white power and, indeed, whiteness. Bunny's call wakes him, disrupting Max's dream so that he can share a newspaper story about Black No More, Junius Crookman's race-erasing treatment that turns both friends white and propels the narrative down to Atlanta—Helen Givens's home city—where a blanched Disher joins a racist paramilitary group, meets Helen again, and marries her in an incomplete fulfillment of his fantasy.

But even before Bunny's narrative imposition and Crookman's racial alteration, the psychic space of Max's fantasy about Helen offers no consummation; sex is thwarted by the threat of lynching. Despite the "dark, satanic cast" with which Schuyler characterizes Max's face and sexual desires, the dream is tellingly sexless. A triptych of dancing, dining, and motoring fills his dream space; even in the most fantastic image, of throned Max and Helen surrounded by white slaves, only the slaves are supine. The couple is seated—clothes on, legs together. But even the chaste self-denial of his fantasy does not save Max from the lynch mob. They storm into his dream, their gray flesh a literal barrier between black and white, and burn him alive. Outside of his dream space, Disher avoids Dotson's fate at the hands of the mob, but he does so only by crossing into whiteness, an act of self-negation so complete that he becomes a leading theorist of black biological inferiority in Atlanta's Knights of Nordica, a Klan-like organization of which Helen's father is the leader. Self-blanching requires suicidal violence.

For Schuyler, the pursuit of whiteness within one's own body is an act of violence, but the pursuit of it in another person's body—like that of his white Southern wife, Josephine Cogdell—was the mechanism of sexual desire and pleasure by which superior children, those with so-called "hybrid vigor," were produced (Talalay 1995, 56). Shades of gray are dampeners of sexual pleasure in Max's racial taxonomy, a requirement for desire that Schuyler seems to have shared. Erotic plenty emerges not in lenticular displacement of dermal difference, but in imbrications of black and white, and penetrations of black *into* white. Schulyer biographer Jeffrey B. Ferguson writes of this psychic phenomenon:

> Difference stands as the center of what it means to desire. Max conflates racial otherness with all of his deepest wants, especially his craving for sex and superordinance. [His] totalizing relationship to race dictates a certain obsessive desire and yet at the same time appears to defeat the essential differentiation on which desire depends. (Ferguson 2005, 231)

That obsessive relationship creates libidinal and narrative continuity for Max's companion Bunny. Once he has whitened, he pursues black women with the same ardor he once pursued light-skinned mulattoes. For two men who fetishized difference, becoming white inspires a new longing, as evidenced in Max's "envious" glance at his friend at the revelation that his lover is a "sweet Georgia brown" in metameric contrast to Bunny's newly-white skin (156). When Disher dreams of traversing these racial boundaries, differences between the character's biography and Schuyler's become evident; Max imagines attraction as unsated without a fundamental alteration of his body that negates the author's figurations of desire.

In his restless bed, Disher encounters what Slavoj Zizek has called "the truth of desire, the knowledge of fantasy" (Zizek 1997, 35). Fantasy, which Zizek reads as radically ambiguous when it comes into contact with "ideological space," performs two functions for the desirous subject, whose fantasy "form[s] an identity" that will make him an object of desire rather than its subject. Within the dream space, fantasy "closes the actual span of choices . . . [and] maintains the false opening" of agency (Zizek 1997, 29). The functions of fantasy enable Max's assimilative drive into white supremacist culture and ideology. The "empty gesture" of becoming white maintains the illusion of choice, treating the coerced choice as real and agentic despite the violence that accompanies it both within Black No More Enterprises and outside of it, where racialized bodies are still subject to specularized violence. Even as the violence promised by fantasy closes Max's span of choices, his desire for whiteness maintains the false opening of assimilation and disappearance into spectral white normativity. The belief in agentic action and the coercion that pushes the subject toward a predetermined choice of racial transformation are autocatalysts for Max Disher's libidinal investments in whiteness.

Like lynching itself, the technology of whiteness that governs Max's transformation is intensely public—flocked by crowds, with a blinking neon sign advertising the possibilities within—and yet, the act of transformation is judiciously hidden by Crookman, a veiling with which the narrative collaborates. When asked by reporters how Black No More works, Crookman glibly says that he "cannot divulge the secret." Certainly both the media and the customers are kept ignorant about the process, which is analogized to violence and the new technologies of both medicine and legal execution, suggesting a parallel between the two. Inside Crookman's machine of "wires and straps, levers and bars," Disher meets his lynchers in a "formidable apparatus [that] resembled a cross between a dentist's chair and an electric chair" (Schuyler 1999, 16). Gazing at the horrible machine, he changes his mind—even "gasping with fright"—and "would have made for the door," but he is detained by "two husky attendants" who strip him naked and bind him to a chair, where he must do violence to "black" in order to live (Ibid., 17). The chapter breaks with the men restraining him, forcing him into whiteness. When the next chapter begins, the audience is immersed in the "after"; there is no present tense to the act of violence, only Max musing that he is "thankful that he had survived the ordeal" (Ibid., 18). The publicness and violence of this racial transformation underscore the relationship between legal execution, lynching, and Max's self-abnegation. These juxtapositions remind the reader that the racially disproportionate application of capital punishment had a directly proportional relationship to incidences of lynching in Jim Crow America, rather than the inversely proportional one claimed by lynch mobs (Tolnay and Beck 1995, 91–93). In the privacy of the machine and the representational void of the novel, the process is also aligned with the scientific quest for racial essence, as underscored by the medical apparatus surrounding Max.

Once his body has been blanched, Max is driven by a fear of disclosure of his past identity, and also by a yet-unlearned cultural value of whiteness. *The Scimitar* newspaper interviews him and gives him a front-page photograph and headline. Frustrated, he confronts reporter Sybil Smith with the fear that "he had undergone the tortures of Doc Crookman's devilish machine" but had not escaped the feeling of "conspicuousness" that accompanied him as a black man. Sybil Smith responds by giving him his first lesson in whiteness, telling him that nobody will recognize him when so many whites look just like him. Herself a white woman, Sybil does not draw on the racist paradigm of people of color as indistinguishable from one another; instead, she assures Max that only African-Americans are immobilized by strategies of surveillance. Whites have a constant zone of privacy around them that no prying eyes will violate.

Learning Sybil's lesson puts Max at immediate odds with his beloved friend Bunny, with whom he had served in France and explored Harlem. Max's whitening is analogous to exile in a foreign country, because a "wider gulf" than the ocean would separate him from his friend. "The great sea of color" makes them permanently and ineradicably different until Bunny follows Max into a suicidal march to the borders of that sea in Atlanta. Within this exchange, race is neither culture nor essence. The quite mundane matter of skin color becomes dramatized by segregation and caste; race *is* racism. The fictions of racial logic are again highlighted in the subsequent chapter, when Crookman's wife, a "beautiful little octoroon" who could "pass for white" is observed by Foster and Johnson, the doctor's assistants. Their sense that she can pass is dismissed by the omniscient narrator, who suggests that her passing "would have been something akin to a piece of anthracite coal passing for black" (Schuyler 1999, 36). Here Schuyler suggests that one's social role constitutes racial essence; the belief in race produces it in opposition to, rather than in concert with, the body. The color of that body should provide—within Schuyler's paradigm of rationality—empirical knowledge, but the pursuit of that truth is blocked by a counterintuitive regime of knowledge that distrusts flesh as evidence.

Like James Weldon Johnson in *Autobiography of an Ex-Colored Man*, Schuyler figures lynching as catalyst for assimilative self-blanching, but his critique emerges in the shift of his satiric tone when lynching leaves dream space and enters public space. The novel's thirteen chapters are bookended by two lynchings—the lynching in Max's fantasy and one in the final sequence, in which, after discovering that they are descended from African slaves, Arthur Snobbcraft, Southern aristocrat and presidential candidate, and Samuel Buggerie, eugenicist and genealogist, adopt blackface costumes to disguise themselves in rural Mississippi. They are met by a lynch mob from Happy Hill, Mississippi, a town that boasts, in Schuyler's words, of an "inordinately high illiteracy rate" as well as a prodigious lynching record. A "sundown," or all-white town, it greeted any black visitors with hanging, broiling, or shooting (Schuyler 1999, 164). Unlike the Atlantans of the 1906 riot, the residents of Happy Hill have, with the help of Black No More, completely cleared the town of African-Americans, resulting in "nothing left to stimulate them but the old time religion and the clandestine sex orgies that invariably and immediately followed the great revival meetings" (Ibid., 165). When Snobbcraft and Buggerie arrive in Happy Hill, the town is collectively praying for African-Americans to return to offer the religious ritual and social cohesion that lynching provides. The men are attacked, and when they insist that they are white, they are stripped naked to provide proof of it. They receive a brief reprieve, until the townspeople see a newspaper story that reveals the African lineage of both men. The men are stripped and their ears and genitals are severed. Their severed appendages are then sewn back on, and they are burned alive.

Here, Schuyler's novel changes from a Juvenalian satire to a brutal expose of racial violence. As in Faulkner's "Pantaloon in Black" and "Dry September," there is an incomplete present tense to the lynching. Though Schuyler's lynching is not as ineffable as those two short stories, the analysands of my next chapter, he is unable to *end* the violence. The account concludes with "AND SO ON AND SO ON," demarcating the traumatic repetition of lynching spectacles that were, even in Schuyler's intra-war period, structurally, visually, and narratively familiar to whites—the audience addressed by their spectacle—and African-Americans, the audience invoked by their violence. The capitalized phrase breaks with Happy Hill, leaving it with embers still cooling in the middle of town, and begins a coda with Junius Crookman, now Surgeon-General of the United States. Jason Haslam reads this conclusion as an "authoritative comment on the society satirized by the book," which transfers the fictional satire from Schuyler's world to the readers' by producing expectations for continued violence (Haslam 2002, 28).

As Jeffrey B. Ferguson notes, lynching rituals "derive [their] power from the juxtaposition of passionate, ritualistic, and primitive bloodlust with a calculating, clinical rhetoric of surgery and dissection" (Ferguson, 2005, 241). The impulse of the lynch mob matches the earlier impulse of Snobbcraft and Buggerie—themselves parodic representations of racial scientists and genealogists—to find a Jeffersonian essence to race. The scene of the lynching became, after nearly four hundred years of such speculative racial science in the Americas, a public laboratory to test the *depth* of racial difference, to see if color went past the superficial haptic layer. The scene evinces the "scientific" process of stripping layers of skin to provide empirical evidence of racial depth, a practice lynching often copied. The men begin in blackface, but are stripped naked to "prove" their whiteness; their pale skin attests to it, but they are again stripped when the newspaper story reveals the black "blood" beneath their white skin, an essence the mob attempts to access by stripping them of their appendages. Finding no origin of race beneath the skin, the lynchers sew the body back together, eliding their failed attempt to harness racial alterity. Finally, they burn Snobbcraft and Buggerie at the stake until the white ash of Toomer's "Portrait in Georgia" affirms both the color and the violence of the mob.

How deep is black? This is the ontological question that racial science shares with the dominant culture of Schuyler's *Black No More*, a culture that Crookman has joined by the conclusion of the novel, when he authors a book that delineates the biological differences between the original Caucasians and those merely dermal whites who were blanched in his machine. As Walter Benn Michaels has written of *Black No More*, the surgical whitening doesn't "make race go away; it just made it harder to find" (Benn Michaels 2007, 25). The means of accessing it travel from the genealogical to the visceral and back to skin, leaving the reader with the image of unbleached Crookman gazing at a picture of Disher and his family in the rotogravure of his favorite newspaper. Convinced by Crookman's "scientific" monograph that bleached African-Americans are "two or three shades lighter than the old Caucasians," the Dishers and the white supremacist Givenses have darkened their skin with *Poudre Negre*, *L'Afrique*, and *Poudre le Egyptienne*, expensive bronzers that differentiate the original whites from latecomers (Schuyler 1999, 179–180). Helen and Max's son Matthew Crookman Fisher sits at his parents' feet in the magazine article's accompanying picture, his dark skin unaltered and nearly the same shade as his artificially bronzed relatives. Notably, the scene in which Crookman looks at the image is confined to his home, a place where he can, with a disinterested, rational, "scientific" gaze, quantify the origins and variations of race. In the public laboratory of lynching, racist fantasy was the founding impulse, the most primal desire that evinces how much of the generic "fantasy" of Schuyler's novel is the racist fantasy of the novelist's America. What Snobbcraft and Buggerie suffer in Happy Hill—and, indeed, what Matthew Williams, stripped, flogged, mutilated, and dismembered in Salisbury, Maryland in 1931, the year of the novel's publication—was the racist desire to pry open, locate, and quantify blackness.[6]

Even before lynching spectacles of the early twentieth century, forced and coerced medical experiments on slaves revealed the quantifying impulse of American racism. Without apparent health benefits for either the slave or the larger society, *medical* might be too generous an adjective to apply to these experiments. It is, perhaps, too much of an honorarium to describe what John "Fed" Brown suffered at the hands of Thomas Hamilton, a doctor who "set to work to ascertain how deep [his] black skin went" by blistering his legs and burning and flaying his skin (Brown 1977, 48). A more famous doctor, James Marion Sims, the so-called father of gynecology, relied on metaphors of illumination and discovery to describe the experiments on enslaved women that led to the development of the vaginal speculum. Upon its first use, he wrote "I saw everything as no man had ever seen before.

The [slave's vesico-vaginal fistula] was as plain as the nose on a man's face" (Sims 1886, 234–35). His eulogist and biographer, W.O. Baldwin, wrote that the light the speculum cast into the slave's vaginal canal illuminated the best impulses of gynecology and "flash[ed]" Sims's name and reputation "over the medical world like a meteor in the night" (Baldwin 1886, 434). Treating these metaphors of illumination and discovery as consistent with nineteenth-century colonial discourses of the exploration and conquest of Africa, scholar Teri Kapsalis has suggested that Sims's imagined his subjects as "doubly dark" because of their "mysterious anatomy and African origins" (Kapsalis 1997, 38). Inserted into the body and casting a reflection to make the cervix visible, the speculum reveals the embedded depth of racial "darkness" even as its light makes apparent race's absent essence, much as the homologous forms and functions of sexed bodies reveal the ideological and discursive construction of "male" and "female." Gazing into the penetrated body, white male racial scientists saw reflected back their own fantasies of radical alterity.

Experiments by doctors like Hamilton and Sims were fundamentally public and hidden, intimate and social. For his own part, Sims tried ardently to hide his experiments, illustrating his medical writings with images of properly-clad white women rather than the stripped, morphine-addicted black slaves on whom he experimented (Washington 2008, 67). The practice of lynching took the intimate oppressions of slavery out of the plantation and into the town square, revealing the inferiority and debasement of the black body by denuding, stripping, and mutilating it, while affirming the power of the lynchers, who occupy categories of whiteness and citizenship by participating in violence, which "highlights whiteness' performative reliance on the existence of blackness" (Haslam 2002, 19). Within the mob in *Black No More*, Schuyler's omniscient narrator recounts, are "two or three whitened Negroes" who must self-blanch in the Black No More machine and within the privileged space of the lynch mob in order to live. The category of whiteness is shored up by both "pork-colored skin" and mob citizenship, two categories that offer access, paradoxically, to both privacy and publicness—the sanctity of the body and access to the privileged public sphere. White skin is both social currency and untrammeled private space, but the lynch mob demands a public recapitulation of private desire and prejudice—often very private desires, as lynchings were ritualistically sexual even when the alleged crimes were not. Readers might consider the escalating interiors the final lynching scene suggests. Religious fantasy piles upon sexual fantasy upon public performance of self-negation, presuming that layers of skin are not reliable indicators of race. Beneath Snobbcraft and Buggerie's black paint is white skin, but beneath that white skin is a fantasy of blackness, believed to be a signifier of interior perfidy invisible to the naked eye, marked not even on a naked body—seen only in a dream.

CHAPTER THREE

"Peaceful and Unfathomable and Unbearable Eyes"

William Faulkner's Elisions of Witness

The "Curious Thing" About Mobs

When asked by Morton Goldman in February 1935 to submit a "lynching article" to *Vanity Fair*, William Faulkner answered aloofly. "Tell them I never saw a lynching," he wrote, "and so couldn't describe one" (Blotner 1977, 89). By the time he negated the possibility of participating in public protest against mob violence, Faulkner had already written the short fiction "Dry September" (1931), the account of the mob murder of Will Mayes for an unknown slight against Ms. Minnie Cooper, an unmarried *femme d'un certain age*, and the novel *Light in August* (1932), which ends with the slaughter of Joe Christmas at the hands of protofascist Percy Grimm. Over the next twenty years, he would represent the violent repercussions of racist ideology again and again—depicting the quasi-legal execution of Rider in "Pantaloon in Black," a story in *Go Down, Moses* (1942), the assassination of abolitionist Calvin Burden at the hands of Colonel Sartoris in *The Unvanquished* (1938), and the threatened lynching of Lucas Beauchamp in *Intruder in the Dust* (1949). The most violent aspects of racism featured in dozens of stories and novels he wrote after his letter to Goldman, ensuring that he is rightly known as the American novelist most fixated on the subject.[1] Considered in light of his response to Goldman, Faulkner's oeuvre seems to make a liar out of its author.

By analyzing two short fictions of lynching, "Dry September" and "Pantaloon in Black," with a briefer treatment of the more explicit representation of lynching and torture in *Light in August*, I examine the narrative strategies that made it possible for Faulkner to reify sight and eschew the other senses as mechanisms of witnessing lynching. In so doing, I also consider the relationship of these occlusions to genre. John T. Matthews, who reads Faulkner's short fiction as "occup[ying], manipulat[ing], and resist[ing]" the conventions of the market, argues for the generic conventions of short fiction as agents of resistance (Matthews 1992, 11):

> The fragmentary nature of the short story form—its necessary sense of compression . . . its foregrounding of moment and anecdote, its attention to minor or marginal phenomenon—these attributes of its very *shortness* make it an effective vehicle for representing material often subordinate in more comprehensive fictional forms . . . The broken, brief form of the short story accommodates the heterogeneity and deformity of the lives of the underclasses. (Ibid., 13–14)

Counter to Matthews, the compression of these stories enables erasures of traumatic memory, while their privileging of moments minor and anecdotal enables the omission of primary action and specular narrative: the violent death of the lynched man. These strategies affirm the experience of the trauma for lynching's (primarily white) witnesses—the audience invoked by the torture and murder of African-Americans in privileged publics—rather than critiquing the practice itself.

In both short stories, lynching takes place as prologue and epilogue, but is refused a present tense; Faulkner places the violence "before the present action or offstage," contrary to the gender division Trudier Harris delineates as men's *authorial* willingness to represent lynching and women's greater reticence (Harris 2002, 464). Indeed, it contradicts Faulkner's own theorization of the short story as a "crystallized instant," as it resists representing the moment that action occurs (Blotner 1977, 345). In "Dry September," this refusal is expressed in the shifting narrative strategies that move the reader from the perspective of Hawkshaw, the barber who refuses to participate in the lynching of Will Mayes, to that of Minnie Cooper, whose hysterical reaction to the news of Mayes's death lends credibility to a story of an interracial violation that is never regarded with seriousness in the community, despite their willingness to kill for the unknown slight. Moving between two unseeing parties, the narrative effectively shields death from the reader's view. The story concludes with the lyncher McLendon gazing into the night from his screen door and narrating his abuse of his wife rather than the violence actuated against

Will. The scene offers nothing more of the lynching. Hans Skei argues that the racist violence emerges offstage, "as in the tragedies of ancient times" because Faulkner is "more interested in the creation of atmospheric detail to portray a landscape, a climate, and a community in a season of drought and a lifeless stasis that threaten to destroy life and all life-giving impulses" (Skei 1981, 91). The formal creation of atmosphere is the necessary corollary of constructing a credible social structure for mob violence and exclusionary citizenship; while the men's motivations constitute the internal mechanism of lynching, the "landscape, climate, and community" are its externalities. By rendering the spaces of lynching private and quotidian, Faulkner abets the will to forget the publicness of lynching.

Like the earlier story, "Pantaloon in Black" narratively shifts from the perspective of Rider—whose aching grief at the death of his wife Mannie leads him on a spiral of pain and recrimination that ends with his lynching—to that of the deputy sheriff, who does not actually see the lynching but offers an account of it to his wife. He can only narrate parts of Rider's story because of perspectival refusals to see black subjectivity that put the reader in mind of Melville's *Benito Cereno* (1855) or Ellison's *Invisible Man* (1953). The connections between Melville, Ellison, and Faulkner return in my third section, in which I explore the trope of invisibility in the literary canon as a way of considering the tradition's privileging of the ocular sense. In both Faulkner stories, omniscience is notably avoided; this strategy is not surprising from Faulkner, who tended to use multiple limited narrators to repeat—but not replicate—the events of the story. Though the readers of his novels are often asked to operate on partial knowledge, at the end, the narrative shifts provide one with so much knowledge from so many competing narratives that no event seems omitted, even if their iterability is constructed as a form of unknowability. In Trudier Harris's taxonomy, the omission of lynching's graphic violence strengthens its resonance as metaphor and warning for black characters (Harris 2002, 464). Faulkner's fictional lynchings, on the other hand, become the trauma that white communities ignore to maintain a sense of diffused responsibility. The short stories are, thus, instruments for Faulkner to maintain the veracity of his claim to Goldman by refusing to be a witness—in either sight or description—to the practice of lynching.

To contextualize these stories in Faulkner's well-traveled critical and biographical histories, I begin by considering his statement to Morton Goldman in light of his public writings about lynching and racial violence. What can readers garner from Faulkner's elision of witness? What relationship does it have to his racial politics? Did Faulkner, seldom protestant in life, if not on the page, utter a falsity to Morton Goldman? A convenient fiction to protect his beloved Mississippi from the memories of Nelse Patton and Ellwood Higginbotham, two men lynched in Oxford in Faulkner's lifetime? Or did he tell the truth, believing that the act of witness implied a responsibility for these deaths that he was unwilling, unlikely, and unable to claim, since claiming and redeeming that guilty legacy would negate his connection to both his state and his "race"? Certainly there is evidence to suggest that Faulkner felt outside the bond of privileged whiteness in Mississippi. Loosed from the geographical constraints of Mississippi, he found an antiracist public voice. This voice was compromised by his less cordial racial sentiments, expressed in an interview with Russell Howe in 1955. "If it came to fighting," he said of the battle over civil rights, "I'd fight for Mississippi against the United States, even if it meant going out into the streets and shooting Negroes" (Meriwether and Millgate 1968, 261). Yet, in June of 1955, at the height of his sympathies with civil rights and attendant pressure from friends and neighbors, he confided in Else Jonsson about his fears of exile:

> We have much tragic trouble in Mississippi now about Negroes. The Supreme Court has said that there shall be no segregation, difference in schools, voting, etc. between the two races, and there are many people in Mississippi who will go to any length, even violence, to prevent that. I am afraid. I am doing what I can. I can see the possible time when I shall have to leave my native state, something as the Jew had to flee from Germany during Hitler. (Blotner 1977, 382)

The language of the letter evokes a long history of white Southern nomadism that began with South Carolinian and fierce abolitionist Angelina Grimke, who described herself—in an aural metaphor that evokes the racial soundscape of Faulkner's fiction—as "exiled from the land of my birth by the sound of the lash, and the piteous cry of the slave" (Smith 2001, 7).

These words, however, compelling and true they might feel to a Southerner who charges against the political grain of white racism, seem less resistant when juxtaposed to the increasing conservatism of Faulkner's public interventions and his obviation of racism's targeting of African-Americans in positioning himself as the "Jew" in Nazi Germany rather than the German. As post-Brown tensions escalated in the South, Faulkner was a less lucid and reliable critic of American apartheid. Carol Polsgrove, noting Faulkner's Cold War rhetoric, argues that his conservative "political statements . . . appear to some biographers [as] an aberration" enabled by his alliances with the State Department, and the international platform and travel that the alliance and the Nobel Prize afforded him (Polsgrove 2001, 95). These divergent political impulses are mediated by his apocalyptic despair following the death of Emmett Till, an event that compelled him to ask if "our desperate culture . . . deserve[s] to survive" (Meriwether and Millgate 1968, 255). Just as he wondered if the South could survive under a new order of integration and federal control, he was certain it did not deserve to: a paradox that saved him from the social ostracism attending an integrationist stance even as it inoculated him against criticism by antiracist activists.

One might dismiss both his directly racist and apologist claims as the rantings of a drunk, a dismissal that Faulkner encouraged in his not-quite apologetic postscript that "no sober . . . or sane man" professes an impulse to shoot African-Americans in the streets in defense of Mississippi (Ibid., 265). One might also attribute them to a man who grew more conservative even as readings of his work grew more politically engaged and sensitive. The gap between his occasional public racism and the content of his novels has been often commented upon, but this gap is not isolated to the tumult of the 1950s. Faulkner's life writing from the time of the composition of "Dry September"—a story that Don H. Doyle sees as "reflect[ing] a distaste for lynching and [an] uncertain faith in white racial paternalism as a counterforce to redneck racism"—offers a dramatically different account of his racial politics (Doyle 1999, 240). The distinction between his work as writer and citizen evinces acute political schizophrenia and deeply wrong-headed engagements with the political and moral problem of lynching.

An editorial letter to *The Memphis Commercial*, a found document from the 1930s, when read with "Dry September"—its close contemporary—evinces a troubling gap between writer and citizen. The letter, discovered by Neil McMillen and Noel Polk in the Tuskegee Institute's lynching archives in 1992, was published on February 15, 1931 in response to a letter printed in the February 2nd edition. In the earlier letter, W.H. James, an African-American man, wrote in praise of the efforts of the Association of Southern Women for the Prevention of Lynching (ASWPL). Faulkner—responding to James's wish that ASWPL president Mrs. J. Morgan Spencer would become governor of Mississippi and James's assertion that African-Americans remain "as humble and submissive" as they were before—excoriates James at length for advocating the extension of citizenship rights to both white Southern women and people of color; Faulkner's response is nearly four times the word count of the initiating letter (McMillen and Polk 1992, 5–6). Written in the midst of personal trauma—spiraling debt, the death of his infant daughter, his renunciation of alcohol—as well as creative productivity, the letter provokes the sense that readers are in the presence of a great mystery, since Faulkner spent much of the 1930s writing on a "Franklinian" schedule for the short story market, a practice with costs and incentives that he compared to prostitution (Carothers 1992, 38). At a time of financial distress, when his short stories financially supported his family and stirred with counter narratives to the paradigms of white supremacy, Faulkner wrote something for free that shames the antiracist critique of his best writing.

The letter, which equates the "sentimentality" of white liberals with the violence of white supremacists, ends with an implied threat and violent wish against W. H. James:

> No balanced man will deny that mob violence serves nothing, just as he will not deny that a lot of our natural and logical jurisprudence serves nothing either. It just happens that we—mobber and mobbee—live in this age. We will muddle through, and die in our beds, the deserving and the fortunate among us. Of course, with the population what it is, there are some of us that won't. Some will die rich, and some will die on cross-ties soaked with gasoline, to make a holiday. But there is one curious thing about mobs. Like our juries, they have a way of being right. (McMillen and Polk 1992, 6)

The interpellative power of Faulkner's "we" disturbs, directed as it is against both James and the presumptively white audience. The "we" makes the reader either mobber or mobbee, thereby suggesting that, unrepresentative as both black criminality and white mob violence might be, there is no outside to mob violence, even though Faulkner discursively creates an ideological loophole. The inevitable death of the deprivileged "some" who die in the lynch fire are as naturalized in Faulkner's formation as dying of old age. Some will die rich, as Faulkner undoubtedly wanted to, but some will die bloody, as he promises in the letter, composed, as McMillen and Polk argue, "hastily . . . zealously . . . and mean-spiritedly" (Ibid., 13). Though I read this line as a threat to James, I make room for the possibility that it is not Faulkner's wish that James die at the hands of a mob, but rather his sense that violent death for black men is as inevitable as any of the myriad ways that a white man's life could end—thereby supporting Ruth Wilson Gilmore's contention that racism is not only "the state-sanctioned or extralegal production and exploitation of group-differentiated vulnerability to premature death," but also the ability of privileged agents outside of state authority to grow accustomed to that vulnerability to violence (Gilmore 2007, 28).

Though he acknowledges that "the standard for a black man is stricter than that for a white man" in both the moral and legal senses, Faulkner is mostly resistant to antiracist or even *racial* analysis of the social crisis of lynching; he prefers to quarantine the practice within individual pathologies—much as other critics discursively quarantined it in the Southern region as a way to recuperate nationalist ideologies and democratic practices outside of lynching rituals. "The people of the black race who get lynched are not representative of the black race," Faulkner writes, "just as the people who lynch them are not representative of the white race" (McMillen and Polk 1992, 4). Denying the possibility of representative violence alleviates the writer of the responsibility to account for social problems, enabling him instead to consider mobs as collections of sick individuals carrying out an understandable, if unjustified, act of violence against a black criminal, who should be banished from the sympathies of the majority of African-Americans, just as the majority of whites should "hold no brief" for the mob's practice. That intense focus on subjectivity and singularity diminishes spatial and social collectivity, inhibiting the reader's ability to locate the scene of the crime (the public sphere), its perpetrators (the community), or its weapon (white supremacy). By indicting the pathological individual, Faulkner and other whites were able to feel unimplicated by violence, just as conservative African-Americans could feel that marginal community members—mentally disabled, criminal, deviant, sexually minoritized "bad" subjects—were solely at risk of carceral violence, a risk that the black middle-class could avoid through the performance of respectability. "The men who are lynched are invariably vagrants, men without property or standing," pronounced Booker T. Washington in 1897, with logic akin to Faulkner's (Dray 2002, 119). The refusal of collective responsibility and insistence on the foreclosure of sympathy for the lynching victim are tendencies shared by gradualists across the color line.[2]

Within both racist and antiracist discourses, an equally troubling but radically disparate tendency exists when scholars and historians remember racist public figures like Thomas Jefferson, Woodrow Wilson, and even Strom Thurmond—notorious segregationist and local hero in my native South Carolina—as solely products of their "time," rather than the ideological labor that remembers that time as monolithically white and white supremacist. In the analysis that accompanies the first printing of Faulkner's lynching letter, McMillen and Polk provide such an apologia, assuring readers that "for all his genius, [Faulkner] was in all kinds of ways as much a citizen of Mississippi as his white neighbors, and necessarily shared, in his personal, communal life, many of his community's values" (McMillen and Polk 1992, 13). The reductions of this analysis require the apologist to believe that Faulkner was somehow *more* of his cultural moment than a close contemporary and resistant citizen like Richard Wright, who grew up in desperate material circumstances far less amenable to resistance against white supremacy. To believe that Faulkner is a son of the South *because* of the racist claims of the letter is to assert that Lillian Smith, Erskine Caldwell, and other white resisters are somehow less Southern and less of their culture because of their antiracist praxis. As my first chapter suggests, I am skeptical of such a claim, as it effectively denies regional citizenship—a citizenship that gives one access to origins, homespace, and vernacular language, all necessities of literary production—based on the most unpleasant of political litmus tests: white supremacy. This litmus test is similarly applied to Hawkshaw in "Dry September," when his communal belonging and nativity are placed under suspicion by the execrable McLendon because he argues for Will Mayes's innocence. Moreover, it also denies the public sphere as a site of contestation, "the *stake* ... and also the *site* of class struggle ... because the resistance of the exploited classes is able to find means and occasions to express itself there (Althusser 2001, 99).

Neither antiracist resistance nor the gradualism for which Faulkner later became famous in his admonition to black leaders to "go slow now [and] stop now for a time" in their quest for civil rights, are present in the 1931 letter (Faulkner 2004, 87). To put a name on the political sympathies of the letter mires the critic further; calling it anti-antiracist seems like a dodge, but calling it racist diminishes Faulkner's powerful literary representations of racial oppression. The unattractive sympathies present in the letter have left the few critics who have treated it with the unhappy task of explanation. So burdensome are these possibilities that McMillen and Polk entertain the notion that the letter is fake:

> The juxtaposition of this letter to the publication of "Dry September" is so bizarre that it is tempting to see the letter as a forgery, to assume—hope—that not Faulkner but someone else wrote it and attributed it to him for reasons unknown. But in fact, we think the letter can be reasonably attributed to Faulkner

himself. It seems hardly likely that anyone would have written such a letter to parody or to embarrass Faulkner this early in his career. (McMillen and Polk 1992, 7)

Eventually, they disconfirm the possibility of a forgery because the letter's "authenticity is not easily denied." However, they do not mention that Faulkner's signature discursive style is imprinted on the letter. Early in the letter, he writes, "no balanced man can . . . hold any brief for lynching" (Ibid., 4). Within the phrase, no balanced man, we find an antecedent to Faulkner's apology for the inflammatory Rowe interview in which he said he would shoot "Negroes" in defense of Mississippi. Recall that "no sober or sane man" would offer to kill African-Americans in defense of Mississippi's racism and that "no balanced man" would defend the mob, though Faulkner evidently does both. In the phrase hold no brief, repeated twice within the letter, there are echoes of Miss Rosa Coldfield's monologue to Quentin Compson in *Absalom, Absalom!* in which she asserts that she holds no brief with herself for the ruin of her courtship with Sutpen, a phraseological repetition that indicates her uncertainty. The letter writer is equally uncertain about the moral necessity of lynching, a practice for which he "holds no brief" and for which he believes that "no balanced man can" hold a brief, despite the fact that mobs are as right as juries (Ibid., 4–5).

The letter has been mostly overlooked by the cottage industry of Faulkner criticism. *The William Faulkner Encyclopedia* (1999) features an extended entry on lynching that offers no analysis of this provocative found document, which is the most extended public statement Faulkner made on the subject (Doyle 2001, 238–40). Those few critics who have written about the letter do not focus on the imprint of Faulkner's language on the document, as that would come to dangerously close to canonizing it. Critical fascination with this letter hinges not on Faulkner's stylistic signature, but his literal one. Mysteriously, Faulkner's name is printed as "Falkner," the spelling from which he had changed it in 1921, a vacillation of which critics have made much. Doreen Fowler, reading the letter in tandem with Faulkner's *Sanctuary* (1931), asserts that the letter's "defining and saving difference" from the antiracist novels is the difference between the "author's text and . . . citizen's public statement" as expressed in the difference in Faulkner's signature (Fowler, 424). Donald Kartiganer sees the name change as a performance of, rather than belief in, white supremacy, asserting that "Faulkner is deliberately adopting the voice of the man he regards as the 'standard' Southern white . . . Faulkner without the 'u' " (Kartiganer 2008, 34). Though both Fowler and Kartiganer's interventions seek to defend Faulkner against the accusation of racism, neither makes a compelling case that his adoption of the normative racist voice is an ethical choice. Asserting that Faulkner adopted a public voice of racism suggests a far greater moral crime, as it makes the racism of the letter into aspirational normativity, a craving for convention and consensus that made passive witnesses of lynching morally blind.

After encountering *Go Down, Moses*, I imagine Faulkner's slight alteration of his name as similar to the evolution of the planter's name—Lucius Quintus Carothers McCaslin—into the name of Lucas Quintus Carothers McCaslin Beauchamp, the black sharecropper who is both the great-grandson and great-great grandson of the planter who raped both an enslaved woman and their daughter. Though registering ambivalence to inheritance—in Lucas Beauchamp's case, of hubris and violence and in Fa(u)lkner's case, of white supremacy—the change itself can neither abrogate nor consolidate that inheritance. Even with the alteration of his name—with a new surname and vowels redacted from the prename—Lucas Beauchamp ultimately inherits Carothers McCaslin's character, becoming, in his white kinsman Ike McCaslin's estimation, "both heir and prototype of all the geography and climate and biology which sired old Carothers and all the rest of us" (Faulkner 1990a, 114). Faulkner's own mild change—from his great-grandfather's *William C. Falkner* to his own *William C. Faulkner*—does not negate the reflexive urge to defend Southern tradition and the privileged ties of whiteness in his own self-interest. If it was not the writer but the citizen, not the private man but the public one, who felt the rightness of lynch mobs, than the ugliness of that urge is not negated; it is the certainty of a distinction between the moral obligations of public and private people, citizens and writers—a replacement of a public demand for justice with a private indifference toward racist blood rituals—that stokes lynching's fire.

Standing at the permeable boundary of public spectacle and private memory are Faulkner's accounts of lynching. As the next section of this chapter considers representations of lynching in his short fiction, it also asks that readers consider the valences of memory in the realm of the senses. Walter Ong wrote that "modern technologized man . . . [takes] the physical world . . . as something visually perceived. The senses other than sight do not count here or count very little, with the exception of touch insofar as it is allied to vision in presenting extension" (Ong 1969, 635). Thus, Ong asks us to imagine that sight, in allowing "extension," enables the modern subject to feel distance from the stimuli of the world around her, in contrast to preliterate and oral cultures that "think of the universe . . . as a sound or group of sounds" (Ibid., 636). Though Faulkner might never have seen a lynching, I argue that it is only this absence of the ocular sense, consistent with Ong's Western paradigm, that enables him to eschew responsibility and discard the onerous burden of witness. Words might have enabled him to offer these denials, but I wager that the psyche had less stable a boundary, since the Freudian primal scene can be twinned with the primal (un)scene: a trauma witnessed without the eye.

Whether or not Faulkner witnessed lynching, I ask that critics consider the function of memory when the eye is excecated. What function might Faulkner's blindnesses—moral, political, and literal—to lynching serve his representations of it? In James Weldon Johnson's *Autobiography of an Ex-Colored Man* (1912), the eyewitness to lynching forsakes his marked racial identity in favor of passing because the spectacle of mob violence made his body vulnerable, a condition he thinks he can forsake by calling himself "white" rather than enunciating, like Homer Plessy before him, that he was a man of color. But it is not only sight that rearranges the psychic life of those who witnessed lynching on all sides of the color line. Just as Plessy and Johnson's speech acts gesture to the power of enunciation, the trauma of hearing and hearing of lynching evinces that the afterimage of violence need not be as ocular as the term suggests. The lynchings that Richard Wright heard of as a child in Mississippi and Arkansas taught him—without recourse to the eye—that violence could "violate [his] life at will" (Wright 1993, 14).

Coming to Atlanta to meet Joel Chandler Harris in 1899, W. E. B. DuBois was turned away because "the news met" him: "Sam Hose had been lynched, and they said that his knuckles were on exhibition at a grocery store farther down on Mitchell Street" (DuBois 1999, 222). The account of the spectacle reached DuBois's ear, driving him away from his previous career as a sociologist because "one could not be a calm, cool, and detached scientist while Negroes were lynched, murdered, and starved" or offer objective truths to a culture that made no "definite demand" of them. At this moment—DuBois's primal (un)scene of recognition that the world needed him as an agitator against racial violence—the aural dimension of witnessing lynching is revealed. The body of the lynched man became a form of prophetic currency between both ocularcentric lynchers and absent aural spectators. The fine sample of the anatomy lab transformed into public spectacle in the butcher's window—a visual joke on the butcher and the barber, the surgeons of the early modern period, before dissection of the human body was a standard part of medical training—and the sight transformed into news that could meet a man who did not come to meet it, ensuring that everyone who saw the souvenir of Sam Hose could give an account that gestated in their listeners' new traumas witnessed only by the ear.

Convenient Fictions

The parched clay and dirt of "Dry September" are miasma around the mechanisms of its plot, rendered with metaphors of dehydration that seep through Faulkner's language like much-needed water. The short story and Faulkner's lynching apologia "appear in print almost simultaneously" despite what McMillen and Polk read as "diametrically opposed attitudes" toward the political valences of mob violence, an opposition they ascertain in Faulkner's willingness to present social causes for lynching and arguments for the lynched man's innocence in the short story (McMillen and Polk 1992, 13). The first sentences of the story enunciate a sixty-two day environmental draught that precedes the action, as does Minnie Cooper's claim of an ambiguous sexual infraction against her by Will Mayes. In the "vitiated air" of the barbershop, the escalating tensions of the debate over Minnie Cooper's virtue transform the community into a mob (Faulkner 1995, 169). One of the men rebuts the barber Hawkshaw's claim of Mayes's innocence, asserting that "this durn weather . . . will make a man do anything. Even to her" (Ibid., 170). After the mob apprehends Mayes in a brawl that wounds his defender Hawkeye, the barber leaps from the car that carries the mob and their intended victim, watching them ride toward the lynching, observing that "the dust swallowed them," an association of dirt and the mob that renders the latter autochthonous. Thus, the weather or, more precisely, the environment, is posited as the cause of lynching. Formalist readings of the story transform its dry dust into the lynchpin for the spectacle of mob violence. In 1954, William B. Bache argued that the lynchers are "urged on by hotness and dryness" conditions that win the rhetorical battle against Hawkshaw's argument for Will's innocence (Bache 1954, 53). John B. Vickery argued that the lynching was a case of "meteorologically induced madness" (Vickery 1962, 11). Two decades later, Hans Skei argued that there exists a "causal connection between climate, landscape, and social conditions and the terror and death that follow" (Skei 1981, 90):

> The men in the barbershop are so ready and willing to accept the story that their readiness must somehow be related to the season of drought, to an unease and a tension that has been building up

for a long time; but the real basis of the immediate reactions of the most active of the customers is obviously their racial prejudices, their absolute conviction that the Negro is inferior, or at least that the social order they have created and maintained takes [Minnie's word above Will's]. (Ibid., 86)

For Skei, the endlessness repetitions of synonyms for heat and dust suggest drought as a cause for lynching second only to white supremacy—the violent regime of racial prejudice that privileges Minnie Cooper's virtue above Will Mayes's body, her cloistered body over his word.[3]

Remarking on the critical tendency to attribute the lynching of Will Mayes to the weather, Cleanth Brooks warned against "identify[ing] the climate of lynching with a meteorological condition" (Brooks 1990, 112). Though I share with Brooks the sense that the attribution of lynching's violence to the weather—or, for that matter, the price of cotton and the ever-popular Oedipus complex—is reductive, I argue that these formalist claims are attempts to delineate collective responsibility for lynching without uttering the phrase. I attribute this uneasiness with the concept of collective responsibility to its associations with the "Denazification" trials of the forties and fifties and, more recently, Jonah Goldhagen's *Hitler's Willing Executioners: Ordinary Germans and the Holocaust* (1996). Arguments for collective responsibility have become almost universally associated with the destruction of European Jewry, an association often avoided because of the intellectual sterility of what Leo Strauss called "reductio ad Hitlerum" (Strauss 2008, 153), what Ron Rosenbaum called "argumentum ad Hitlerum" (Rosenbaum 1998, xxii), and what one of the Internet's insistent neologisms names "Godwin's Law." In short, arguments are intellectually vacated at the moment individuals and phenomena are compared to Nazis. For contemporary academics, citing collective responsibility for racial violence treads close to naming America as fundamentally corrupt in a time when comparing—or being seen to compare—American racial violence to European genocide is enough to land one on David Horowitz's academic blacklist. For their colleagues four decades ago, the aforementioned environmental determinisms tread between two possibilities: firstly, attempts to hold individuals, rather than larger communities, responsible for lynching and, secondly, to hold American culture responsible for the actions of the mob. The second is avoided because of the infelicities of the Holocaust metaphor, while the first is jettisoned because it is disproven on first sight of a lynching spectacle or photograph, where hundreds of people gather and participate.

Unfortunately, the median space between determinism and free will, the "meteorological madness" described by Bache and Vickery, does little to theorize the potential for justice in the aftermath of community violence, because social constructions—phenomena scholars now discuss as truisms—become immoveable, fatalistic, totalitarian, and, most troublingly, organic. Troubled by this tendency toward "abstraction" in "Dry September," Irving Howe described the text as "a paradigm of all lynching stories . . . populated not with men but with Murderer and Victim" who become pawns in totalizing analyses (Howe 1951, 127). Ignoring the political and social labor that created white supremacy and its attendant violence, formalist critics read the racism of Faulkner's world as an exotic plant indigenous to the least hospitable regions of the Republic. Because of their investments in the humanist elevation of the subject—not so different, I argue in my next chapter, from contemporary reclamations of the resistant, agentic marginalized subject—these readings also draw too sharp a distinction between perpetration and witnessing. In most early readings of "Dry September," with the exception of W. B. Bache's "Moral Awareness in 'Dry September'" (Bache 1954), Hawkshaw, who argues for Will Mayes's innocence but does nothing to save him, is located as the story's unproblematic central consciousness, a hero for the reader only when contrasted to the monstrous McLendon, who leads the mob despite his indifference to Will's guilt or innocence. Drawing sharp distinctions between McLendon and Hawkshaw, as well as the latter and Minnie Cooper, who he reads as an unambiguously evil Delilah, John K. Crane praises the "humble barber . . . [who] surely possesses the Faulknerian virtues of the heart but who is severely tested . . . and nearly discovers himself to be morally dry" (Crane 1985, 419). Perhaps I have too few sympathies for Hawkshaw's dilemma, but I reject Vickery's construction, which valorizes Hawkshaw, despite the fact that he leaves Will for dead because, in a struggle against the mob, the captive flails and accidentally strikes him. Abject and nigh apologetic for his intractability against mortal racial violence, Hawkshaw leaps from McLendon's car with two voices piercing his memory. McLendon calls him "niggerlover" and Will Mayes pleads for "Mr. Henry" to stay with him (Faulkner 1995, 179).

Between Hawkshaw's retreat and the post-lynching codas, which show Minnie Cooper's hysterical breakdown and McLendon's violence against his wife, the audience "sees" no lynching; they share that blindness with Hawkshaw, who hears Will Mayes's pleading in the dark, but refuses to see the consequences of his inaction at the scene of the lynching. But his failure to see the lynching does not make Hawkshaw an innocent man. Though he might have chosen not to look, the psyche is permeable to sound. While the mob leader McLendon's voice inveighs him to take responsibility for the real or imagined infraction that Mayes committed, the voice of the intended victim asks that he take responsibility for preventing lynching rather than reveling in its punishments. Structurally, the audience is protected from sight, but no comparable protection is afforded to Hawkshaw, whose aural sense rings with the echo of the plea and the denunciation. Though he leaps from the car to save his eye, it is a logically hidebound and ocularcentric definition of the role of witness that enables that protection.

As Mark M. Smith has argued in his sensory histories of the American South, the often-discounted aural sense is not the apprentice of the visual. Indeed, as firm color lines diminished because of immigration to the United States and miscegenation in the plantation South, Smith argues, race migrated from vision to the other senses, reifying "sensory fingerprints" of race in the ear and the nose, rather than the unreliable eye. Because skin color is evidently an ordinal difference within racial groups as well as between them, white supremacists posited other senses as sources of verification for racial alterity (Smith 2006, 41). Bridging the gap between what he sees in the car and what is hidden by the weeds and darkness into which he falls as the mob and their captive Mayes speed away, are two aural fingerprints that cannot abrogate accountability. Will Mayes's pleas and McLendon's denunciation mark the ways that Hawkshaw has been incomplete to each man's purpose and reading of his racial identity; he has failed as the righteous lyncher with McLendon, and the paternalistic savior to Will.

As "Pantaloon in Black" attests, the white man's *eye* on the black man can be as devoid of sympathy as Hawkshaw's ear. The story offers a split narration from the sensoria of two characters: first, Rider, with the aid of a nearly anaffective omniscient narrator, accounts for his transformation from "Spoot"—the hard-drinking small-town playboy—to the husband and eventual widower of Mannie. When she dies, he feels profoundly suicidal grief at her absence. Second, the sheriff's deputy, who assists the coroner that found Rider "hanging from the bell-rope in a negro schoolhouse" after he murders the gambler Birdsong, recounts the same story—with several degrees of separation between his account and the first narrator's omniscience—in an almost uninterrupted monologue to his wife (Faulkner 1990a, 149). Each man has a vastly different relationship to his senses; for Rider, sight is revelatory. He falls in love with Mannie when "he saw [her], whom he had known all his life, for the first time," a sight that so transforms him that he announces that the life that preceded it is over, in a scene repeated twice within the short story (Ibid., 134, 146).⁴ But the deputy's sensory apparatus has been transformed by white supremacy to look for difference rather than intersubjectivity. Signs of Rider's grief—his desire to bury Mannie with his own hands, in intimate communion with a body he loved; his decision to return to work rather than live in the house with her ghost, who refuses his request to take him to her afterlife; his cognitive disappearance into alcoholic stupor; his violence against Birdsong; his suicidal refusal to flee from the town where he committed murder; and his near plea for the deputies and other inmates to kill him—stimulate the senses enough to reveal to the deputy that "niggers . . . ain't human" (Ibid., 149). In *Light in August*, Gavin Stevens narrates Joe Christmas's death as suicide at Grimm's hand, calling it passivity that "defied the black blood for the last time" (Faulkner 1990b, 449). If we follow Stevens's logic in both texts, than Rider's refusal to survive and the passivity of his eventual surrender are symptoms of whiteness in defiance of the brutal self-preservation Stevens considers inherent to blackness.

But even within the deputy sheriff's racist construction in "Pantaloon in Black," Faulkner accounts for the possibility of a transformative story, an account of violence that circumvents the toxic reflexivity by which only one's own subject position—however pernicious, however racist—is affirmed in the making of language. Though the deputy sheriff seems to offer the story as a way to transmit knowledge of difference affirmed by racist logics, he interrupts his own story before the lynching, before the arrival of Birdsong's family to kidnap and kill Rider. The lawmen watch through the bars of the cell as Rider takes on a crowd of men, "a big mass of nigger heads and arms and legs boiling around on the floor"; even inside of his grief, Rider's instinct to preserve his life is not quite dimmed as "every now and then a nigger would come flying out and go sailing through the air across the room" as he strikes back against the group (Faulkner 1990a, 154). When the deputy's friend Ketcham peels the men off of Rider, he finds a stricken face under the pile of flesh, with "tears big as glass marbles" falling onto the floor with a "popping sound." Repeating Rider's words in a Faulknerian pidgin dialect, the deputy sheriff says that he punctuated his tears with laughter and a plaint: "Look lack Ah just cant quit [thinking]" (Ibid., 154). At this moment in his story, the deputy sheriff does not try to resolve the paradoxes of violence and grief, laughter and tears, with an aphorism about the atavism of African-Americans of the sort offered by Gavin Stevens in *Light in August*. Instead, he reveals to his wife that, much as he would like to resolve it, he cannot. "What do you think of that?" he asks her, but he gets no response. Indeed, the wife—who has already denounced the laziness and stupidity of lawmen who turn a blind eye as posses kidnap and lynch men—tells him that she prefers the voyeurism of the picture show to an aural postmortem on Rider's destruction. Yet, the deputy sheriff shares Rider's inability to "quit thinking," as Hoke Perkins argues, residing in a state of "near empathy [and] honest anguish" in which he can tell a story in the language of the racist, but with the feeling of someone whose racist ideology is in a state of upheaval (Perkins 1987, 232).

Structurally, the story provides an interruption of the narrative in *Go Down, Moses*, which is most often read as a novel in short stories. The story of Ike McCaslin's rejection of his patrimony has only a tenuous relationship to Mannie and Rider's parting in death; the only evidence the reader has for cohesion is that Rider used the marriage of Lucas Beauchamp, McCaslin's black kinsmen, as a model for his own. Just as Beauchamp lit an eternal hearth fire for Molly to signify their marital bond, Rider marked the end of his life as "Spoot" and the beginning of it as Mannie's husband by bringing flame to their sharecropper's cottage. Aside from this narrative detail, very little links "Pantaloon in Black" to the larger story of *Go Down, Moses*. One might read this interruption as a refusal of master narrative; a certain contentment with the minor literature of Rider's story, both in its heart-rending account of love and its violence set in a "cramped space [in which] the individual concern . . . becomes all the more necessary, indispensable, magnified, because a whole other story is vibrating in it" (Deleuze and Guattari 1986, 17). Existing at the margins of the grander narrative, Rider's story "accommodate[s] fugitive energies not welcome within the central enterprise" of white supremacy or the novel itself (Weinstein 1987, 170). Within Rider's account of his own grief, the tragedy and moral crime of lynching "vibrates" within, contesting lynching's cultural logic and the sharply delineated boundaries of personhood under racial apartheid.

Setting the account of Rider's downfall in domestic space suggests parity between the home and the lynching site, rendering both quotidian. Faulkner is aware enough of the pedestrian nature of posse lynchings in rural Mississippi to repeat the common coroner's verdict—"dead at the hands of a person or persons unknown"—without his own metaphoric or narrative reimagining (Faulkner 1990a, 149). The common phrase is not made new; it sits mutely and flatly in the center of a paragraph, with no authorial thumbprint smudging its vacancies or deceptions. Yet, the phrase's refusal of art or embroidery, and the adhesion of Rider's tragedy to the deputy sheriff's narrative—the archetypicality of which troubles a contemporary reader, much as "Dry September" troubled Irving Howe—reveals the instability of vision.

Contesting the bare sociology of the ledger books and family trees that flutter through the pages of *Go Down, Moses* to give evidence of miscegenation and incest, the minor sightless moment and the telling aural interruption trouble the grander account of white men's violence and lust.

The short fictions share what I have come to think of as the tyranny of the section break—a structural upheaval that my own chapter approaches warily. Within both narratives—written a decade apart, in vastly different political contexts—section breaks fulfill an ideological and sensory function. To preserve Faulkner's ocularcentric claims to Morton Goldman, the reader and narrator are protected from the sight of lynching. Because Faulkner plays at verb tense and chronology, lynching is neither a closed book nor a present trauma. Like a cinematic flashback from whose violence the spectator erroneously believes chronology has protected her, it is erased from narrative past and present; it is, therefore, always imminent. If Faulkner, Hawkshaw, and the deputy sheriff privilege the ocular over the aural as evidence for firsthand witnessing, it is a position that protects all three from the obligation of militating against the violence of lynching.

Though Hawkshaw and the deputy sheriff remain frozen in place—one eternally watching his crime retreating in the dust, the other structurally resisting the totality of the McCaslin *begats*—Faulkner does not. Between "Dry September" and "Pantaloon in Black," Faulkner offered his most complete epistemology of race and the senses in *Light in August*. The narrative of Joe Christmas is, like the short fictions, placed in the racial sensorium, but it takes place in a canon of literatures of the visible and invisible; the deployment of this trope to theorize race does not begin with Ralph Ellison's *Invisible Man*, but instead pervades American literature—a canon peculiarly fixated on racial alterity and dermal variation. In the section that follows, I undertake the ambitious project of tracing a brief history of the trope of invisibility from Ellison's ancestors to his heirs, considering the ethics of the eye in a broader history than this section has considered the ethics of representing the primal (un)scene.

High Visibility

In the beginning was not the "ocular modernity" that, according to Mark M. Smith, transformed the soundscape of the Old South into the "worldview" of contemporary sensory paradigms (Smith 2001, 6). In the beginning—contiguous to that modernity, but rendered in a dramatically different language—was the mirror evoked by William Apess in "An Indian's Looking Glass for the White Man," an essay from *The Experience of Five Christian Indians* (1833). Writing with vernacular oral memory of the Pequot War (1637) and King Philip's War (1675–1676), Apess recalled the genocide that had transformed the Massachusetts Colony from a multiracial space to a white monolith, with an indigenous population numbering in the hundreds rather than its previous millions (Drake 2000, 110). Apess, a "praying Indian" and Methodist minister with Abolitionist inclinations, wrote of the disappearing Pequot tribes—the target of America's first genocidal war—and other indigenous people as reflective surfaces in which a white colonial minority scrupulously avoided seeing themselves:

> Assemble all nations together in your imagination, and then let the whites be seated among them, and then let us look for the whites, and I doubt not it would be hard finding them; for to the rest of the nations, they are still but a handful. Now suppose these skins were put together, and each skin had its national crimes written upon it—which skin do you think would have the greatest? (Apess 1992, 157)

Which skin, indeed, would be the darkest with the text's imagined inscription? The metaphoric conceit transforms the unmarked "white" flesh into paper onto which criminality and violence can be inscribed. Without acknowledgement of the crime of genocide, the flesh and nation remain white, but the lingering few New England Indians, and the diasporic Africans who were "rob[bed from] another nation to till their grounds and welter out their days under the lash" remain a truer mirror than any blank whiteness (Ibid., 157). However much Apess's white contemporaries might have cursed dark skin as the mark of Cain or the curse of Ham, it is, he argues, the truest reflection of their "national crime," a mimetic stain that the invention of whiteness obviated. In destroying and containing dangerous difference, whites exiled themselves from the mirror, and discovered in its absence a citizenship "link[ed] . . . to the abstract identity of white manhood" (Nelson 1998, 182).

As the Beat poet William Burroughs incants in "A Thanksgiving Prayer" (1986), people of color provided "a modicum of / challenge and danger" to the white colonial; the challenge of exterminating, enslaving, and silencing these dangers shaped American culture more than any European forebear. Thus, it is not an accident that Melville's *Moby Dick* (1851), written two decades after Apess composed the metaphor of the mirror, is set on a whaleship called *Pequod*, which is inhabited by disparate colors that create American fictions of metamerism—Ishmael's, Tashtego's, Queequeg's, Fedallah's, and Daggoo's. Surveying the ships in Nantucket, Ishmael chooses easily between the *Devil-Dam*, the *Tit-Bit*, and the *Pequod*, choosing the latter, because it was "the name of a celebrated tribe of Massachusetts Indians, now extinct as the ancient Medes" (Melville 1992, 100). To serve the dogma of absence— the exile of the indigenous, the containment of the African—delineated by Apess, the "vanishing Indian" motif developed in Melville's era to make "the theme of a dying race congenial" at the moment of genocide (Dippie 1991, 11). Before that, the "empty land" ideology persisted to excuse the American colonial project.[5] Both are tropes of invisibility. Ishmael's monologue in Nantucket and the eventual utopian cooperation on the ocean, allow for multiple readings of the relationship between disparate races and the American continent. A conservative reader might imagine the *Pequod* as a place of interracial cooperation and justice between the "colors" that created the early Republic, or a story of "the free world's triumph over a totalitarian power" (Pease 1986, 415). A more sensitive reading can consider the ship's contact zone as symptomatic of the leveling of difference in an ersatz democracy—or even a "ruthless democracy," in Melville's own words—whose downfall is relayed by a "narrator who only dimly and partially comprehends the clash of cultures unfolding everywhere around him" (Powell 2000, 155). Ahab must get the men in line by lying, wheedling, deceiving and resorting to violence until they sacrifice life, subjectivities, and identities in pursuit of whiteness, a trait that causes Ishmael "terror to the furthest bounds" (Melville 1992, 274). In our national literature, as Toni Morrison argues, the language imposed on haptic whiteness is "mute, meaningless, unfathomable, pointless, frozen, veiled, curtailed, dreaded, senseless [and] implacable" (Morrison 1993, 59).

If the canonical imaginary has so constructed whiteness, then Ralph Ellison's *Invisible Man* contested the literary history that preceded it, offering an account of racialized looking that draws from Apess and Melville's accounts of genocide and assimilation while providing an ocular confrontation rather than an elision. The trope of invisibility is used as both a critique of America and the articulation of one man's condition as an appendage of the national body. The tension between assimilation and syncretism, best represented in the Liberty Paints sequence, is not unresolved in the text or in Ellison's oeuvre since, as Morris Dickstein has written, Ellison "never tired of describing how different cultural forms, high and low, classical and vernacular, eastern and western, northern and southern, were braided together into an authentic American creativity" (Dickstein 2004, 129). But Ellison's narrator nonetheless encounters cultural forces that dwindle away Dickstein's list of adjectives into the unitary "American." At Liberty Paints, the Invisible Man learns that the "right white"—a startlingly colorless paint called "Optic White"—is made by adding "ten drops" of black tint, though the end result is a diamond white that covers the walls of major political and social institutions like the White House and Capitol Dome without a hint of the "blackness" within (Ellison 1995a, 205). The ability of these "democratic" institutions to function in light of the history of oppression depends on the disappearance of color. The nation, covered with Optic White and white nationalism, subsumes color, creating "a dumb blankness, full of meaning, in a wide landscape of snows—a colorless, all-color of atheism," demanding assimilation and invisibility (Melville 1992, 282). But the whitewash of the paint does not match the conditions of oppression faced by the narrator; a man is not merely a pigment.

After all, the Invisible Man can be seen. In his opening précis on invisibility, he tells the story of a white man mistaking him for a mugger as the exemplary incident of his condition; yet the man could see enough to approach him in the dark and shout at him an "insulting name" (Ellison 1995a, 4). All told, the Invisible Man suffers from "high visibility"—he is conspicuous everywhere he goes, from the Golden Day to the paint factory to the Men's House, once he is detected as a laborer. Black nationalist Ras the Exhorter—the narrator's sometime political antagonist—does not realize that an African-American man need not mount a white horse, as Ras does in the novel's final chapters to attract attention; the "scopic malice" that Maurice O. Wallace delineates in *Constructing the Black Masculine* will follow wherever he goes (Wallace 2002, 50). Black invisibility, in fact, means that skin is seen but subjectivity is not. Within the political confines of the cryptosocialist Brotherhood, the Invisible Man makes the horrifying observation that he had joined them because they did not see race, "when in reality it made no difference because they didn't see either color or men" (Ellison 1995a, 508). While that formulation might articulate the visual obstacles barring the sights of the Brotherhood, the logic of American race prejudice forces any black skin to stand in for another. Hence, the Invisible Man is looked at, but never seen. This mode of invisibility is expressed, in shifted terms, in James Baldwin's political memoirs in the decades that followed Ellison's novel: *Nobody Knows My Name* (1961) and *No Name in the Street* (1972).

In the racial formations of each of these writers—Apess, Melville, Ellison, Baldwin—the marked and marginalized subject is looked at but never looking, a position that feminist theory articulated in notions of the gaze and sexual surveillance. Film critic Laura Mulvey wrote that "in a world ordered by sexual imbalance, pleasure in looking has been split between active/male and passive/female. The determining gaze projects phantasy [sic] onto the female figure which is styled accordingly," thereby offering a language to a discipline's worth of feminist readings that followed (Mulvey 1998, 837). But, emerging from these nineteenth century antecedents and influencing the twentieth century texts with considerable self-awareness, William Faulkner consolidated his most iconic, paradigmatic, and, indeed, cinematic, scene of racial violence around the gaze of the violated man at his oppressors—shifting the violence into a private domain so that the public space of the fictional Jefferson, Mississippi remained unimplicated. The posse lynching of Joe Christmas—the parchment-colored, possibly biracial murderer of Joanna Burden—is a moment of radical severance in the (too-brief) literary history offered here, as it offers a reversal of the gaze while maintaining Faulkner's self-protective diminution of the aural sense as the mechanism of witnessing violence. Rather than imbue a black character with the gaze that has structured so many of these iconic American texts, Faulkner offers it to Joe Christmas only at the moment of death, in a narrative that, like the short fictions, resists and elides the present tense.

When racist whites look at a marginal subject they see nothing but his function as placeholder for racial anxiety. Despite their own failures of vision, lynch mobs understood the power of looking. Hence, multiple visual rhetorics were produced by collective violence. The first rhetoric was spatial, as Leon Litwack argues in *Trouble in Mind* (1999). Black men were brought to their own neighborhoods to be lynched, sometimes outside of their own homes or near the homes of family members. The tortured, lynched body then served as a visual warning, like the sea monsters drawn at trading borders on old maps: do not pass beyond this boundary. The second visual rhetoric was the publication and distribution of lynching photographs, postcards, and posters (Litwack 2000, 284–86). Images of lynching proved to be endlessly readable and writable surfaces, which enabled lynchers who saw death to witness it again and again, and distribute it to those who lacked their superior eyeline. Yet, the lynchers of *Light in August* have no grand designs on posterity or publicity. Indeed, they bypass the demands for public death by Christmas's grandfather, who shows up in Jefferson long enough to "preach . . . lynching" as the appropriate punishment for the perceived abomination of miscegenation (Faulkner [*Light in* August] 1990, 463). Rather than bring Christmas to public space to face his death, Percy Grimm and the uniformed, deputized lynchers that he and the sheriff organized bring the exterior public space of

Jefferson—the courthouse, the town square—into the "stale and cloistral dimness" of Hightower's house, evincing the permeability of private spaces (Ibid.).

In the chase with Christmas, Grimm is blinded by the "glint once like a flash of the heliograph as the sun struck the handcuffs," and seeks the man not with vision, but with the sound of difference in the "panting and desperate breath" that leads him from the "negro cabin" to the preacher's house (Ibid., 461). With his ocular sense diminished, he follows almost by instinct, simultaneously chasing and following Christmas. At the sight of him, Grimm, who had previously advocated "order [and] justice" befitting the "uniform of the United States," becomes feral with rage, emptying a gun into Joe's body, and then using a knife to it to remove his genitals (Ibid., 453). The deputies that follow him are shocked by the violence and the spectacle, but their ability to see—to structure hierarchies of vision around the power dynamic delineated by Apess, Melville, and Ellison—is diminished by the fact that it is Christmas who looks at them with eyes "empty of everything save consciousness" (Ibid., 465). Even in his long passage describing the gaze of the lynched man on his attackers, Faulkner's ability and willingness to describe the present tense of the violence are as muted as they are in the short stories; the narrative shifts from the present moment of castration to the future of the men upon whom Christmas gazes. With his eyes upon them, the white men are extracted from the living present; the gaze occupies the same imminence of lynching's trauma in the short fictions, dispersing and "soaring into memories forever and ever . . . in whatever peaceful valleys, beside whatever placid and reassuring streams of old age . . . they will contemplate old disasters and newer hopes" (Ibid.). Thus, even in the moment of lynching's violence, Faulkner temporally displaces his reader, enabling a construction of the violence that is an imminent past and a deterministic future, with a vexed relationship to the present. Indeed, this construction also resides in a vexed relationship to race. As Philip M. Weinstein has argued, "there are very few actual blacks in this race-obsessed novel." With so few named black characters and narratives offered about their "flesh-and-blood reality," the novel becomes instead a "lifelong nightmare of a white man *imagining* himself (and imagined by others) to be a black" in a "murderously projective state" (Weinstein 1987, 177–78). Indeed, the visual metaphor of projection persists in the death scene, unless readers are persuaded that the account they have of Joe Christmas's gaze is one seamlessly communicated from the face of the dying man to the futures of the men who murdered him.

Though Joe's eyes promise the deputies lives of haunting uncertainty, guilt, and grief, the spatial dynamic that Faulkner constructs forecloses accountability for the offense to the smaller circle of individuals, rather than to the larger community of Jefferson, which has tacitly condoned the violence—or to American structures of apartheid, which created in Christmas the certainty that the barest trace of black "blood" would doom him to a life of fetishistic sexual violence and wounded subjectivity. Lynching's cultural logic is ignored when the person who serves as its instigator and agent is not a figure of community authority—but a reckless, fascistic bundle of sexual pathologies; under these conditions, literature lies. Yet, Faulkner's avoidance of social commentary against lynching is most evident in the fact that it is not a black man who is castrated and killed on the floor of Hightower's house. From his first appearance, Christmas is a racially ambiguous figure, with "level dead parchment color[ed]" skin that provokes Mississippians to *ask* if he is a foreigner, not assume that he is a black man (Faulkner 1990b, 33–34). Contrasted to the marked bodies of Rider and Will Mayes, Christmas is pale; by every available cultural lens, his skin is white, even if his fatherlessness and marginality make him racially suspect. Whatever present tense Faulkner constructs or avoids, the "pale body" on Hightower's floor, with blood pouring out like a "rush of sparks from a rising rocket," is not the specularized body that organized the mob dynamics of lynching in Jim Crow America. That lynching—the racial lynching—is one that Faulkner and his intended audience "never saw" and "couldn't describe." Indeed, to preserve privileged sight and space, it cannot be represented.[6]

In a stunning triptych in *Without Sanctuary: Lynching Photography in America* (2000), Frank Embree stands naked in front of a lynch mob in Fayette, Missouri. Taken in 1899, the three photographs show him, in ascending order: (1) hanging from a tree with dozens of men crowding around him to touch the bark as an extension of his body; (2) alive, revealing his flogged buttocks and back to the crowd; and (3) gazing with startling forthrightness at the camera, with his manacled hands cupped over his genitals. When I first saw this photograph, I was struck—perhaps like the men who follow Grimm into Hightower's house with curiosity that turns to horror and sickness as they witness his mutilation and corporeal destruction—by his gaze, certain that it challenged and complicated the sight of the lynching in the space that surrounded him and the one that surrounded me eleven decades later. Perhaps, as a literary critic, I saw in him some real-life avatar of Joe Christmas, whose death is transformed into a crucifixion by Faulkner's craft and attention to the unsettling potential of the senses. Looking at Frank Embree's face three years later in tandem with the literary death of Joe Christmas, I see less of a challenge than a foreclosure of witness. In his eyes is not an accusation, but the unknowable imminent muteness of death. Sight, powerful though it may be in Western conceptions of sentiment and sensibility, is not the only sense; whether or not it is the most powerful, the sine qua non of witnessing violence, is an unanswerable question.

In Faulkner's constructions, the ocular is the witness's only sense; the account of Christmas's death ends with the assertion, once again, of aural insufficiency. "Again from the town, deadened a little from the walls," Faulkner writes, "the scream of the siren mounted toward its unbelievable crescendo, passing out of the realm of hearing" (Ibid., 465). Concluding with this description provides Faulkner a chance to reassert the power of the lynching, the thing he did not see in Oxford, but its power cannot be contained in sound, whose intensities are "unbelievable," whose stimuli "pass . . . out of the realm" of the senses, while sight lingers in the "memor[y] forever and ever" (Ibid.). In the final dimension of my argument, I consider Faulkner's own excecated vision and aural witness to the crime of lynching. His powerful insistence on vision as the definitive sense is an elision of witness, a salve against memories that pass through the other senses.

Son of Mississippi, Child of the South

On the morning of September 8, 1908, Nelse Patton, a trustee at the Lafayette County Jail in Oxford, Mississippi, brought a message to Mattie McMillan, the wife of another prisoner. According to the contradictory news stories that followed, he either raped her or had his sexual advances repulsed. All sources agree that he used a razor to cut her throat so thoroughly that she was nearly decapitated. A broken piece of the razor stuck in McMillan's exposed vertebrae, and was used to identify the weapon found in Patton's pocket when he was apprehended. The wounded Patton was taken back to the courthouse, where he was again jailed. A mob gathered and W. V. Sullivan, former United States senator from Lafayette County, urged the crowd to break down the walls; his presence assured them that they participated in a "good lynching," in which the mob was "few in number and recognized leaders maintained relatively tight discipline" (McMillen 1990, 242). Several children, including Faulkner's friend John Cullen, were boosted through the windows of the prison to let the grown-ups enter. Once the mob had Patton in their grasp, they shot him, castrated him, and mutilated his face and head. His body was hanged from a tree in front of the courthouse, and left hanging until morning. A fusillade of bullets was emptied into the corpse and, for the sake of propriety, overalls were placed on his body to obscure his mutilated genitals. For his own part, Senator Sullivan, speaking with the voice of authority, said that he had "led the mob which lynched Nelse Patton" and was "proud of it. I directed every movement of the mob and I did everything I could to see that he was lynched. Cut a white woman's throat? . . . Of course I wanted him lynched . . . I don't care what investigation is made . . . I will lead a mob in such a case any time" (Ibid., 225). The lynching, with its unimaginable noise and odor, happened fewer than one hundred yards from the bedroom window of eleven-year old Billy Faulkner. One wonders what he heard, what he saw, what he thought of the spectacle and, indeed, what recollection child witnesses of lynching carried with them into adulthood.

Native of Montgomery County, Kentucky, poet and literary critic Allen Tate witnessed a lynching in July 1911. In the poem "The Swimmers" (1963), Tate, as transfixed by Southern history as Faulkner, recounts the story. Tate passes a posse on the road and follows in the "cloudy hearse" of horse-hoof dust as the sheriff and a stranger drag the body through town and dump it in front of the courthouse. Gazing at the corporeal remnants of the lynching, Tate reflects on the distinction between public and private violence:

> My breath crackled the dead air like a shotgun
> As, sheriff and the stranger disappearing,
> The faceless head lay still. I could not run
>
> Or walk, but stood. Alone in the public clearing
> This private thing was owned by all the town,
> Though never claimed by us within my hearing. (Tate 1997, 135)

In a white supremacist paradigm that prized the private sphere containing the sexually guarded bodies of children and the sacralized bond of racially endogamous marriage, the public sphere became the site of regulatory violence. To maintain the sharp distinctions between the violent work of men and the world of women and children, silence surrounds the common practice of lynching in Tate's poem. Silence is necessary to "manage the rupture to identity posed by the memory of lynching," argues Anne P. Rice in her analysis of the role of white children in acts of mob violence (Rice 2005, 48). The violent sites and sights of lynching are to be preserved in the memories of African-Americans, who are required by white supremacy to live within the trauma, inscribing it on segregated communities and carcerally-contained bodies. But white children were asked to half-remember: to recall the violence that could be deployed against African-Americans, but forget it so that they could associate home, community, and the public sphere with the pleasures of conventional, rather than mob, citizenship. "You shut the bad away and remember only the pleasant," wrote antiracist activist Lillian Smith of her relationship to her native North Carolina (Smith 1994, 71). To both banish and remember was the task of the passive lynching witnesses—often children—who looked and listened without touching or maiming.

For John Cullen, a friend of Faulkner's and an "apprentice lyncher," as Rice calls the male children who participated in the ritual capture and torture of lynching victims, such forgetting would obliterate the pleasures of memory that he evidently felt when recounting his story to Floyd C. Watkins more than fifty years after Nelse Patton's death. His narrative, putatively linking Nelse Patton's story to Joe Christmas's in *Light in August*, places his own acts of teenage heroism at the center of the story. Reading the ghost-written account in *Old Times in the Faulkner Country* (1961), we are to believe that Cullen fearlessly faced Nelse Patton, who is transformed into two caricatures of black men, the criminal and the minstrel, capable of murder even as he implores, in the language of Stepin Fetchit: "Mr. Jenks, you knows I'se a good nigger" (Cullen and Watkins 1961, 90). In his self-aggrandizing account, Cullen faces Patton twice: first in the woods, where he was "ready to shoot him between the eyes" and then in his jail cell, filled with gunpowder and smoke from the efforts of the lynch mob. Twice he is able to stare down the accused murderer, armed first with a razor and then with a "heavy iron coal-shovel handle," without receiving a wound (Ibid., 91). The only action of the lynching from which Cullen's narrative bars him was the least "heroic," the mutilation and dragging of Patton's corpse. Even at his privileged vantage point, Cullen claims that the excesses of the lynching were committed by persons unknown. Cullen makes the inarguable claim that Faulkner interpolated parts of Patton's story into *Light in August* and *Sanctuary*, but evidently believes that the portrayal of Percy Grimm, who he compares to Senator W. V. Sullivan, is a heroic one, despite the evidently jaundiced view that Faulkner takes of him, when he says that Grimm had "a sublime and implicit faith in physical courage and blind obedience, and a belief that the white race is superior to any and all other races and that the American is superior to all other white races . . . and that all that would ever be required of him in payment for this belief, this privilege, would be his own life" (Faulkner 1990b, 451).

Cullen, the onetime human projectile and catalyst for the lynching, did not grow into a racial progressive, but a racist who believed that the scandal of Emmett Till's death was not the murder itself, but the "hysteria" of the

North, that white and black Southerners "have more fun" if they live in segregated circumstances, and that the white Mississippian was the "friend" of the African-American (Cullen and Watkins 1961, 56–60). Troublingly, he transfers all of these prejudices to Faulkner, claiming that they are the community standards that Faulkner practiced, even if his public speeches "are stronger and more liberal than his personal opinions" (Ibid., 59). Perhaps it is a failure of imagination on my part, but I can see Faulkner as neither a human projectile nor an ardent "seg;" it takes a greater leap than I can make to imagine the young Nobel Laureate leaping through a jailhouse window to do the work of adult lynchers. I cannot imagine him as so active a *witness*, the kind of witness that he eschewed and denied in his letter to Morton Goldman. But I imagine Joe Christmas, Lucas Beauchamp, Will Mayes, and Rider as remnants of memory heard but not quite seen, remembered if not quite touched.

If Faulkner managed to avoid an immersive relationship to the mob, he might yet have been unable to close his ears, though an apprentice lyncher might have been able to close his eyes. The abstraction of hearing makes for a more troubled and ambivalent Faulkner. Encountering a primal (aural) scene—the primal (un)scene—compels the listener to reconstruct, visualize, and invent; in short, deferred sight enables the mechanism of fiction. The other senses are, like vision, hazy shadows of memory laboring toward its reconstruction. A hundred years after Faulkner's primal (un)scene, my questions linger. Was his "Mammy Callie"—Caroline Barr—with him on the night of Patton's death? Was her body, and the bodies of other African-Americans in Oxford, hazarded by the violence of the mob? What does one hear a hundred yards away from a fusillade of bullets? What sound emits from "four hours of hard work . . . to break through the thick walls of steel and masonry" necessitated by the police's refusal to provide the mob with keys to Patton's cell (Ibid., 95)? What can one *avoid* hearing? It strains the imagination to think that Faulkner heard nothing, since sound is created by proximities to motion, to congestion. "There is a geographical quality to listening," writes Diane Ackerman in *A Natural History of the Senses* (1991). "But it all begins with quivering molecules of air, each being jostled into the next like a crowd pressing forward into a subway" (Ackerman 1991, 178). Without immersion in the crowd, hearing becomes exaggerated because the other senses are choked and blocked. Memory creeps, moving from the external crush of bodies to the interior of the listener.

If we return to Faulkner's letter to Morton Goldman, questions proliferate. What formations of cognitive dissonance are required for the hearer to attest that he could not describe such traumatic violence? In my imaginative reconstruction of the night of September 8, 1908, I have preserved Faulkner as a speaker of truth: "I never saw a lynching," he told Morton Goldman. If he did not see, he might—*must*, in fact—still have heard. The ocularcentrism of his memory formation preserves his refusal to accept responsibility for his place in the social order of white supremacy. If the role of children under lynch mob rule was, as Anne P. Rice argues, to learn the lessons of racial oppression while forgetting the violence that shores up the system, Faulkner fails. But within the formal spaces of fiction, he succeeds in hiding violence in plain sight, shifting it to narrative aporias in the stories, and private spaces in *Light in August*, to omit the community-wide approval of lynching itself, despite Mississippi's reputation as "the land of the tree and the home of the grave" (McMillen 1990, 252).[7]

CHAPTER FOUR

The Lynched Woman

Kara Walker, Laura Nelson, and the Question of Agency

Regarding Pain

In the coldest months of 2000, sixty black-and-white postcards were displayed in the Roth Horowitz Gallery in New York City. Of the exhibition, organizer Andrew Roth said that he hoped that no crush of visitors strained the capacity of the small gallery, but crowds formed nonetheless—piling into "a [claustrophobic] black room [with] coarse red carpets," its starkness underscored by images of horrifying racist violence (Hale 2002, 990–91). Castrated bodies, tormented faces, and grinning perpetrators greeted the crowds of five thousand a day who attempted to squeeze into the 22 x 14 gallery, where Witness: Photographs of Lynching from the Collection of James Allen and John Littlefield, was exhibited for the first three months of the new millennium. Some who saw these images thought they "promot[ed] healing" between races (Tucker 2002). Others responded differently. "To commercialize the suffering of black people is to do the ultimate disservice to black people," argued Michael Dyson. "To make coffee tables out of that kind of pain is highly problematic" (quoted in Apel 2003, 464). Historian Grace Elizabeth Hale, who visited the New York exhibition space to review it for The Journal of American History, later wrote that "viewers [were] left with an exhibit that is too close to the spectacle created by the lynchers themselves" and demanded that stories of black resistance and activism accompany the images to contest their "intended" conflation of blackness with victimization (Hale 2001, 993).

At the exhibition's website, which assembled all of the images for free—perhaps in response to Dyson's claim about a profit motive—viewers used the forums to claim that "hatred is part of our human heritage" (DSB), and in the longest thread, angry white men argue that "black strippers" in league with "black racists" did unto Duke University's lacrosse team as white juries once did to the Scottsboro Boys (John R). That accused rapists Reade Seligmann, Collin Finnerty, and David Evans served not a day in jail, while six of the seven Scottsboro Boys were sentenced to death, is not mentioned in this post, nor is the fact that the longest-serving of the Scottsboro Boys went to jail for thirteen years and committed suicide upon release. Responses to these images—web denizens dreaming of a vast conspiracy of black radicals, professors shaking their fists at the money that exchanges hands for consumption of artifacts of atrocity, and journalists contemplating the triumph of the human spirit actuated in their presence—vary, perhaps revealing that images are glyphs in search of a translator, endlessly flexible interpretive objects demanding an agent to imbue them with meaning.

In the space of one chapter, I cannot offer a complete genealogy of each view, as it requires reservoirs of optimism, which I lack, to transform lynching photographs into catalysts for post-racial reconciliation, dimensions of cynicism which I eschew to call the exhibition of lynching photography a get-rich-quick scheme by James Allen, and because I am loath to spend another moment in the presence of white racial paranoia, particularly when it is paired with gleeful misogyny. But I am compelled to return to Hale's contention that the exhibition ought to contain a refutation of "victimization as the defining characterization of blackness," paired with her sense that the photographs were taken with the intention of communicating that condition (Hale 2002, 994). While Hale and I agree that violence ought to be "foreground[ed] . . . as a defining characteristic of whiteness" within these exhibitions, we differ on the mechanism of foregrounding that violence.

This chapter asks for reconsiderations of two dimensions of critique; first, it offers a genealogy of critical deployments of "agency" as a means to contest their obfuscations of dimensions of victimhood and oppression. Second, it hopes to save voyeurism rather than bury it, to contest Hale's desire to diminish the participatory violence of spectatorship. My own position treads dangerously close to irrelevancy because Hale has, seven years after her initial critique, triumphed. Responding to her criticisms, the Allen/Littlefield images were collectively renamed *Without Sanctuary: Lynching Photography in America* (2000) and juxtaposed to a plethora of primary and secondary sources—the lyrics of Abel Meeropol's "Strange Fruit," the anti-lynching pamphlets of Ida Wells-Barnett, and the text of James Baldwin's short fiction "Going to Meet the Man"—to diminish spectators' experience of voyeuristic consumption in the subsequent traveling exhibition. "The black voices of lament," wrote Dora Apel, "provided a sense of black subjectivity that worked as counterweight to the largely faceless black corpses and smug white mobs in the photos" (Apel 2003, 472). The reclamation of agency and critique of the gaze are orthodoxies within these criticisms, echoed by Hale and Apel in their sense that it is undifferentiated subjectivity—a condition equivalent, rather than ancillary to, to corporeal violence—which constitutes the crime for which the photographs are evidence. This chapter attempts to put Hale's critique into conversation with comparable objections to Kara Walker's work, theorizations of pornography, and debates over the agency of marginalized subjects, to consider what I call "anxieties of audience," rather than influence: the fear that the "wrong" spectators—ones pruriently aroused by violence or invested in easy racial reconciliations—will consume these representations, thereby colonizing the sensorium with racialized logics and flattening the subjectivity of the photographed subjects at whom they gaze.

Voyeurism often comes to infamy in critical theory, since racism and misogyny can themselves be read as logics of surveillance deployed against the oppressed by the dominant society. Yet, forcing privileged spectators to step into the position of the lynch mob is, in my estimation, the benefit of Allen and Littlefield's efforts, as it prevents identificatory conflations between spectator and lynching victim that "increase . . . the difficulty of beholding black suffering" (Hartman 1997, 20).[1] Conflations between lynched men and white gallery spectators offer the latter a balm against considering their vested positions in structural violences and inequities inherited from American apartheid, because they are able to consider themselves potential victims rather than potential perpetrators, as Susan Sontag argues of war photography in her final book, *Regarding the Pain of Others* (2004):

> The imaginary proximity to the suffering inflicted on others that is granted by images suggests a link between far-away sufferers . . . and the privileged viewer that is . . . yet one more mystification of our real relations to power. So far as we feel sympathy, we feel we are not accomplices to what caused the suffering. Our sympathy proclaims our innocence as well as our impotence . . . To set aside the sympathy we extend to others beset by war and murderous politics for a reflection on how our privileges are located on the same map as their suffering, and may—in ways we might prefer not to imagine—be linked to their suffering . . . is a task for which the painful, stirring images supply only an initial spark. (Sontag 2003, 102–103)

Instead of sympathy and identification—feelings an audience can inherit or co-opt from narratives of black resistance to lynching, a political position that has reached near unanimity in contemporary America—white spectators ought to consider the more troubling possibility of parity with the lynch mob as they crowd into exhibition halls, much as lynchers crowded into town squares—pushing and struggling for eyeline, for coverage, for totalities of vision—so that the exhibition can critique consuming visions as privileged inheritances of American culture.

When she treats lynching explicitly rather than implicitly in her reading of atrocity photographs, Sontag's position is more ambiguous and perhaps more closely aligned to that of Hale. "Intrinsic to the perpetration of this evil is the shamelessness of photographing it," she writes of *Without Sanctuary* (Ibid., 91). This position is one that she shares with curator James Allen, who called the photographer "more than a perceptive spectator" but something closer to a perpetrator of lynching (Allen et al. 2000, 204). Sontag asserts not only the sense of photography as crime— a position shared by the United States Armed Forces, which convicted soldiers at Abu Ghraib for photographing a corpse, but not interrogators for killing the man pictured in these postmortem photographs—but also the sense that looking at images of war is *more* necessary in the post-9/11 context of imperialist foreign policy, where critique is "regarded . . . as a most unpatriotic endeavor" (Sontag 2003, 94). Positing something close to a zero-sum struggle between racism at home and nationalism abroad, Sontag suggests that the emphasis on justice for African-Americans siphons energy from the international struggle for peace, since the antiracist position has become "a benchmark of civic virtue" in domestic, if not international, policy (Ibid., 93). While I disagree with the stakes that she posits, I would agree that certain kinds of memory occlude others. In the final sections of this chapter, I consider the longstanding invisibility of lynching in American scholarship—a period that stretches from the NAACP's 1940 conference on the status of anti-lynching legislation to "Lynching and Racial Violence in America: Histories and Legacies," a symposium held at Emory University in 2002—as a function of the iconic status of slavery in American life, a status that enables racist claims that the institution's temporal remoteness requires neither reparation nor restitution, and antiracist critiques that have posited the freedom of slaves to act on their own behalf in the space of the plantation; this agency is more difficult to locate in the carceral containments and blood rituals of Jim Crow.

Within Hale's critique, the quest for agentic subjectivities comes into contact with a theoretical truism emerging from forty years of feminist interventionist scholarship: the notion of the marginalized subject as target of a violent gaze that functions as part of their oppression. As Laura Mulvey wrote in "Visual Pleasure and Narrative Cinema" (1975)—the essay that launched a thousand citations—"in a world ordered by sexual imbalance, pleasure in looking has been split between active/male and passive/female. The determining gaze projects phantasy [sic] on to the female figure which is styled accordingly" (Mulvey 1998, 837). Truth and truism that Mulvey's claim has become, does not address the necessary corollary of the deployment of the gaze against men, whose effects are delineated by Susan Bordo in "Reading the Male Body" (1993):

> Outside of homoerotic representations . . . the penis has grown more, not less, culturally cloaked over time. The phallus, of course, is always *symbolically* in evidence, from metaphors of war and weaponry to contemporary worship of pumped-up muscle. . . . But only in pornography and homoerotic representations do we see the phallus embodied in the erect human penis—insofar as it is capable of being soft as well as hard, injured as well as injuring. (Bordo 1993, 698–99)

Since mainstream texts—from Maxim to Cosmopolitan, from late-night advertisements for Girls Gone Wild to mid-afternoon chat shows that parade the bodies of teenage girls and transsexual women—traffic in the spectacle of the social threat and commodity of femininity, it is pornography—the hidden text of popular culture—that reveals the male. Even in the last ten years, which have authorized the so-called mainstreaming of pornography in a "raunch culture" in which exhibition of the female body is "not extraordinary [but] emblematic," the cultural sense that the naked male is the sine qua non of abjection, of filth, of smut, has not diminished (Levy 2005, 17). One knows they are looking at pornography at the sight of the penis—and perhaps more-so at a flaccid penis, since patriarchy makes no room for soft male flesh. Therefore, however necessary the pornography debates of the 1980s, they remain theoretically incomplete insofar as they seldom treated the cultural meaning of the male body when transformed from the possessor of the gaze to its target in violent, sexualized spectacle—a transformation accomplished and inflicted upon the bodies of men of color pictured in lynching postcards. If the penis is imagined only "as a weapon in intercourse with a social inferior," then the exposure and mortification of the male body are erased, preventing productive confrontations between feminist models of the gaze and spectacles of racist violence (Dworkin 2006, 24).

The privileged gaze in a gallery space filled with images of lynchings doubles the gendered stakes of visual power, placing it on the racially-marked body, which is almost always male, and often represented with visual cues that tease at the potential for more complete exposure. Frank Embree's nudity is barely concealed in the 1899 photographs of a lynching in process (Allen et al. 2000, plates 42–44); Abram Smith is covered with a Klan robe draped over where his trousers had been before they were torn away in the frenzy of genital violence (Ibid., plate 32); and the mob gathering below Jesse Washington's charred body does nothing to conceal the murder committed, though they diaper the corpse to hide his genitals (Ibid., plate 24). Centuries of antiracist activism in which the public sphere has been the site of pleading for "manhood rights" for African-Americans spectrally reappear in the gallery spaces that hosted *Without Sanctuary*. The Abolitionist plaint, "Am I not a man and a brother?" morphs into the demand that the white man's zone of corporeal privacy be extended to the men of color in these images, as if their exposure heightens the pain of their deaths, a possibility hinted at in the title of the exhibition, whose denial of sanctuary refers as mimetically to the flesh's exposure as to its mortification.

One might ask, in response to a demand for coverage—which would diminish the white and male particularities of privacy—that spectators process these images not as pornographic spectacle, but as evidence. Imagine a person indicted on federal charges of possessing or trafficking in child pornography; in this case, the distinction between evidence and pornography becomes negligible. Presumptive guilt is brought into being by a juridical tautology: pornography is evidence of a crime, yet evidence is pornography and therefore erased from the sight of his accuser. By juridical convention, his accusers include every reader of this chapter, who are nonetheless protected from an encounter with pornographic evidence of wrongdoing. The hypothetical case transforms each subject into a blinded agent of the state, required by convention to react with a frenzy of outrage at a spectacle to which they cannot bear witness. The tautology that posits spectacle as crime, and crime as a spectacle to be concealed is consistent with Catharine MacKinnon's argument in *Only Words* (1996), in which she argues that pornographic text can never serve as evidence, since its evidentiary weight reproduces not only the traumas of sexual violence, but also its motivating ideologies. Addressing a hypothetical "you" brutalized by intimates and pornographers, MacKinnon writes:

> [Viewers] do not feel your pain as pain any more than those who watched as they hurt you to make the pictures felt it. The

pictures, surrounded by a special halo of false secrecy and false taboo—false because they really are public and are not really against the rules—have become the authority on what happened to you, the literature of your experience. (MacKinnon 1996, 4)

Though curator James Allen circulates lynching photography—a position perhaps akin to the pornographer, in the most absolutist critiques of their distribution—he seems to agree with MacKinnon, arguing that photography at the scene of the lynching "facilitate[ed] an endless replay of anguish" (Allen et al. 2000, 205). Laws against pornography—and, indeed, Allen's curator's note—thus reveal a contradiction. The viewer—whether a juridical authority or a subject under law—is corrupted by the act of looking, though one of those categories must remain incorruptible in order to sanction or pass sentence against the other.

To see pornography is not to become its preferred subject, as anti-pornography theorists—who often voraciously watch pornography to report on its excesses—assert. Robert Jensen, author of *Getting Off: Pornography and the End of Masculinity* (2007), quotes at length from so-called "gonzo" porn, clarifying for the concerned reader that while he looks at pornography for his research, he no longer "uses" it. One assumes that the verb *to use* is a euphemism for an act far more nefarious than masturbation: the formation of an aspirational relationship between pornography and one's already-existing relationship to the Gaze (Jensen 2007, 40–41). The paradox of Jensen's approach emerges in the two questions with which he concludes the prologue: "can we bear to look?" and "can we afford not to?" (Ibid., 11). Thus, anti-pornography interventions imagine their target as a text with inherent intention, requiring a carefully-trained eye to locate its utility, but lacking the tension that enables skeptical reading of any other text, visual or written. Though I regard anti-pornography critiques with great sympathy—believing, as many assert, that the economic conditions that create pornography and the industry that produces it cannot find a space outside of coercion—the flattening of the visual field is a limitation of their analysis, and one that produces a troubling anxiety about audience that infects the discourse around lynching photography.

Since Grace Elizabeth Hale assumes that lynching photography is—as many feminists have argued of pornography—a text with inherent intention, she asks that contemporary audiences valorize resistant agency—the proposed opposite to "victimhood"—an embarrassing condition of oppression from which much so-called "third-wave" feminist and antiracist criticism attempts to save their objects of study. But we ought not accept Hale's sense that lynchers ask photographic spectators to experience the lynched man or woman as a "victim"; they ask, instead, that we look at them as criminals—an inexact opposite, but a very different assignation nonetheless. As Judith Butler argued of images of Rodney King being beaten by four officers of the Los Angeles Police Department, "the visual representation of the black male body being beaten on the street . . . was taken up by that racist interpretive framework to construe King as the *agent* of violence, one whose agency is phantasmatically implied as the narrative precedent and antecedent to the frames that are shown" (Butler 2004, 205). For the purposes of undermining this narrative, the next section treats two very different lynching photographs—those of Frank Embree and Laura Nelson—with no narrative of their alleged offenses, because I believe that we ought not structure our experience of these photographs around a sense of the crime of which the lynched man or woman was accused.

Such a narrative reinscribes the association of blackness with criminality; the status of the "criminal" is the only potential identity recognized for marginal subjects under discriminatory legal constructs (Hartman 1997, 41). It is that condition—not victimhood—that enables a spectator to look at the lynched man and ask, "what did he do?" The question comes dangerously close to asking, "what did he do to deserve this?" even though no crime warrants torture as a punishment. Associations of violence and corporeal threat within those questions enabled lynch mobs to imagine their violence as the pacification of immense danger and violence: his strength and power, after all, affirm *their* strength and power because they are able to subdue him. Both tasks—"confirming a collective identity" and the "oblatory, efficacious goal of giving up something valuable" and powerful—are the primary modes of collective violence (Pizzato 2005, 8). Their violence is dependent, therefore, upon a preexisting agentic narrative of the threat of that lynched persons pose with their marked bodies, pathological desires, and iron wills.

Arguments for agency are, I fear, closer to the "intended" message of lynch mobs than the one Hale posits. Her critique takes place against the backdrop of the critical history of agency—the extension of resistant personhood to marginal people—from American slaves to sweatshop workers in the developing world to porn stars and prostitutes—all seen, by various theorists in varying social contexts, as finding an outside to oppression in the practices that might seem to reify or reiterate the conditions of their exploitation. In the next section of this chapter, I consider this question of agency for the scholars and artists that have "looked at" and "used" the images of Frank

Embree and Laura Nelson—to borrow Robert Jensen's verbs—and found in images significantly different agencies dependent upon the gender of the lynched person.

Debates over the question of agency emerge from the renaissance of scholarship on American slavery in the 1960s—from Eugene Genovese to Kenneth Stampp to Stanley Elkins—and have created what Hugh Tulloch called a "Teflon slave" immune to any indignity of the peculiar institution, with ideological constructions of subjectivity that mask the material conditions of oppression (Tulloch 2000, 64). In the third section, I trace the trajectories of these arguments through the work of Kara Walker, whose self-described "inner plantation" and images of sexual abuse of male and female slaves have evoked long debates about black women's sexual agency and the permissibility of reproducing taboo images of racialized sexual violence. In the argument's final sections, I argue that the baroque scenes of violence in Walker's art should be considered in relationship to lynching as well as the plantation, because mob violence reveals the circumscription of agency—a condition that the field of slavery studies works to deny—and therefore problematize volitionary models of oppression emerging from new social history. In the fourth section, I practice a "new" context for Walker, arguing for her self-portrait "Cut" as a lynching silhouette that challenges the ambiguities and limitations of prevailing models of subjectivity and enslavement.

The Ethics of Voyeurism

A man stares. A woman dangles. I stop short of direct objects in my attempts to describe photographs of the lynchings of Frank Embree (1899) and Laura Nelson (1901) to gesture discursively and desirously toward the fiction of neutrality. But, with a sentence's worth of hindsight, I begin to question even the verbs. What ideologies of the enslavers and the lynchers do I emplot when I deploy these terms—one laden with agency, the other with inertia? I would not be left alone and shivering in a shy corner of critical inquiry if I decided to let these verbs remain, since the Mulveyan formation—men act, women appear—continues to reside in critical writing on these two lynching photographs. Rather than posit the authority of action or agency as the solution to the problem of voyeurism—its embeddedness in power, its vexed relationship to empiricism—I would like to suggest the radical potential of "looking at" lynching photographs—thereby risking voyeurism—rather than "using" them for the ideological aims of locating resistance within the visual field, as the tripartite photographs of Frank Embree have so often been used.

I am a recovering "user" of lynching photographs. When I began this project more than two years ago, I argued, in an essay subsequently published in *Psychoanalysis, Culture, and Society* (September 2007), that Frank Embree's eyes could militate against the problematic of the gaze, charging their viewer with the task not of looking, but of looking back (Lightweis-Goff 2007, 294). In that formation, I believed I had located an entry into debates that could clear the field of assumptions about ocularcentrism. Here was a paragon of resistance who could reveal the ideological diversity and potential of first-generation lookers—the lynchers who saw his body destroyed, the antilynching activists in the Northern cities who militated against mob violence with exhibitions of lynching artifacts, the African-Americans who fled North from mob terror, with mental images of violence interpellating them.[2] The theoretical intervention I offered, though, was no radical refiguring of the gaze, as it echoed the perceptions of scholars who saw and critiqued *Without Sanctuary*, particularly Jacqueline Goldsby and Dora Apel.

Here, I practice three descriptions of Frank Embree as an introduction to Goldsby and Apel's readings (Allen et al. 2000, plates 42–44). A black man stands, revealing his strong torso and arms, but concealing his genitals, thereby revealing the phallus and concealing the penis that "haunt[s]" it with the threat of flaccidity and violability which patriarchal models of masculinity deny (Bordo 1993, 697). As he grasps his penis, he seizes white masculinity, a condition determined by bodily concealment; his eyes dare and challenge the spectator. Most importantly, they deny them access to the black penis, the prized souvenir of lynching spectacles, the erotic trophy of fetishists from photographer Robert Mapplethorpe to serial killer Jeffrey Dahmer who "incorporate [and] eat through the eyes" in a process that, according to David Marriott, elides the distinction between "appreciating and destroying, loving and hating" (Marriott 2000, 27). But we might journey, without a long walk, to seeing Embree as the paradigmatic human sacrifice as delineated by George Bataille. Writing of the Chinese practice of "death by a thousand cuts," Bataille remarked that the face of the punished man transforms—even as his torso and arms are shredded by the knife-wielding elite of his community—into a mixture of "these perfect contraries, divine ecstasy and its opposite, extreme horror" (Bataille 1989, 208). Drifting into a Bataillian interstice between pain and knowledge, Frank Embree locates resistance and sacrifices himself with ecstatic, messianic determination, using his eyes to say, as Christ did in the Gospel of Luke: "into thy hands I commend my spirit" (23:46). The sacrifice shores up the utility of the image for black spectators who have sometimes argued, like Gwendolyn Brooks, that "the loveliest lynchee was our Lord" (Brooks 2006, 70). Or, we might see Embree as controlling and haunting memory—accusing, like Joe Christmas does at the end of his life in *Light in August* (1932)—marking the white spectator as perpetrator and witness, just as American ideologies of color marked him as black and therefore disposable.

Looking at the lynching images of Nelson and Embree side-by-side reveals vastly different photographic conventions and scholarly responses. Embree's lynching-in-progress unfolds over three images: the first reveals his shackled hands and forthright gaze; the second reveals his mortified back and buttocks; and the final shows his hanging body, with men gathering around it to touch the hanging tree's bark as though it is an extension of Embree's brutalized flesh. In the proliferating responses to *Without Sanctuary*, scholars have commented on these images—remarkable not only for their revelation of the lynching process, but also for the sense of contemporary spectators that Embree's eyes are interrogating the response of the comparatively privileged audience in the rarefied air of an art gallery. In an unsigned editorial in *The New York Times*, the reader is sternly instructed that the gallery space "sanctioned" a different gaze than the one privileged by the mob, in part because of the photograph of Frank Embree, who "looks back at us, beyond us too, challenging our moral imagination across the years" ("Death by Lynching" 2000). Art historian Dora Apel writes that "a nude Embree stands on a buggy and faces the camera with calm defiance, as if challenging our historical imagination a hundred years later to look and see" (Apel 2003, 467). In a similar vein, Jacqueline Goldsby writes that Embree "glare[s] directly into the camera lens and rebuff[s] its gaze with an indignant grimace," his "courage call[ing] to mind the mob's readiness to exploit his vulnerability" (Goldsby 2006, 237). The revelation of Embree's "resistant" eyes and body simultaneously provoke and feed the critical quest for agency—the desire to find in marginalized and violated subjects some freedom *within* the experience of oppression.

That this impulse is located by critics in the eyes and powerfully muscled body of a man is not, I think, a coincidence, since the terms of agentic arguments are so often invested with the language of masculinized power. Within two vastly different sources—postcolonial theorist Homi Bhabha and feminist bell hooks—this narrative persists. In "The Postcolonial and the Postmodern: The Question of Agency" from *The Location of Culture*,

Bhabha seeks to disrupt the essentialism of locating the agent as prior to action and suggests that both agent and action are called into being within discourse, arguing that "the agent who 'causes' the narrative becomes part of the interest, only because we cannot point unequivocally to that agent at the point of outcome" (Bhabha 1994, 189). Bhabha suggests that developing a relationship of control to narrative figurations of oppression creates the subject as a resistant one. In a very different style and context—a printed conversation with Cornel West—bell hooks defines agency as "the ability to act in one's best interest" (hooks 1990, 206). The definition seems meaningless if one considers the experience of Frederick Douglass, who rebelled against slavery in the interest of freedom, but whose escape plot was revealed by enslaved people who believed that currying the favor of the overseer and owner was within *their* best interests. Using the term *agency* to delineate the relationships of both Douglass and his antagonists to the experience of oppression reveals something of the word's limited utility, and its mystifications of the relationship between the subject and the power that injures her. Both hooks's and Bhabha's definitions constitute demands for marginal subjects to control experience, to self-govern, and to exercise personal responsibility—regardless of the fact that they do not create the conditions of their oppression.

It is in a very different spirit and tone that writers respond to the lynching of Laura Nelson and, less directly, to that of her son Lawrence, who hangs beside her but is seldom mentioned in these accounts (Allen et al. 2000, plates 33–34). The American folksinger Woody Guthrie, who grew up in Okemah with a father who had been among Nelson's murderers, described the sight of her death in 1938: "A negro mother . . . hang[ed] by the neck from a river bridge, and the wild wind whistl[ed] down the river bottom, and the ropes stretched tight by the weight of their bodies . . . stretched tight like a big fiddle string" (Guthrie 1940, 7). The memory of Nelson's lynching appears to have haunted Guthrie, who wrote about lynching, perhaps less obliquely than his friend and collaborator Huddie "Leadbelly" Ledbetter, whose song "Where Did You Sleep Last Night?" (1944) simultaneously addresses and speaks as a faithless lover, revealed to be the widow of a lynched man who was disarticulated. For Guthrie, the memory of the lynching is metonymically represented in the figure of the bridge that replaces the more iconic "skeleton tree" of American lynching practices; the metonym reappears in at least four of his songs from the 1930s (Jackson 2005, 672–73). The national character of mob violence seems not to have been lost on Guthrie—author of the sing-along travelogue "This Land Is Your Land"—whose pencil illustrations (now collected in the Smithsonian

Folkways Collection) feature an American landscape dominated by a bridge bending in the horizon, with a line of hanging bodies as far as the eye can see (Ibid., 672). From California to the New York Island, this land(scape) is dominated by harbingers of death.

Sharing a reverential vocabulary with Guthrie, curator James Allen—the "picker" who assembled the images in the *Without Sanctuary* exhibition—imprints his memory of Nelson's body in a strangely beautified (and beatified) recollection. He imagines her "caught so pitiful and tattered and beyond retrieving—like a child's paper kite snagged on a utility wire." The sight of her is transferred from the bridge in Okemah to a contemporary house, where he sees a woman who serves as somatic reminder of Nelson, as a narrative of her life and death replay in her revenant's "deep-set eyes." In the presence of this woman—as well as imagined avatars of lynched men John Richards and Leo Frank—Allen wonders if he is given access to a rough sketch of their subjectivities, in encounters that at once recall the photographs and insist upon the necessity of their replication. That Allen concludes with a sense that the photographs reveal "the cold steel trigger in the human heart" undermines his call for justice and empathy, when the unmarked human of this final sentence suggests an intrinsic drive to violence that might excuse its existence with a blanket claim to human nature (Allen et al. 2000, 204).

Fiction writer Stephanie Dickinson describes the image in similarly poetic language in the story "A Lynching in Stereoscope" (2004), where a contemporary African-American woman finds a postcard whose visual and spatial dimensions evoke the image of Nelson and her son Lawrence. The story switches between the contemporary narrative of Jelly and Ciz—the lynched woman—asserting a parity between them in descriptions of the "hot gingerbread" of Jelly's skin and the "lips full but not to bursting" of Ciz's mouth; their pulchritude is rendered without ambiguity in the text, with the danger and violence of the lynchers established, in their first appearance, with an uncharitable assessment of Ciz's sexual prowess (Dickinson 2005, 96–97). The postcard of Ciz's death is found among the treasures and beloved objects of Jelly's elderly white employers, described in language that affirms the beauty the lynchers attempted to diminish: "The calico skirt seems to take the wind and still it. Hanging with her head to the side, the woman is graceful like a ballet dancer at rest. Her toes point downward, her tiny feet, like lilies below her hem" (Ibid., 108). Rendered by Guthrie, Allen, and Dickinson—Nelson is music, yet she is the dance; she slumbers, but reveals the tension of rope against the wind. She is a flower, a kite, a tattered dress.

One might reasonably critique the language of each looker, since they attempt to garner sympathies for Nelson not by describing the violence of the mob or the mortifications of her flesh but by specularizing her body along lines that reify it as the focus of empathy qua eroticism.

Considering these profoundly aestheticized readings of Laura Nelson's body, one might ask why I object to Apel and Goldsby's accounts, and to my own of three years hence. At the risk of forgetting the tripartite structure of the Embree photographs—front, dorsal, dead—each of the journalists and scholars (myself included) suspended the narrative at the moment of Embree's gaze in order to save contemporary spectators from voyeurism—in order to allow them to "look" without "using." The interventions transform the image into a story of resistance that "effect[s] a meditation between events and certain universally human 'experiences of temporality' "; we fail, nonetheless, to mediate the encounter between the lynched man and his violent, imminent death (White 1990, 173). The photographic moment seizes these readings, holds them with his eyes—until I forgot that Embree died and is dead and, indeed, that his eyes contain an awareness of death's nearness. These accounts have—as I argue of Faulkner's short fictions in the previous chapter—a premortem and a postmortem, but occlude the *mortem*. For Faulkner, this occlusion suspends guilt; for contemporary lookers at lynching photographs, it authorizes memory of death at the hands of the mob as volitionary, as sacrificial. The profoundly different image of Nelson activates a kind of tenderness rather than an (imagined) militant demand on the part of the dead, provoking in Guthrie, Dickinson, and Allen a poetic reverie that one seldom hears in descriptions of lynched men. Though this discursive space is activated by what we would rightly call "the Gaze"—the sense that every function of the female body is sexualized and aestheticized—I would argue that their readings also benefit from that logic, which inscribes passivity as the corollary to looking, thereby diminishing the quest that so many social historians have charged, to find in these images what we now call "agency," and what Western philosophers have long called "free will."

Looking at the images with these constitutive tensions in mind—rather than the sense shared by Hale and MacKinnon that an image can resist and bypass interpretation—offers the looker an opportunity to feel the gap between the "intention" of the mob—a belief in black criminality with a preexisting narrative of agency with which the contemporary critic need not imbue the subject—and the mortification of the body, a vulnerability inherent to flesh, rather than the sexing and racializing practices imposed upon it. When we look at Laura Nelson—with associations about the cultural meaning of the female body intact—we tread close to voyeurism, a condition posited as inherently violent by theorist David Marriott. The relative benignity of photographer Robert Mapplethorpe's attractions to the black male body, Marriott has argued, shares an ontology with the relentless violence and torture of the murderous Jeffrey Dahmer, who photographed the suffering and death of his (mostly black) victims (Marriot 2000, 34). Perhaps I would be more compelled by the attendant violence of this desire and the analogous modes of looking—an analogy that Marriott confesses is an "outrageous association" (Ibid., 34)—if they shared an epistemology, a method of sating their desire. As a counter to Marriott, I am not even sure that Mapplethorpe and Dahmer shared a fetish, since dead and living bodies are profoundly different loci of desire. Perhaps they felt similar triumphs in the moment of its satiation, but this constitutes a troubling snapshot of the "naturalness" of violent and pathological sexuality for the wounded subject. I resist a totalizing system that invalidates desire, a feeling that motivates the pursuit of justice as surely as the pursuit of sex or of violence.

Looking at Laura Nelson and aestheticizing her body as a representation of her lost life does not transform Guthrie, Allen, or Dickinson into lynchers. At the moment of active looking—which we might call voyeurism, though I avoid the more evaluative "scopophilia"—we are not close to justice, nor to empathy; we are close, as it turns out, to desire. Laden as it is with power, *desire* is a verb without a direct object, like *stare* and *hang*, the verbs with which I begin these readings. If men act and women appear, then with regards to images of lynching, one might prefer to appear, since the agency imposed upon Embree's face and eyes aligns him with the agents who acted upon him, but the appearance of Laura Nelson as a (passive) catalyst of affect enables every feeling except *no* feeling. One might look at Nelson and desire her death, or retribution for that death, or a language of sorrow that will not cleave the tongue. Desire is a feeling with which I might authorize any action, or none; it can justify the action that wounds *me* most or that which wounds *you* most. For my own part, I hope it is not the latter. Imminent, unsatisfying desire dangles before me and is, as a section break looms ahead, all that I can offer in resistance to the seductions of Embree's gaze by which so many spectators have been deflowered.

Against Agency

From the tragically real images of lynching and the "false mimesis of pornography," I turn to cut-paper murals of Kara Walker, which traffic, as her critics have argued, in similarly unreliable representations of the sexed and racialized body (Gilman 2007, 30–31). Before she turned thirty years old, Walker had exhibited at the Whitney and at the Istanbul Biennale, presented solo shows domestically and internationally, and earned the MacArthur Genius Award. Despite these achievements, Walker's career was plagued by controversy. Feminist artist Betye Saar, known for her critique of the marketing of black women's bodies in *The Liberation of Aunt Jemima*—which replaces the commercial icon's culinary accoutrements with a rifle and the Black Power fist—circulated a petition warning women of color that "these images might be in your city next," with pernicious ideologies of race and class in tow. The work, Saar argues, is "selling [African-Americans] down the river" with artistic success that assumes and invokes a "white, elitist audience" (quoted in Bowles 1998, 4–5). Meanwhile, Kara Walker teased, telling an interviewer that she drew her inspiration from her "inner plantation," that African-Americans "want to be slaves a little bit," and that oppression was a category to which slaves had adapted, transforming contemporary black people into self-abjuring masochists (Saltz 1996, 84).

In the decade that has followed Walker's meteoric rise and critical controversy, incidents of outright censorship have followed, most notably at the Detroit Institute of Arts, which removed her work from *Where the Girls Are: Prints by Women* from the DIA's Collection under the advice of the Friends of African and African American Art, who objected to images of "racialized sexual depravity" (Shaw 2004, 103–104). More solo exhibits and retrospectives followed, often upping the ante from her early work; troubling and graphic content continued to flood her catalogs: a seemingly-dead lynched man ejaculates on the face of a spectator, personals advertisements in search of BDSM sex with racialized overtones are pinned beneath the faces of antebellum politicians, and Abolitionist hero John Brown, painted in muddy charcoal, breastfeeds a black child. The recursive nature of public controversy, in which artists grow more intractable and shocking in response to criticism, is perhaps revealed by this catalog of offenses and responses, but I am interested in the ways it evokes a longstanding critical debate about the politics of representation. Though previous sections of this chapter have questioned whether violence is mediated or reproduced by artistic and literary uses of it, subsequent sections consider whether or not the agency of injured parties can be located in these representations. For the purposes of time, space, and focus, I treat only the question of the agency of the enslaved, a critical controversy that has followed from the renaissance of scholarship on American slavery in the 1960s—from Eugene Genovese to Kenneth Stampp to Stanley Elkins.

Writing in the wake of the Nuremberg Trials and early Holocaust scholarship, Elkins argued that both plantations and concentration camps were "closed systems" wherein "a society of helpless dependents" was trained in non-resistance to the violence of their everyday lives by abusive, patriarchal tyrants (Elkins 1959, 98). Elkins argued for the relationship between the plantation and the concentration camp as locations of biopolitical containment that radically constrained agency. Abuses had "disintegrative effects" on the prisoners and slaves; the psychic alienation of capture, transport, and forced labor infantilized slaves and prisoners, turning the captive into a parasite (Ibid., 107). Because he cited as evidence of this circumscription the surprising dearth of slave rebellions (and, in fact, underestimates the number of such incidences), subsequent critiques of Elkins have often reframed less direct forms of rebellion as resistance: work slow-downs, voluntary sterilization and the allegedly "softer" confinements of concubinage and domestic slavery. The controversy emerging from Elkins's comparison between the Holocaust and slavery is not simply a contestation of the attendant analogy between America and Nazi Germany, but also of the sense that to become a subject under power—a victim—is to lose some moral standing. At his moment of realization that he is no "freak of nature, nor of history," Ralph Ellison's *Invisible Man* reflects on this supposition, confessing that he once hated his enslaved family for their surrender. "I am not ashamed of my grandparents for having been slaves," he says. "I am only ashamed of myself for having at one time been ashamed" (Ellison 1995a, 13). To mitigate that hatred-in-hindsight, scholars have worked to find some freedom within slavery.

One of the ethical uncertainties of that quest is its relationship to the ideology of slavery. In "A Flight from Freedom," anthropologist Elizabeth Povinelli cautions theorists against reducing subjectivity to a flight to freedom and urges against forgetting the irreducible relationship between *subjectivity* and *subjection*. Discourses about freedom elide the "social nondetermination" that "freedom" pleads for; this radical separation reduces the potential for social action and, consequently, limits the aims of "subjugated social groups" (Povinelli 2005, 145–46). Freedom is necessarily the twin of unfreedom; once one loosens the social bonds that limit freedom, subjectivity is born from a necessity of self-management. In short, freedom replaces old limitations with new ones. Povinelli claims that flights toward individuation and freedom are inseparable from Enlightenment projects; she refers to Marx's typology of the "bourgeois revolutions" that emerge in the seventeenth and eighteenth centuries which "transform . . . radical social projects into liberal individual contracts" (Ibid., 149). Subjectivity is born during the heyday of the Atlantic slave trade, a synchronicity hidden by contemporary accounts of self-determination *born* within the experience of enslavement. In a specifically American context, Saidiya Hartman has argued that the language of liberation and rights-bearing citizenship became, when extended to slaves, a "new form . . . of bondage enabled by proprietorial notions of the self" that should enable critics to "interrogate terms like 'will,' 'agency,' 'individuality,' and 'responsibility,'" all terms used prescriptively to militate against resistance by freedmen (Hartman 1997, 5–6). Povinelli's flight from freedom, however, is a circuitous one when *agency*, the privileged term of critical theory, is not subject to the interrogations offered by Hartman. One seldom hears academics talk about freedom, except as it regards freedom of speech and dissemination of ideas; agency, on the other hand, is omnipresent. Supplanting "agency" for "freedom" avoids confrontation with these proliferating discourses.

Among the pitfalls of critical deployments of agency, I argue, is the loss of the enslaved person under the weight of related discourses of subjectivity and choice. Though designed to illuminate the margins and "restore" personal freedom to oppressed minorities, celebrations of agency lose the margin when all subjects are imagined as free actors, when the word *agency* is applied to both the colonizer and the colonized, both the slave and the overseer. Like the terms *desire* and *identification* in psychoanalysis, *agency* is often present in postcolonial, feminist, and cultural studies, but seldom with any fixity of definition. Consider the definitions offered in the previous section by bell hooks and Homi Bhabha in conversation with the definition of Srinivas Aravamudan, who, in the introduction to *Tropicopolitans*, a text that seeks to reclaim agency for the colonized, vaguely defines agency as "the active resistance . . . to discourses and practices that silenced and disempowered various groups," thereby begging for specificity in regards to the strategies of resistance in question and the trajectory by which yearning or desire for freedom crosses the line of delineation from passive to active (Aravamudan 1999, 10).

Between Elkins's totalities and Aravamudan's ambiguities, sixties-era new social historians responded to victories of the Civil Rights Movement with the rallying cry to "give slaves back their agency" (Johnson 2003, 119). Since then, scholars have responded by locating agency in the cultural and artistic production of slaves and their descendants. Early attempts to restore slave agency, Walter Johnson argues, enabled scholars to "advertise . . . their good will" to oppressed peoples—slaves, brutalized colonials, sweatshop workers, with women over-represented in all three categories—by claiming agency on their behalf (Ibid., 120). Considering how frequently discourses of personal responsibility do battle with progressive pushes for social responsibility, I believe it would be a far greater gesture of good will for academics to distance themselves from what I would call "agentic singularities," definitions that advocate for a single agent, a rugged individual.

Yet I am unwilling to fully reject the potential of agency, insofar as the term can be applied to productive formations of culture and collective action. After the publication of LeRoi Jones/Amiri Baraka's *Blues People* (1964), Ralph Ellison responded by urging Baraka and the Black Arts Movement not to forget that slaves fell in love, gave birth to children—that they loved, and created art, music, and culture.

> "A slave," writes [Jones/Baraka], "cannot be a man." But what, one might ask, of those moments when he feels his metabolism aroused by the rising of his sap in spring? What of his identity among other slaves? With his wife? And isn't it closer to the truth that far from considering themselves only in terms of that abstraction, "a slave," the enslaved really thought of themselves as *men* who had been unjustly enslaved? (Ellison 1995b, 254)

While some might read this injunction as a restoration of agency, I read it differently; I think Ellison warns Baraka and his general audience to find personhood in creation, and most especially in the places where lives touch and transform singular subjectivities into radically dispersed selves capable of collective action and formations of community. Granted, these domains of privacy and the quotidian were permeable to white supremacy, but they also reveal that "a space of freedom" can look like "a space of captivity" and vice-versa (Hartman 1997, 9). Though he allows that slavery was not "a state of absolute repression," Ellison goes on to argue that the "group experience" of African-Americans enabled laughter and creation as strategies that resisted the admittedly "dehumanizing pressures" of being owned by another (Ellison 1995b, 254, 256). Perhaps the most productive figurations of agency allow for transformation in the locations where the lives of the oppressed touch and comfort, resisting radical autonomies that benefit hierarchies of power.

After Ellison, I am inclined to consider reclamations of radical, individuated agency pernicious in comparison to collective group resistance, because the former shifts the cultural endowments of the unmarked subject—possessor of free will and actuated agency—to the marked one in an attempt at color-blind neutrality. Art historian Gwendolyn DuBois Shaw's *Seeing the Unspeakable: The Art of Kara Walker* (2004), locates agentic singularity within

Walker's silhouette, *The End of Uncle Tom and the Grand Allegorical Tableau of Eva in Heaven* (1995), trying to find sexual desire in the representation of sex between a "master character" and a child:

> The silhouette of an adolescent slave girl ending at the waist [is] raising her buttocks in the air and grasping a corn stalk with both hands for support. Resting on her back is the enormous belly of a legless master character that stands with the aid of a wooden leg and a saber that is thrust into the body of a small child on the ground behind him. The two larger characters merge, and the slave girl's legs become a substitute for the man's missing limbs. They are further connected by his abdomen, which is physically and metaphorically supported by the labor of her back. . . . She is complicit in the act of domination; she is taking in the body of her oppressor; she is becoming one with him. (Shaw 2004, 54–55)

For Shaw, the agencies of the master and slave become coterminous in the act of sexual intercourse, where the girl is imagined as searching the man's face for pleasure, rather than for perdition or impending punishment at his hands. This formation is not so far from claims of nineteenth-century whites who kept slave concubines; the "imputation of lasciviousness" and reciprocity on women of color "effaced the violence of property relations" to "obscur[e] violence and conflat[e] it with pleasure" (Hartman 1997, 25). The "simulation of consent," Hartman argues, is fundamental to the spectacle of enslavement, an ocular logic that informed the practice of lynching as well (Ibid., 38).

Here, Shaw seems to forget how much space pleasure and punishment shared in the psyche of the master class, and how it was inflicted upon—rather than created by—the enslaved class. One need only recall Frederick Douglass's Aunt Hester, whose repeated floggings at the hands of the overseer Plummer offer a somatic spectacle of suffering that becomes a public corollary to the private crime of rape:

> I have often been awakened at the dawn of day by the most heart-rending shrieks of an own aunt of mine, whom he used to tie up to a joist, and whip upon her naked back till she was literally covered with blood. No words, no tears, no prayers, from his gory victim, seemed to move his iron heart from its bloody purpose. The louder she screamed, the harder he whipped; and

where the blood ran fastest, there he whipped longest. He would whip her to make her scream, and whip her to make her hush; and not until overcome by fatigue, would he cease to swing the blood-clotted cowskin. (Douglass 1994, 18)

The spectacle of the abused woman enables Douglass to be born into the consciousness of a slave, to learn what awaited him, if not to become inured to it.[3] Again, the act of looking might provide vastly different impulses. For Douglass, they awaken fear. For Plummer, they actuate pleasure. Though Hester's desires are unknown—a silence that, according to Saidiya Hartman, renders Douglass's account pornographic (Hartman 1997, 81)—we are in a dangerous place if her silence becomes an excuse to assume her complicity. If the agentic slave woman can "becom[e] one" with the master, then we might look at Hester and tell her to stop hitting herself, or to Walker's young girl and demand that she cease and desist an act of autonomous sodomy.

In her formative praise of Walker and figurations of agency, Shaw shares a critical impetus with Grace Elizabeth Hale, whose critique of lynching photography is treated in the first section of this chapter:

> Unlike the recent touring exhibitions of lynching photographs, Walker's art does not give viewers a clear sense of the victims and the victimizers, the people we are supposed to love and the people we are supposed to hate. In Walker's art, all these complicated layers of the oppressed and the repressed, old and new historical narratives, and the dreams, desires, and nightmares these histories express and deny come together. (Hale, 2008)

For whatever reason, both Hale and Shaw seem invested in finding a space to make slaves the agents of their own oppression—and potential victimizers of whites. These agentic claims create volitionary models of enslavement and assault that amount to a denial of atrocity. With such defenders, Kara Walker requires no opponents.

Reclamations of agentic singularity tread dangerously close to racist claims about the responsibility and blame for slavery. When I taught about American literature and culture in a small Southern town, I frequently heard students "reclaim" slave agency to advertise their *ill* will toward contemporary antiracist politics. Their claim did not involve connecting African folk traditions to American plantation pottery or sorrow songs; instead, they wanted to blame Africans for slavery. The racist claim that Africans sold other Africans into slavery is asserted as a truism in conservative circles and publications, and in David Horowitz's sustained attack against the reparations movement:

> Black Africans and Arabs were responsible for enslaving the ancestors of African-Americans. . . . The claim for reparations is premised on the false assumption that only whites have benefited from slavery. If slave labor created wealth for Americans, then obviously it has created wealth for black Americans as well, including the descendants of slaves. The GNP of black America is so large that it makes the African-American community the 10th most prosperous "nation" in the world. American blacks on average enjoy per capita incomes in the range of twenty to fifty times that of blacks living in any of the African nations from which they were kidnapped. (Horowitz 2001)

Is this not reclamation of agency, a desire to find independent will and volition in the actions of Africans—colonial, enslaved, subject to sexual concubinage? Influenced by forty years of scholarly gestures toward agency, Horowitz refuses to call slaves "victims," despite tremendous suffering in the New World and the subsequent depopulation of Africa that weakened its borders and cultures, making it ripe for European domination after the cessation of the Atlantic slave trade. These arguments are not so different from Shaw's figuration of the adolescent slave girl, in that they create volitionary and contractual economies of desire and labor that indict equally voracious demand and nonconsensual supply. The by-product of our conservative political climate is the consensus of progressive academics and conservative ideologues, who so fear the possibility of limited choice that they jettison the word victim as an insult, rather than a description.

In response to the demand for agency shared by racist and antiracist forces, I caution against making an unmarked agentic subjectivity portable across boundaries and barriers enforced by power. Even if Gwendolyn DuBois Shaw could document the pleasure of a single slave woman who consented and felt desire for her master, I ask what other options were available to her, when she lived both *for* her master's pleasure and at his pleasure, in the old feudal conception of vassal and lord. The silencing of slave voices makes this evidentiary material impossible to attain; I am more likely to believe that the white power structure silenced slaves' cries of pain than their cries of pleasure at violation and enslavement. What could these hypothetical Africans have known of the Middle Passage, when all who had experienced it were dead or six thousand miles away? Their will and volition were created in concert with power and subjection, conditions of oppression whose locality has been absented in the desire to render agency an unmarked, human universal. Even if Horowitz could document the sale of Africans by Africans—which he does not and probably could not were he to make an attempt—I would again suggest that a choice cannot be free if it is neither informed by foreknowledge of likely consequences nor selected from a range of other possible choices. What could these hypothetical Africans have known of the Middle Passage, when all who had experienced it were dead or six thousand miles away? Their will and volition were created in a concert with power and subjection, conditions of oppression whose locality has been absented in the desire to render agency an unmarked, human universal.

The End of the Rope

As Dinah Holtzman has argued of Walker's detractors and defenders, the latter often intervene against the former by locating humor and satire in Walker's representations of violence, but authentic, solemn self-narration in her public statements on the "inner plantation" and pleasures of sexual slavery (Holtzman 1997, 377). What if, instead, critics found satire in her words and critique within her images? I am inclined to think of the relationships between word and image as comparable to that of Carrie Mae Weems's project Ain't Jokin, in which images of lynching and grotesque Black Americana are juxtaposed with the text of racist jokes. To signify on a Romantic notion of artistry, I argue that both Weems and Walker hold a mirror up to culture, enabling figures of minstrelsy and more pernicious propagandas to leap from the technicolor of a sanitized history to the stark black-and-white of the photograph and the silhouette. Walker's images—of white Southern belles standing in piles of heads with African phenotypes, of black women vaginally penetrated by the slender necks of swans, black men giving birth from their rectums, white men disemboweled with spoons, animals crawling post-natally from the wombs of slaves—provoke a dry and bitter smile rather than a belly laugh, but the contrarian proclamations—like Walker's "proposal for a summer work camp for assimilated, middle-class black children . . . which takes place on a plantation"—tweak respectable aesthetics and politics with remarkable acuity and comedy (Garrett 2002, 29).

Though she is no comedian, Walker seizes a relationship between the tragic and the comic for which there are black antecedents in popular culture. In African-American cultural production, there is an intimate connection between sorrow and laughter; one need only watch Richard Pryor performing as *both* his agonized body and his dying heart in a routine about cardiac arrest in *Richard Pryor Live in Concert* (Jeff Margolis, 1979). His heart sneers that he shouldn't have eaten so much pork, taunting him with racial epithets as it brings his racked body to the ground. As Walker suggests in her interview in *I'll Make Me a World*, art produces a talisman of desire and fear that enables the black artist to perform both as himself and the force that can kill him. Yet, this interstice between the serious and the comic is the location of critique, not a locus of containment. Like Pryor, Walker reveals what has been concealed by elisions, lies, and layers of muscle and bone. She lures the spectator with humor—a seduction as certain as the one provided by Frank Embree's eyes—only to dangle a brutalized body in front of them. Critics who locate either pure comedy or pure volition in her work see her silhouettes and name them *only* black or *only* white, rather than noting where the two meet and create palimpsests of their history against the stark backdrop of the Other.

In Gwendolyn DuBois Shaw's *Seeing the Unspeakable: The Art of Kara Walker*, Walker's putative self-portrait *Cut* (1998) is imagined as an ambiguous construction of artistic agency, a corrective to representations of Walker in mainstream art criticism and a private joke on the way some African-American critics imagine Walker as controlled by white Svengalis. Paralleling *Cut* to Noe Dewitt's photographs of Walker in *Interview* (November 1998), Shaw suggests that Walker, ashamed of her acquiescence to the magazine's admonition to "jump," reconstructs her leaping body as a place of shame and blood-letting, as well as a control, in the form of the male puppeteer that Shaw sees in the "upper line of the silhouette" (Shaw 2004, 133). I confess that, after hours of squinting, I do not see a man lingering under the skirts of the Walker figure. Whether or not there is an agency in Walker's self-representation, I see no narrative *agent*. The facelessness (and, thus, absent differentiation) of the figure undermines any attempt by Walker's critics to find an African-American agent within them. This abdication of narrative agency creates a pervasive discomfort in spectators who expect the Gatesian "speakerly text" to "concern itself with the possibilities of represent[ing] the black voice in writing" and offer a narrative "self-consciousness" that establishes a "hybrid character" in literary incarnations of multiple consciousness (Gates 1992, xxvi). This expectation of black artistry persists in the treatment of Walker in the Public Broadcasting Service (PBS) documentary *I'll Make Me a World*, where she is troublingly juxtaposed to the spoken word, and poets and rappers and MCs—most of whom are fixated on black vernacular traditions that Walker eschews in favor of attentive mockery of a once-standard white English. As if to foreground her dramatic differences, she is the only artist featured in the documentary whose hostile critics—Betye Saar, Ossie Davis—are given equal screen time; her danger is punctuated with a sinister musical beat that introduces her, bent at the waist and chalking white lines on black construction paper—in sharp contrast to the flattering images and joyful sounds that introduce artists like Spike Lee, Julie Dash, and Bill T. Jones.

The traditions that inform and influence Kara Walker stand at a far remove from the Gatesian "black literary tradition" and the canon-formation attempted by PBS. In a conversation with Thelma Golden reprinted in *Pictures from Another Time* (2002), Walker argues for the relationship between her work and the cultural productions of nineteenth-century whites:

> Narrative is very important to my work. I appropriate from many sources . . . frontispieces for slave narratives, authentic documents, as well as a novel or a great sort of artistic spectacle. I was really apprehensive the first time I gave one of my large pieces a title. . . . I love historical paintings, and I also love the cyclorama and these other kinds of touring versions of art or non-art entertainment, and I love the language that goes with them. It's a little bit overblown, a little bit pompous, and I've been trying to acquire that sense of confidence. (Dixon 2002, 47)

The rich, early sources of African-American expression provided within slave narratives are not listed as an influence. Rather, their "frontispieces"—the spaces where white patrons and editors attested to the veracity of the former slaves—are given primacy in Walker's self-creation. Thus, Walker presents herself as identifying not with the slaves, but with those who structured the audience's response to their self-expression. The response seems to deliberately poke art critic Juliet Bowles, who imagines Walker's art and subjectivity as dependent upon the white male gaze and the approval of the art world and accuses her of using her "waist-length, auburn braid extensions" to embody "her self-described identity of 'wench,'" specifically the "nigger wench" of many of Walker's written works (Bowles 1998, 7). Unfairly conflating Walker's artist's statements with her body and relationships to race and gender, Bowles argues that "the controversial Kara Walker phenomenon . . . extends from her art to her entire persona. . . . Underneath all of the sassy impudence, behind the occasional brilliant flash of insight, and within the worldly woman, there is a dejected girl" (Ibid., 7). Because even her ethically questionable artistic production evinced her intellect and daring, Bowles argues, she might one day "ris[e] to the challenge of producing art that is 'great,' " provided she allows for the "totally transforming experience" of motherhood to diminish her aggressive provocations against an older generation of black artists (Ibid., 7–8).

Though imagining Walker's narrative influences through her own self-description is productive, it also feels dangerous to take her solely at her word—as her statements are provocations, as Bowles points out, with a deliberate doubleness that is too often ignored. Walker, like the Signifying Monkey of the black vernacular tradition, delights in playing her black critics against white institutional spaces like the Guggenheim and MacArthur Foundations. While her artistic production highlights the moral ambiguities of the white spectators of her work, her language seizes the position traditionally occupied by whites in relation to black artists. While she has received financial support from these institutions, she has gestured to the paternalism of that support. She hints at the tension in her relationship with the white art world in the invitations to a 1998 exhibition, in which she writes:

> Missus K. Walker
> returns her thanks
> to the
> Ladies and Gentleman
> of New York
> for the great *Encouragement*
> she has received
> from them,
> in the profession
> in which she has practiced
> in New England. (Walker, quoted in Shaw 2004, 138)

The invitation features a woodcut in which a white slave driver terrorizes two black slave women in the cotton fields. He cracks a whip in the air, and it is level with the first slave's face; the illustration captures a moment before the slave is stricken by one of the most brutal implements of slavery. That image, side-by-side with the above text, uses a tragic moment to accomplish an ironic, combative stance against white patrons. The italicized word encouragement serves a double function, referring to both the patronage of the white art world and the driver's "encouragement" of faster production with the threat of violence. She thus aligns white patrons with slave drivers, demolishing the moral foundation of their seemingly benign acts of patronage.

Resuscitated after a half-century of silence, the accoutrements of American mob violence return in *Cut*. If we are to imagine this work as a portrait of a black artist's ambiguous subject position under observation by both black critics and white spectators, then it might be useful to imagine *cut* as a verb rather than a noun, an imperative—an order—rather than a descriptor. Imagine the word barked as a command, as Shaw imagines the word *jump* in the images accompanying the article in *Interview*. If it is an order, than Walker both issues it, by giving it titular centrality, and follows it, by spilling blood. As Shaw argues, Walker simultaneously occupies the position of oppressor and victim. The affective- and effectiveness of *Cut* is accomplished by the spectator's inability to differentiate the figure within it. In defiance of both the African-American speakerly text and the Western conception of a discreet self, the image is faceless. The face could belong to Walker; *Cut* could represent anyone or no one.

Though silhouettes by definition lack facial differentiation, many are racially differentiated by their evocation of stereotypical African physiognomies circulated in both popular and pseudoscientific circles of the nineteenth century. *A Work on Progress* (1998) shows two female figures with enormous, gaping mouths, broad noses, and sloped brows. Walker's most ambitious silhouettes offer parades of raced faces; yet *Cut* has little potential for either racial or facial differentiation. Because of the placement of the figure's left arm, the face is obscured. The lips and mouth, the key features of racial differentiation in the tradition of eugenics—as well as the primary instruments of self-expression—are invisible. Even in a painting labeled a self-portrait, there is no mouth to narrate experience, nor a long title and captions to tell the spectator what they should think or how they should react to the violence they witness. I imagine Betye Saar or Juliet Bowles looking at this image, and seeing no black woman looking back; herein resides the source of their discomfort. The spectator is denied a referent for Walker's self-creation.

Walker draws spectators further into whiteness by illustrating racist fantasies and paranoias—lascivious black women licking each other's breasts, violent children wielding axes with unawareness that the weapon is self-directed, and emasculated black men giving birth. This is part of her function as an artist; by adopting traditionally white modes of narration, expression, and ideology, she can say what whites no longer do in a "post-racial" world in which a call for open dialogue against racism can itself be read as racist. The iconography of racial violence can nonetheless provoke a moment of pause and recognition for racist subjects who have learned to conceal an ideology that has been rendered impolite, but not irrelevant or invisible. Outside of the academy, discussions of racial violence do not pivot around whether slaves were virtuous resisters or debased into cooperation. Outside of the academy, the assumption is that slavery has been overdramatized, that it is talked about too much, and that it is in the past—strategies and rhetorics of avoidance that have become hallmarks of white identity politics. When I look at Kara Walker's silhouettes, I do not see a dredging-up of old racist stereotypes but a necessary corrective to the sanitized past one encounters in American public spaces—from the former slave market on Wall Street, to the bull-dozed and bombed black neighborhoods of Tulsa, to the monuments to the White League once displayed on New Orleans' Canal Street but now stowed in warehouses—that have erased evidence of white supremacy without correcting the social inequalities that it has wrought.

Despite my earlier critique of Gwendolyn DuBois Shaw, we seem to agree on the premise that Walker is working toward a corrective of accounts of the past in texts like *Gone With the Wind* and *Uncle Tom's Cabin*, but we disagree on what constitutes the history of slavery. In her introduction to *Seeing the Unspeakable: The Art of Kara Walker*, Shaw vacillates between dismissing representations of slavery as full of "predictable horrors" and arguing that Walker's representations of the unspeakable constitute "horrific accounts of physical, mental, and sexual abuse that were left unspoken by former slaves as they related their narratives, the nasty and unfathomable bits of detritus that have been left out of the familiar histories of American race relations" (Ibid., 5–7). Yet, the narrative that Shaw sees as repressed within the story is one in which every person in the tableaux, whether slave or enslaver, is "guilty of vile acts and intentions" that necessitate a guilty legacy "regardless of racial self-identification" (Ibid., 64–65). Here, we are left with an account of yet another volitionary model of enslavement that attempts to disperse guilt between slaves and the owners who expropriated their labor; it provides a model of agency that fully imbricates the artist with the text, projecting subjective and sexual pathology onto both the artistic text and the history of slavery, an institution that Shaw posits as having neither victims nor innocents, only compromise, shared guilt, and a collective "traumatic legacy" (Ibid., 65).

Though I contend that *Cut* could represent anyone or no one, I would like to suggest that it evokes a very different context than the "forgotten" texts of slavery evoked here by Shaw. The "self" in self-portrait is brought into critical being through imbrications of the artist and her text. Hints at

Walker's sexual history—sexual relationships featuring debased interracial fantasy, a long marriage to a white man—are sprinkled through the critical body on her work in backhanded suggestions that her investments in representations of agency within violation and miscegenation are deeply personal; her sexual experience and romantic history would, I wager, be entirely her own possession if she was a male artist. Meanwhile, her detractors evince an obsession with her body, which becomes a mechanism with which to aestheticize racial violence. Journalist Julia Szabo commented on her "Botticelli-brown" hair extensions (Szabo 1997, 49), and Juliette Bowles attacked the same "straight, almost waist-length braid extensions" as embodying the alter ego of the "nigger wench" with which Walker has sometimes toyed. In response to these claims against her character, Shaw argues, Walker uses *Cut* as a space to strip her extensions, bundling the remaining hair into the short braids of a "pickaninny" in radical opposition to the brown temptress of Bowles's and Szabo's imaginations (Shaw 2004, 133).

But what happens if we also strip the "self" from self-portrait, questioning the association of the artist's body with the labor that has produced Walker as receptacle of anxiety and extra-textual fetish? What would happen, too, if we discarded the logic of the female artist as spectacle, thereby withholding the immensely personal attacks that Kara Walker has faced? What if we similarly shifted the critical focus from slavery—a critical space that, now infused with agency, works to render violence and death invisible in favor of forms of everyday resistance? Produced in 1998, the exhibition of *Cut* at the Brent Sikkema Gallery in New York City precedes that of *Without Sanctuary* at Roth Horowitz by more than two years, but echoes and rhymes with Laura Nelson nonetheless. The figure's tense feet and legs—which must be held close together to produce the orientation of the arched feet—hardly seem capable of the leap that Shaw describes. The self-mutilating hands hack away at each other with suicidal intent, in the logical endpoint of an account of agency within oppression, what Saidiya Hartman has called the "willed self-immolation" of the slave agent (Hartman 1997, 53). Like Primo Levi, who survived Auschwitz only to commit suicide, the traumatized woman of *Cut* accomplishes the goal of the oppressor by destroying her own body. Even if her strategies are her own, rather than theirs, this moment of bloody volition strikes me as cold comfort. She swings in the wind, dying but unbound by the noose that killed Laura Nelson.

Because of the association of Walker's work with the inner plantation of slavery's aftereffects and, indeed, of the space for agentic narrative that slavery studies has carved out, Shaw sees in the leaping body the apron, petticoats, and dimity frock of an enslaved woman. What if, instead, we saw it as the fin de siècle dress of Laura Nelson, a woman lynched in Okemah, Oklahoma in 1911? What if critics, who have spent so much energy locating resistance in neo-slave narratives and reading it into the original documents of chattel slavery, considered the ruthless "death sentence" of Jim Crow in tandem with the "life sentence" of American slavery? Nelson faced this sentence in its most brutal manifestation. When Sheriff George Loney came to her door to arrest her husband for petty theft on the morning of May 15, 1911, she was home with her teenage son, who allegedly shot the police officer when he wielded a gun in threat against her. After Loney's death the next day, a lynch mob came to apprehend the Nelsons and made the woman watch as her son Lawrence was hanged. She was then gang-raped, tortured, and hanged from a bridge. When juxtaposing the image of her—most especially Stephanie Dickinson's description of her as "graceful like a ballet dancer at rest"—with Walker's *Cut*, we might see a lynching silhouette sans rope, tree, or even bridge (Dickinson 2005, 108). Without embodying those machineries of death, Walker tempts us to imagine agency in the figure's hacking hands, but critiques it by positing that the trajectory which critical visions impose upon an oppressed will shares a destination with the will of its oppressors.

These violent images, narratives, and bodies disappeared in American social and intellectual life in the latter half of the twentieth century, a period that produced a tremendous body of scholarship on the experience of slavery. That the surge of scholarship emerging from new social history overlaps with the nadir of attention to lynching in the American academy is—at the risk of evoking Susan Sontag's zero-sum game between violences international and domestic—an indication of a profound paradigm shift in determining the contexts that defined the experience of racial oppression in the United States. From bureaucratic documents like the Moynihan Report on the Negro Family to bestselling novels like *Roots*, the American question of race was refocused from the anti-lynching campaigns of the 1920s–1930s to the examination of slavery's lingering social consequences. Lynching, meanwhile, faded like a political campaign from another epoch—as recherché as the Glass Steagall Act, the Sherman Anti-Trust measures, or the long-dead gold standard. Reflecting on that disappearance, Fitzhugh Brundage argues that "nothing about the history of mob violence in the United States is more surprising than how quickly an understanding of the full horror of lynchings has receded from the nation's collective historical memory" (Brundage 1993, 258). The crime, Joel Williamson argues, might have disappeared from American public spaces and scholarly journals, but it lived "in [the] bones" of African-Americans, roaring to the fore in the 1990s in Supreme Court Justice Clarence Thomas's denunciation of his "high-tech lynching" at the hands of the United States Senate during his confirmation hearings (Williamson 1997, 1228–29). The period of lynching's erasure stretches from the NAACP's 1940 conference on the status of anti-lynching legislation to Lynching and Racial Violence in America: Histories and Legacies, a symposium held at Emory University in 2002, where Fitzhugh Brundage issued his injunction. Lynching reappeared in American political life first as specter with the lynching of Michael Donald in Mobile, Alabama in 1981, then as metaphor with the self-protective accounts of Clarence Thomas, and finally as memory in *Without Sanctuary* and the mass of criticism that has followed its exhibition.

Regardless of its ethical value—as pornographic replication or avenging restitution—the postcards recovered a text so hidden and yet so foundational that any literary historian who has ever found a discarded manuscript or a forgotten author would be jealous at its success, as evinced by the sudden reappearance of the noose in American culture. Before the Jena 6, there was a remarkable surge of workplace racial harrassment in which the noose was integral—increasing from ten thousand reported cases in the 1980s to fifty thousand in the 1990s. By 2000, the year that the exhibition debuted in New York City, noose-related incidents constituted one-fifth of all lawsuits filed by the Equal Employment Opportunity Commission—in a series of cases that stretched from San Francisco to Chicago, from Detroit to Auburn, Alabama (Apel 2003, 470). As Dora Apel argues, the most remarkable dimension of lynching's discursive reappearance is that it has been deployed against ethnic minorities who were not descended from African slaves, thereby affirming the portability of the lynching spectacle now in use to again delineate racial boundaries of citizenship; these uses require a counter-narrative to which I hope this book will contribute.

Calling for more discussion of the issue of lynching is, I suspect, a very modest aim. The less modest claim that histories of slavery have accounted for some of lynching's erasure is one I do not rescind. Yet I do not contest the vital importance of slavery to the experience of racism in America; no reasonable person could or would; one might cite David Horowitz as a counterexample, but I would reiterate my interest in rationality. There remains more to be said, more to be written, and more to be argued about chattel slavery, though the field seems crowded with accounts that diminish the violence of everyday life, and of the racializing practices that created the plantation system.

When I began considering the possibility of writing a dissertation on lynching, it was in response to the culture's long silence on the subject. I was writing an M.A. thesis on Nazi propaganda and saw the exhibition catalog for *Without Sanctuary: Lynching Photography in America*. The project radically changed the way I thought about the erasures of violence in the context of genocide against Jews; though Hitler never uses the words *Jew* or *race* in *Triumph des Willens* (1935), racist propaganda in the same epoch of American life resists his elisions. Lynchers pose with the kill in a way that Nazis did not; the perpetrators of the destruction of European Jewry were its first deniers, but American white supremacists took great pride in the slaughter they perpetrated. Yet, in the decades that followed the Civil Rights Movement, the erasure of lynching from American politics and scholarship was accomplished with remarkable success that deniers might have admired.

A few months before my first encounter with *Without Sanctuary*, I took a seminar on Literature and Arts of the Holocaust. In a class of thirty-seven students, I was the only one writing about the violence that genocide had done to Jewish communities; the others seemed to pride themselves on finding counterintuitive stories of the violence—half-Jewish Nazis, collaborators in the ghettos, priests who died at Auschwitz—at the end of which I wondered if there was anyone to whom the Holocaust had *not* happened, any definitive means by which we could say that there were perpetrators and targets and affirm—like Frederick Douglass—that our "tongue[s] should cleave to the roof[s] of [our] mouth[s]" should we elide the distinction (quoted in Blight 2002, 106). Are we looking for an outside to oppression? Trying to find a model that adds complexity to the experience of victimization for contemporary subjects, even if the originary experience felt like total power pressing against the its victim? My questions remain, as I read reclamations of agency like Gwendolyn DuBois Shaw's and bell hooks's, but my context is new. Though I do not wish to rid African-American Studies of either agency or enslavement as referents and analysands, I offer images of lynching as a complication that troubles and challenges contemporary witnesses, asking them to find their own subjectivity within the visual field and admit, with the sigh of failure, that they can—and yet cannot.

CONCLUSION

Vacant Lots

Public Memory and the Practice of Forgetting

For Jonathan

> But where does the outside commence? This question is the question of the archive. There are undoubtedly no others.
>
> —Jacques Derrida, *Archive Fever*, 8

What the Map Conceals (Greenville, South Carolina) Willie Earle, 1947

The Pickens County Museum—formerly the Pickens County Jail—is constructed from red brick and copper, design features once associated with the bureaucratic and functional. Thirty years since the election of Ronald Reagan and his libertarian ethics of care began the inexorable decline of small-town life—with occasional flashes of gentrification for those lucky enough to live in proximity to major cities—its red-on-copper exterior lends the building the look of expensively refurbished condominiums. Metal awnings and a glass-and-concrete extension unsettle the seamlessness of its Victorian architecture.

Through the double doors and to the left an exhibit begins on the antiquities of the county, once part of John C. Calhoun's upcountry South Carolina holdings. As an eighth grader, I, like every Sandlapper, took a class on the state's history. Beginning with a unit called "South Carolina Before Man," we learned that the Pleistocene Coast of the state once reached Columbia, its geographical center and current capital. Encouraged to gasp with wonder at the possibilities of those prehistoric days at the beach, we nonetheless never learned about lynching. My teacher, Rosemary Wise, was younger than either of my nonnative Southern parents, but had mysteriously been part of a small contingent that integrated Seneca High School, where I later spent four years of more quotidian difficulties.[1]

The museum, located fifteen miles from where I grew up in Oconee County, makes no attempt to correct this omission in the official record of the state's history. When Clemson University, funded by the Morrill Land Grant Act, was founded in 1889—the surrounding county was still the frontier, far from the imperial splendor of Charleston, the tat and trash of Myrtle Beach, or the gridded streets of Columbia, burnt by retreating Confederates in 1865, but still swearing that Sherman did it. Emerging from so recent a frontier past, the history of the area has been shaped by the relentless media friendliness of Clemson University, an institution that aestheticizes its profound conservatism with two distinct symbols—Bowman Field, where military decoration abounds but contemporary political protest was until recently forbidden by university policy, and Tillman Hall, named for Pitchfork Ben Tillman, nineteenth century governor and subsequent senator from the state, who often boasted that he would lynch members of the race that must "remain subordinate or be exterminated" (Kantrowitz 2000, 258). The museum, located in the Pickens County seat, seven miles from the university, makes no mention of lynching. Indeed, why should it, when there's so much space to dedicate to Ben Robertson, an obscure memoirist who authored *Red Hills and Cotton* (1983), the cornerstone of the local canon?

Yet, with the frontier of the recent past came so-called "frontier justice," executions and trials strangely divorced from state sovereignty and juridical authority. Perpendicular to the museum's front desk, where volunteer docents sell crystals and postcards, the jailhouse's original cell is intact. Inside is a mannequin clad in iconic black-and-white stripes. Above him dangles a noose. Killer of two men, tool of local authority, the noose was the central prop at the county's legal executions in the the late nineteenth and early twentieth centuries. Today, it artfully covers a sepia photograph of the execution of Haas Butler in 1900, leaving his suffering to the imagination. Despite the exposed viscera of the visual display, the accompanying text is remarkable mostly for its chastity. The perpetrator, it says, killed a farmer named James Hendricks and forced his wife to "spend the night and make his dinner." Rape requires euphemism, but state-sanctioned murder dangles shamelessly from the ceiling.

I visited the museum on August 4, 2008 and found the curator less than forthcoming about violence than the bare, dangling noose would suggest. On February 17, 1947, Willie Earle, accused of assaulting Thomas W.

Conclusion 147

Figure 1. A noose is on the left side of the photograph of the execution of Haas Butler in the Pickens County Museum.

Brown, a cab driver who had stopped in Greenville to pick up a fare bound for Pickens, was kidnapped from the cell by a mob that formed a caravan for the seventeen-mile one-way trip. Jailor J. E. Gilstrap released Earle without a struggle, intimidated, perhaps, by the mob's casual use of profanity in front of his wife. An indicted conspirator, Jesse Lee Sammons, later told FBI agents that Gilstrap, when facing the caravan of twenty cars, said "I guess you boys know what you're doing, don't you?" ("Jessie Lee Sammons Statement"). The mob took Willie Earle to the Saluda River Dam, where they tortured him in search of a confession, though Sammons attests that he had already admitted his involvement in Brown's injury on the drive toward the water (West 2006, 250). A few hours later, an anonymous caller informed the African-American undertaker in Pickens that there was "a dead nigger in need of his offices" in the slaughteryards of the Southern Provisions Company (Ibid., 2006, 253). Earle's body was found a mere mile from the river, across the county line in Greenville County, near what is now the Cherrydale district of Greenville city proper. Knives and guns had been deployed against his flesh; pieces of his brain splattered the bushes nearby (Ibid.).

The crime of Earle's death is one shared by the two counties. Pickens, home to Earle and the location of the assault on cab driver Thomas W. Brown, released the twenty-four year old epileptic into the hands of the Greenville mob, who left his slaughtered body in proximity to the abattoir, undoubtedly aware of the bloody meaning even as they ignored the appropriateness of the murder site's address: Gethsemane Road. *Father, if you are willing, take this cup from me; yet not my will, but yours be done*, read scenes from the Gospel of Luke in the Garden of Gethsemane (22:42). Though no curtain rent or foundations trembled at the moment of Earle's death, his killers were raised on diets of scripture in baritone, hymn in soprano, yet felt no pause at the indication of parity between the blood they venerated and the blood they spilled.

Just as the borders of the South prove remarkably porous, county lines, too, are arbitrary. In the twenty-three years I lived in South Carolina's "Golden Corner," I felt no change in season when I crossed into Greenville County from Pickens, or from Pickens to Oconee, but the museum's curator insists on a difference. The lynching is Greenville's problem, not Pickens's. Bristling as though I had suggested that she arrested, released, tortured, and murdered Willie Earle with her own hands and that, given permission to reconnoiter the premises, I would find his mutilated corpse under glass, she ended the conversation by whipping on her sunglasses and brushing past me. She need not open the door or ask us to leave to communicate that we had asked the wrong questions.

Our overtures at conversation rejected, my partner and I drove across the county line, navigating with the help of James Shannon's article "How a 1947 Greenville Nightmare Changed South Carolina," in search of the "forlorn patch of asphalt" where Willie Earle died. We find the intersection with difficulty, but it feels neither forlorn not lonely. The neighborhood is residential, with a cluster of tidy trailers and a white-steepled church. Despite its proximity to the city center, tracts of land sit sprawling and empty, covered in rolling kudzu vines and new-growth white pines that do little to conceal the cleared acreage that once housed the Southern Provisions Company. The proprietor of a tiny garage sale, a woman in her forties, tells us she cannot remember the slaughterhouse, which would have bordered her property. A man of roughly her age passes me on a scooter as I screw my camera onto my tripod. He gives me a long, appraising look; I hear his motor as he circles around Old Easley Highway to Old Bent Bridge Road, back to where I am standing at the intersection of Old Bramlett and Gethsemane.

Figure 2. The intersection of Gethsemane and Old Bramlett Roads in Greenville, South Carolina.

Smoothing his shaggy blonde hair into a ponytail, poor protection against the heat of August, he asks me if the camera plugs right into a computer; I confirm that it can. I confess that I was, at the moment, certain that I was going to lose my camera, my wallet, or the long Indian kundan around my neck. It's the necklace that caught his eye, he tells me. I am neither mugged nor mistreated; he tells me he likes that people take more pictures these days and that digitals are getting cheaper. When he was a kid, you took pictures on special occasions and, thus, lost the day's pleasurable inanities when the sun went down. At last, he asks me why I am photographing his neighborhood. Grateful for the cover story provided by my partner Chip, I respond that I am a paranormal researcher investigating the sighting of a ghost in the ruins of the old slaughter yard. The mild deception was motivated by the curator's hostility, as well as my vaguely anthropological sense that I should ask about traumas other than lynching, because a general question yields a more precise answer than a narrow one. "You're close," my nameless interlocutor tells me, pointing to the telephone pole that casts slender shade against the garage sale. Then he bids me a good day, speeding away with the pleasant "brrrr" of the scooter's engine.

Returning to Oconee that afternoon, Chip and I reflect with surprise on the remoteness of the lynching site. "It's one of those places," I tell him, "where you have to know where you're going long before you get there." This dainty tautology is not true of all the South's locations, distinguished as they are by geographies of accidents. A day after our adventure, still dehydrated by the enervating heat, we look at satellite maps of the area and find something curious. For all the limits of living memory at the lynching site, the land has been empty for at least ten years. All the growth at the clearing looks new and the images from ten years ago look like nothing—not even intrepid kudzu—was growing over the foundations. Outside of the Gethsemane loops, satellites reveal the massive parking lots and gargantuan structures of the big box stores strangely close and congested in juxtaposition to the insularity of the looping neighborhood. New geographies—signs of civilization, however commodified and boring—at the site of the lynching change the narrative of emptiness and loneliness, of rural malfeasance, promoted by contemporary conceptions of racial violence.

Scholars of early American literature or narratives of settler colonialism might recognize fantasies of lynching's rurality as some version of the empty land ideology, the British notion of *terra nullius* in Australia, the Puritan conception of colonization's "errand into the wilderness" (Miller 1956). To justify expansion, settlers posited the land as already empty, as though the one hundred million indigenous peoples living in the United States at the time of first contact were a scant presence, that the continent was spread open in invitation, simultaneously virginal and wanton. Reading "The Gift Outright" (1942) at Kennedy's inauguration in 1961, Robert Frost gave voice to this particular fatalism:

> The land was ours before we were the land's.
> She was our land more than a hundred years
> Before we were her people. She was ours
> In Massachusetts, in Virginia,
> But we were England's, still colonials,
> Possessing what we still were unpossessed by,
> Possessed by what we now no more possessed.
> Something we were withholding made us weak
> Until we found out that it was ourselves
> We were withholding from our land of living,
> And forthwith found salvation in surrender.
> Such as we were we gave ourselves outright

Conclusion

Figure 3. Under kudzu vines and new-growth white pines is the slaughterhouse where Willie Earle's body was found.

> (The deed of gift was many deeds of war)
> To the land vaguely realizing westward,
> But still unstoried, artless, unenhanced,
> Such as she was, such as she would become. (Frost 1969, 348)

The possession—the destiny, both manifest and latent—to which Frost gestures is belied by only the word war to hint at the traumas of conquest and the preexisting occupation of the land by a resistant, native population. The myth of empty land and Frost's iteration of it fairly accomplish a bloodless narrative of the colonization of the American continent.

Contemporary memory of lynching reveals another kind of empty-land motif. In 1998, James Byrd, hitchhiking along a road in Jasper, Texas, accepted a ride from three men who beat him, chained him to back of their truck and dragged him until seventy-five pieces of his body spread across a three-mile stretch of road. They took his head to the gates of the black cemetery, spray-painted the word "head" in orange next to it, then went to a barbeque. John William King, one of the three murderers, wrote a letter to a coconspirator that read: "Regardless of the outcome of this, we have made history. Death before dishonor. Sieg Heil!" ("Closing Arguments Today in Texas Dragging-Death Trial"). Perhaps King was lucky since, a year after his sentencing, *Without Sanctuary: Lynching Photography in America*, was exhibited for the first time in New York City. The exhibition reintroduced the country to something they had never quite forgotten: the noose, which made subsequent appearances in Jena, Louisiana and at the University of Kentucky, where Barack Obama was hanged in effigy before the 2008 election. Suddenly, in the early days of the millennium, evidence of lynching staged spectacular interventions in galleries as well as the United States Congress, which drafted an apology for the practice; indeed, searching for *James Byrd* and *lynching* yields 8,100 search results on Google. John William King's crime was exemplary, a useful reminder of the persistence of prejudice.

Locating the paradigm of lynching in the rural, lonely unwitnessed death of James Byrd, contemporary representations of lynching, as in the film *The Great Debaters* (Denzel Washington, 2007)—in which a team of orators from a historically-black college turn a wrong corner on a school trip and become unwilling witnesses—define the crime as something unannounced and irrational, an act of violence one could happen upon on an empty road. The paradigmatic empty lynching site is evacuated of witnesses and, therefore, perpetrators; the absence of urban or rural "main street" architectures registers resistance to the alignment of modernity with lynching thoroughly evinced in Jacqueline Goldsby's *Spectacular Secret: Lynching in American Life and Culture* (2006). Within these representations, the noose might also be wielded by the marginal subjects—mocked in popular culture as both NASCAR dads and the redneck rapists from *Deliverance* (John Boorman, 1972)—figured as primitives without a hint of romance, acting only on instinct and impulse. But these images do not even represent the triumvirate of Byrd's murderers, who had close connections to Confederate Knights of America, a national white supremacist organization, and who meticulously planned and enacted their violence.

Reflecting on the map's more literally empty land, Chip and I headed first to the Greenville County Historical Society and then to the Greenville County Library, where we consulted maps from 1930 to 1970 and found that the former site of the Southern Provisions Company was once the urban archipelago of a rural county, not, as it currently stands, the rural isolate of an increasingly urban location: Greenville, home to BMW, Duke Power, Furman University, and the execrable Bob Jones University. Sometime after Willie Earle's death at the hands of the mob, the county cut Bramlett Road's legs off, removing those sections that once crossed over the Saluda River, the remains of the railroad, and the junction of state Route 123 and Interstate 85.

Staring at the loop of Gethsemane extending to what is now the highway on an obsolete map, I begin to see the remote neighborhood, home to Scooter Man, Yard Sale Lady, and the ghost of Willie Earle, as it once was: a road that connected the outbacks of Oconee and Pickens Counties to the urban center of Greenville, which had four functioning slaughterhouses, five cab companies, and twenty-five millionaires at mid-century (West 2006, 25). So few remain. I wonder now if development has joined in a conspiracy against memory—or if, in fact, they share a trajectory of destruction, of occlusion, of ruthless erasure occasionally shaken when a severed head is thrown at the gates of forgetting.

The Transitive Property of Railroads (Port Jervis, New York)
Robert Jackson Lewis, 1892

What three things, Katie asks at midnight, do you need in a city to make it home? Our answers diverge—public space is twice repeated, as is Indian food and international airports. We carve out necessary spaces for two very beloved men—my Chip, her Burke. Among the four of us, magicians are listed once, as are jazz musicians, and each other. Our folie à quatre, I should mention, stretches peripatetically across a length of the Northern Metroline Railroad in Port Jervis, New York, past a restaurant called the Blue Parrot, the stunning Immaculate Conception Catholic Church, which skimped on exteriors with a hollow, plastic Virgin Mary, and up Sussex Street, where Robert Jackson Lewis was dragged to the site of his death on June 2, 1892.

None of the four of us list violence and vigilantism as a requirement for homespace, but, as I have discovered in the process of writing this book, there is no place without it, no location in the urban North or the American flyover without "a spectacular secret" (Goldsby 2006). James Allen reported in his 2005 lecture at University of Rochester, that the first exhibition of *Without Sanctuary: Lynching Photography in America* in Chicago was greeted with a request by an African-American family to hold a family reunion in the exhibition space. Having never seen an image of their progenitor, who died before his time, they were hopeful that an image of him might be among the gruesome memento mori that Allen had collected. The curator assented, allowing love in proximity to death. Perhaps out of curiosity, but, I hope, also love, my partner and dear friends followed me to Port Jervis in October 2008 to observe how Lewis's life and death are written on the landscape and architecture of this tiny town, which sits on the borders of three states.

According to *The New York Times* printed the day after Lewis was lynched, "two young negroes and a crowd of [white] children" witnessed him assaulting Lena McMahon, leaving her in an "insensible condition" with mortal injuries. Following the path of the Neversink River by canalboat, Jackson found his way to Cuddlebackville, where he was apprehended by a small posse who brought him back to Port Jervis ("Lynched at Port Jervis"). According to Seward B. Horton, one of Jackson's escorts, the captive frankly told the posse that he had been encouraged to assault McMahon by her suitor Peter Foley, who had fallen out of favor with the McMahon family when he was arrested for failing to pay a hotel bill. Perhaps seeking revenge or a comparable incident of public humiliation, Foley told Lewis that "if he wanted a piece go down and get it" (Testimony of Seward B. Horton, quoted in Goldsby 2006, 246). Though Foley was never brought to justice for his role in McMahon's death, Lewis was dragged the length of the town to First Baptist Church, where he was hanged once to kill him and once, in a much higher tree, to display the corpse. In the coroner's inquest that followed, Judge William Howe Crane, whose brother Stephen Crane would later draw from Lewis's story to write the novella *The Monster* (1899), proved unable to identify any member of the mob that he claimed to have resisted at the spectacle of death, which took place a block from his private residence (Ibid., 123). However furious they might have been at the illicit cross-racial bond between Foley and Lewis, the residents of Port Jervis slipped into greater shame as major newspapers of the day descended upon the town, shocked at the novelty of a lynching spectacle outside the hinterlands of the defeated Confederacy. Compelled by the quest for relics and forgetting, the citizens of Port Jervis hacked the tree where Lewis hanged to splinters, sold his clothing and possessions to Worth's Museum in New York City, and fell into frenzied silence about the violence of the day (Ibid., 124).

Twelve decades and three months later, I made reservations for two rooms at the Erie Trackside Manor, a two-story building with a nineteenth-century basement and a twenty-first century second floor, a composite structure created by a fire in the 1980s. As soon as I hung up the phone, I was struck with worry about who would hold open doors, run our credit cards, and give us our keys, since Lewis was a hotel porter at the Delaware House Hotel—which burned to the ground in 1902—two blocks from the Erie Trackside Manor. I wanted a memorial, not a visitation of spirits. When we arrived, no spectral face appeared to us in the lobby, since there was neither a lobby nor a clerk. We checked in at the crowded bar in the adjoining restaurant, where a ragged bartender handed us our keys and hurried back to her post to distribute pitcher after pitcher of Blue Moon to the locals.

After climbing the very narrow stairs—also original, and well-suited to the Gilded Age bordello the local antiquarian bookseller assured us the Erie had once been—we found two closet-sized rooms where we had space to either stand or sleep. If the bar was open, sleep was out of the question, since the neon light casts the mirror image of the word *Erie* in glaring red against the wall. Though we arrived at midnight and spent a half-hour jockeying for position at the bar, sleep was far away as long as light from the malicious cursive *E* filled the room.

Blocked in our quest, we return to the hotel bar to watch a bar fight between a man covered with Nazi tattoos and his more pedestrian opponent. After the police intervene to end their fun, we head to the night air of Port Jervis. A man follows us into the cold of October, stumbling through the narrow doorway onto the street, which looks much as it did in the Gilded Age. Brick storefronts with beveled silhouettes lay flatly against the starless sky, its murky gray brightness sure indication of our closeness to New York City and Philadelphia. Jeff, who has followed us onto the street, knows we're not from around here—a term I had until that moment thought of as the exclusively Southern social kiss of death. He leans into Katie's body, reads the logo on her jacket, and says, "you're from the North Face?" Then he swoops into my tattooed chest and announces that he cannot read Hebrew, a statement punctuated with a wink that lingers between the flirtatious and predatory meanings of the word *wolfish*.

Immediately, he assumes that we are visiting from New York City, a mere eighty-three miles southeast. When he hears that we are not, his gait straightens and the slur evacuates his voice. For the next fifteen minutes, we four talentless small-talkers return desperately to the convenience of the weather in avoidance of his helpful assertions that he is interested in everything to which we express loyalty: literature, photography, science fiction, mythical creatures, critical literacy. One suspects, considering his studied acquiescence, that he would have responded to Burke's magician-and-jazz-musician priorities with a vigorous nod. "You like magicians, man? I can find you magicians." We have the feeling we are being artlessly hustled—perhaps for sex, perhaps for whatever drugs he is carrying, perhaps to become recruits in his Acai Berry energy drink pyramid scheme. Chip—the bravest of us, in that his beard and stature often cause terror in men who cause terror—with no impulse toward revealing our purpose, reveals half of it. "Do you know any town secrets?" he asks.

My dread spills into the gap the question creates, leaving no room for silence. "The secret is," Jeff tells us conspiratorially, "that this town filled up after 9/11. Lots of people saw what they saw *there* and moved *here*, to the country, five minutes from Jersey, two minutes from Pennsylvania, with a train to the city." As a child in Seneca, South Carolina, the only trains I ever saw hauled wood from the mountains to the shore or oysters from the ocean to the foothills. As such, Port Jervis does not feel much like country to me. It feels, as Burke observes, that it "define[s] itself by various kinds of proximity . . . we're this far from NYC which is far enough but not too far" (Scarbrough to Lightweis-Goff, personal correspondence, March 3, 2009). Remembering the ease of travel between Ridgefield, Connecticut and New York City, and Manomet, Massachusetts and Boston—trips that characterized his childhood falls and summers—Burke says that Port Jervis is made "city" by the transitive property of railroads.

The cold air, the bar fight, and the eagerness of Jeff all feel like invitations, urgent urgings, to retreat up the two flights of steps to our hotel rooms, to wake at what passes as early for us, to find the lynching site as promised, on the ground between two churches. What Jeff didn't tell us—what, indeed, I found out later, only when I had a desk at which to find the secrets that the Internet yields—was that a far dirtier secret followed 9/11. On November 12, 2006, Adrean King, a New York City police officer who served the Bronx's forty-fourth precinct but lived in Port Jervis, was beaten by a gang of white men who stomped, kicked, and punched until, as a witness reported, King's leg was "twisted and shaped funny." The racial epithets rained down like blows ("Port Jervis police searching for men who beat NYPD cop"). After the indictment of Matthew Howell, James Conklin, Michael Gurliacci, and Shawn Kurtz for "second-degree gang assault," the local newspaper contained quotes from locals who believed the crime was motivated by a desire for fame and fueled by drugs, but who were reluctant to call it "a hate crime." A local woman who asked the newspaper not to print her name "for fear of retaliation" admitted to discomfort at the thought of her daughter walking home unchaperoned. In the comments on the newspaper's website, another dirty secret or, perhaps, a rural legend, appears: "this isn't the first time Gurliacci has attacked a black person" ("Police Searching for Men Who Beat NYPD Cop"). After his convalescence, King granted an interview to the local paper that affirmed Jeff's story; the officer and his family had "moved from the Bronx [to Port Jervis] to escape a fast-paced life" ("Officer Tells His Story of Being Attacked"). Port Jervis proved not to be the refuge that King expected, not the peaceful country oasis away from the chaos of the city.

The morning after our conversation with Jeff, a breakfast of lox and fancy omelets convinces me further that this is no country for country people, but far more like the deregionalized suburbs that surround the District of Columbia, places Republican vice-presidential candidate Sarah Palin denounced as the insufficiently Virginian parts of Virginia in the anti-American regions of America. At the risk of sounding like Palin, I will withhold such judgments about Port Jervis and assert only this: it felt like an unsafe place to *eat* lox, but not an unsafe place to *order* it. Too far from the ocean to eat fish without hygienic neurosis, but not too far from the city to require the concealment of Jewish identity. The public space of Port Jervis—notably Orange Square—feels strangely urban, too, if only because shining marble memorialization is not a mode of conservatism available to cash-strapped Southern towns. A martial culture of memory persists in this place, much like District of Columbia or Richmond, Virginia, and marks, at the corners of Orange Square, wars major and minor to which Port Jervis has offered blood sacrifice. At the furthest corner of the square from First Presbyterian Church is a memorial to the War on Terror: not to the fragmentation of the nation indoctrinated into a hypervigilant patriotism that polices its internal borders, not to the demoralization of a nation certain that its founding documents are living ones only insofar as they take away the rights therein enumerated, not to the cynicism of a nation that shrugs at the revelation that "we don't torture" means we neither kill nor administer beatings hard enough to cause organ failure in detainees indicted and convicted of no crime, not the apathy of a nation that politely avoids talking about politics. Instead, etched on the memorial are the names of four soldiers killed in Iraq and Afghanistan—Brian L. Pavlich, Irving Medina, Louis E. Allen, and Carlos Gonzalez—of interest to the chisel only because they lived in Port Jervis before they died with sand and blood in their mouths.

I am moved, I confess, by any stone or marble even remotely resembling a grave, by carved names—dented, worn, and interior—that beg the looker to touch what remains of the human. It was a pleasure and communion that had been denied to me at the ancient Jewish cemetery in Prague, where moss has grown into the angular shapes of the Hebrew letters, closing the gap in which I feel so somatically and psychically touched. But in Port Jervis, the space is open, the monument new, the copper letters raised, requiring me to feel the carved space as periphery. When I place my fingers there, I feel some modest hope that Robert Jackson Lewis will be memorialized, too, that somewhere, I will find his name and touch it as memory of his life and a remnant of his death.

We stop briefly in the First Presbyterian Church, where our wide-open faces and camera lenses attract the attention of the parishioners who are beginning to spill out into the square. The church is white and gold and red; skin saturated by the light from the stained glass windows, Katie looks like an Orthodox icon, glowing from scalp to throat. She disappears down a small flight of steps, following a chattering middle-aged congregant who is pleased at the sight of a camera, certain as she was that it was only the old folks who found the church beautiful. I follow at a distance and find, in the smaller chapel—three short steps down from the altar—that cooler light prevails, filtered through blue stained glass that offers me a "crown of life" in exchange for an obeisance I will never offer to a God in whom I will never believe.

Chip wanders away to look at the museum of information in the church's narthex, where walls are lined with photographs of previous ministers, including William H. Hudnut, who presided the day in 1892 when Robert Jackson Lewis was dragged past the structure. Had he stood at the pulpit on the day of the lynching, Hudnut would have been twenty feet from long, narrow Sussex Street, which ends at Main, where Lewis met his end. I move from Chip's side back to Katie and Burke's to listen to the outpouring of generosity and pleasure from their host. She is passionate about the church, frank in her desire to replace its aging columns and roof with something more modern, but remarkable mostly for her guilelessness. The sound of her voice, the look on her face, puts Katie at an ease she didn't expect in a town she later describes as "stale, tardy, wayward, truant, webby . . . yardsalish . . . [and] eternally Halloweening" (Van Wert to Lightweis-Goff, personal correspondence, April 27, 2009).

Kind, generous, and churched: these are traits I am resistant to link together. A childhood in the South taught me to distrust people who believed in a Brotherhood of Believers, rather than the essential dignity of all people, even those who do not share belief in their god. The kindness of these folks, I have often observed, does not demonstrate a fundamental generosity of spirit, but rather a self-protective normativity. The psychic work of assuming everyone is Christian is far less taxing than looking into another's eyes at first contact and imagining them consumed by the fires of hell. Even the most fundamentalist of Christians, I suspect, do not want it to be true. When I confess to them—friends, family, though not the good people of Port Jervis—that I am the one Pascal references in his famous wager, the one God made so he cannot believe, a storm builds in their eyes and they tell me, sadly, that if it were up to them, it would not be so, but since it is up to God, whose ways are mysterious and greater than ours, I might just have to burn in the fiery heat of his superior wisdom and limited

Conclusion 159

Figure 4. The First Baptist Church in Port Jervis, New York. Robert Jackson Lewis was lynched near the church's current location in 1892.

imagination. Failing that, they tell me they do not believe in Hell, but a universal heaven—a little piece of heterodoxy that could, I am certain, land them in the fires governed by the tyrannical God of their co-religionists' fevered fantasies. When faced with C. S. Lewis's famous "trilemma" of Lunatic, Liar, and Lord, I inevitably chose a combination of the three (Lewis 1952, 55). If the world is governed as the Bible says it is, then the categories are not mutually exclusive. God is a fetching combination of a tyrant and an animal that eats its young at roughly the rate it gives birth. The Tyrant is a fetching combination of Vladmir Putin, and an animal that eats its young at roughly the rate it gives birth. I will be an irritant in that Invisible Kingdom, demanding regime change and sovereign transparency, because silence about the violence of religion—a price demanded of non-Christians in the West, as Jewish theologian Hyam Macoby has argued—is a collaboration with atrocity (Rosenbaum 1998, 326).

They hanged Robert Jackson Lewis on a tree between two churches, in shouting distance of three more. Frankly, I expect Christians to take responsibility for this if only because no one else will, rather than earnestly assert that the real Christianity is just not being practiced in these dark corners of the earth. In return for them owning up, I will take responsibility in the unlikely event that there is a lynching at a beading store, a Marimekko retailer, an art gallery, a bookshop, or any of my other ports of ecstatic call. In this oasis of God and its adjoining street, I feel no separation: not a moment in the open air that tells me "this is a lynching town," or a foot inside the church doors that tells me "here is the house of God." The town and the structure are seamless, as are the lynchers and what they believed. After walking alone at night past the "tarpy brown sides" of a dozen unlit houses, Chip attested that he felt a blast of existential cruelty. he town "sleeps in might-have-beens," he tells me, "like the fading high school football star. You can see the longing in glittering eyes in the cabs of pickup trucks that slow down imperceptibly at the sight of a stranger; it's less than a threat, but more than a coincidence." "Do the eyes stare at you from a past full of racial bloodletting?" I ask him. "Do they contain the force of Port Jervis's history?" "No," he says, "but you cannot wash away a bloodstain" (P. Lightweis-Goff to J. Lightweis-Goff, personal correspondence, November 21, 2008). Attempts to scrub the stain repeat its dimensions in a frenzy of repetition that changes the surface and texture that surround it.[2]

Port Jervis has, nonetheless, tried. If you are new to lynching travel, you might be surprised to find its location is zoned for commercial use, a Kentucky Fried Chicken built where the crowd would have stood to watch Robert Jackson Lewis flail against the bright June sky. But this surprises us not at all. Close to Chip's hometown of Florence, South Carolina, is Lake City where, in 1898, Frazier Baker, a postmaster appointed by William McKinley, was lynched for speaking in a "braggadocio manner" (*Fairfield News and Herald*, March 2, 1898, quoted in Waldrep 2006, 208). The land where Frazier Baker was burned out of his home for the atrocity of being a black postmaster in a Jim Crow town—where he faced the mob, watched his infant daughter shot out of his wife's arms by a shotgun blast and his remaining children shielding their mother from injury, before he himself died from bullet wounds from dozens of guns—is not cursed earth, but commercial land in use by Dollar General. In Greenville, Willie Earle's resting place is for sale in hopes of finding one more big box store to price out Yard Sale

Lady and Scooter Man. We pace out the size of the mob—Burke measuring from memory of fire drills at the high school where he taught—in the parking lot of the KFC, across from the Baptist Church, in what might have been eyeline for Robert Jackson Lewis's suffering. Here we four stand at the axis of the lynching, the crucifixion, and the deep fryer. Such juxtapositions remind Chip that "there are forms of obsolescence waiting for renewal that will enable them to forget" (P. Lightweis-Goff).

Behind the church is a parking lot and a tree grown to look like a broken heart exchanged by schoolgirls to commemorate their friendships—a bauble I would give to all three of my traveling companions for the service done to me this day, for their willingness to stave off loneliness in the Valley of the Shadow of Death. We sit on the asphalt, toying with the remnants of a chimney. Those of us who smoke, smoke more frantically than usual. Mostly, we wait to feel. While Katie meditates and Chip paces, I ask for wisdom from Burke, who like "The Student" of Marianne Moore's poem "renders service when there is / no reward, and is too reclusive for / some things to seem to touch / him; not because he has no feeling but because he has so much" (Moore 1994, 102). He tells me that "it's the most complex form of erasure when the very old borders the very new and the not-so-new." We debate the utility of this amalgamation to capitalism, its likeliest cause, but Burke's face tells me more than the words we exchange. Every little ambiguity of a life is illuminated by his look, until I suspect that a still face and a sincere mouth are the only memorials I can offer to the dead, since Burke's face promises prelapsarian fairness, the option of remembering a lynched man for a moment longer than it took him to die.

Vatican West (Marion, Indiana)
Tom Shipp and Abram Smith, 1930

The air did not change when Chip and I traversed the Ohio River on January 3, 2009, crossing from Kentucky to Indiana, though the liquid border between slavery and freedom is fraught with meaning in American literature and culture. It is the site where Sethe gives birth to Denver in Toni Morrison's *Beloved* (1987), where Stephen Foster heard boatmen singing "doo-dah, doo-dah" as he struggled to write "Camptown Races" (1850), where Eliza flees across treacherous ice in Harriet Beecher Stowe's Uncle Tom's Cabin (1852), and the sight, in the days before the Fugitive Slaw Law (1850), that awoke escaped slaves to the imminence of freedom. Surely the topography changes in that Kentucky rolls over while Indiana just lays there, but this is no regional marker, since we had seen a more dramatic shift three hundred miles earlier, when we left the foothills of Alabama near Auburn to meet I-65, where the sand and pine scrub of Birmingham greeted us. Looming over the floodplains beneath the elevated clover interchange between Route 280 and I-65, I am struck by how much the steep view downward looks like New Orleans's I-10, where so many residents waited for death on the asphalt's higher ground after the levees breached on September 1, 2005.

I was tempted to imagine a last gasp of the South exiting our lungs as we entered the Midwest, but the closest I had was a glimpse of Muhammad Ali Boulevard in Louisville. I smiled, thinking that the vibrancy, boastfulness, and righteous political anger of Ali was the departing spirit of *my* South written on the landscape. Moments later, I thought of native Peorian Richard Pryor, a man with the same traits in more dazzling hues, and the remembered cadences of his incendiary monologue "Bicentennial Nigger" warned away from regional exceptionalism and the desire to delineate Southern boundaries, a game that had kept me awake for the first five hundred miles of excruciating boredom from Auburn to South Bend, Indiana. Once Pryor disconfirmed my relentless delineations of Southernness, I had nothing to do but stare at the ever-flattening horizon on Route 31, a road that Notre Dame students take from Indianapolis to the church-and-circus enclave of their campus, famous for its sports and basilica. Seven McDonald's, nine Steak-and-Shakes, and seventeen radio references to the Hoosiers later, I find myself thinking that I have found hell, and it has a remarkable basketball team, though no discernible sense of irony.

For the next three nights, we sleep on the floor of our friend Keith's house in South Bend, where I correct my earlier elision of self and Other, South and Midwest. Gazing at the wax statue of Saint Severin in the reliquary at Notre Dame, I feel far away from the South, where Catholicism is strange and exotic, though that definition changes as the demographic of the region shifts, making room for Latinos, a population relatively new to the South that stretches East of Texas. This gilded dome, this statue of Mary, these thousands of bits of bone trapped in dangling brooches behind glass, I think, create an aura more like Vatican West than the American frontier. But I cannot decouple the curious relics of the saints' bodies from the somatic souvenirs grabbed by witnesses in lynching's violent aftermath. James Allen, curator of the *Without Sanctuary* project and "picker" of history's secrets, found just such a relic in a frame that secured the image of Tom Shipp and Abram Smith's lynching in nearby Marion, Indiana. Locks of their hair are trapped between the glass and the mat in a reminder that purity is preserved by stasis, by latency, by Otherness (Allen et al. 2000, 177). At the same time, lynchers "gathered souvenirs—small bones, ears, toes, and fingers—for use sometimes as watch fobs or for display as curiosities in service stations or general stores," in a drive to memorialize the dangerous body and celebrate the community's triumph over it in a language they had learned from Christianity (McMillen 1990, 233).

After a night spent listening to a neighboring table defend the virtues of priests charged with molestation against a conspiracy of atheistic accusers in the Fiddler's Hearth, a microbrewery that aspired to Irishness—an ethnic affiliation that increasingly signifies unreconstructed whiteness—we hit the road once more, travelling through South Bend to towns called Peru and Mexico, and, finally, to Marion, where Shipp and Smith were lynched on August 7, 1930. The day before the lynching, Claude Deeter and Mary Ball had parked in Lover's Lane near the banks of the Missinewa River, which winds and weaves through the plains between Marion and the Ohio border. According to Ball's account, three men in a battered Ford ambushed them, shooting Deeter and raping her. Though Ball survived to give an account to the police and the mob led by her father Hoot Ball, Claude Deeter died on August 7. Plans to lynch the men were announced in advance—by flyer in Marion, over public address system at a dance in nearby Kokomo, by street signs emblazoned "Necktie Party in Marion" between there and South Bend (Carr 2006, 46, 115). Plans to lynch the accused—Shipp, Smith, and James Cameron—were announced in advance. A crowd formed at the jail, demanding the keys to Shipp, Smith, and Cameron's cells. Marion mayor Jack Edwards estimated that the mob had fifteen thousand members (Ibid., 13). When law enforcement resisted, a struggle ensued between the police and the mob. Several dozen men—as many as one hundred or as few as thirty, depending upon who tells the story—fought against the swinging billy clubs and canisters of tear gas. Armed with tools from the Marion Machine Foundry, they broke into the jail and enacted furious revenge against Shipp. They hanged him from the window of his cell, tying his arms to end his struggle against them, and stabbing him to ensure that he was dead. Afterwards, they stripped Smith and dragged him through a gauntlet of braying men to the lawn of the Grant County Courthouse, where he was hanged from a maple tree. Part of the mob returned to the cell to retrieve Shipp's body for display next to Smith's. They returned for the third prisoner, James Cameron, and brought him to the tree. As they slipped the noose around his neck, someone intervened. Some say that Sol Ball, the uncle of the raped girl, or Rex George, the head of the American Legion, protested that he was not one of the guilty parties; Cameron later said that it was God—for whose help he had prayed—that stopped the hand of the mob (Madison 2001, 7–11). He lived seventy-six more years, dying in 2006, after a long life of activism, in which he founded the Black Holocaust Museum in Milwaukee, Wisconsin; wrote his memoirs, and consulted the Senate about civil rights legislation.[3]

During the night, photographer Lawrence Beitler took a picture of the two bodies and the remnants of the mob, capturing a moment of violence juxtaposed to mundanity that could have illustrated Hannah Arendt's *Eichmann in Jerusalem*, in which she imparts the "lesson of the fearsome, word-and-thought-defying *banality of evil*" (Arendt 2006, 252). Beitler—no hero of the Civil Rights Movement—took the photo in a burst of entrepreneurial ambition, and, on the morning after the lynching, began a "brisk business selling [copies] for 50 cents apiece" (Madison 2001, 64). Copies traveled as far as Terre Haute, though protests to the state police by the NAACP were compelling enough to order Beitler to desist, making the image the sole province of newspapers, including the *Chicago Defender*, which published it with the trenchant caption "American Christianity."

Songwriter Abel Meeropol saw the image in *The Crisis*, the house organ of the NAACP, with the caption "Civilization in the United States, 1930," and was inspired to write the song "Strange Fruit," later popularized by Billie Holliday (Ibid., 112–13). Considering its source material, the song begins with curious misdirection:

> Southern trees bear strange fruit,
> Blood on the leaves and blood at the root,
> Black bodies swinging in the southern breeze,
> Strange fruit hanging from the poplar trees.

The song, inspired by brutal violence not in the South or the North, but the Midwest, repeats the regional marker three times in its twelve lines. Like Meeropol, second-generation witnesses to the Shipp and Smith lynching have remembered it as an image of the South. As James H. Madison points out, the image is reproduced in three museums—the Birmingham Civil Rights Institute in Alabama, the DuSable Museum in Chicago, and the Museum of Tolerance in Los Angeles—with no identification of the setting or date, leading visitors to believe, considering discursive quarantines of racial violence in the American South, that they are looking at the death rattle of the Confederacy (Ibid., 114). In the film *The Chamber* (James Foley, 1996), the photograph is reproduced as the page of an imaginary history text called *Southern Negroes and the Great Depression* with a caption reading "Lynching in Rural Mississippi, 1936."

But the image, like the practice of lynching, is ordinary, mundane, and American without regional specificity. A cluster of women—one pregnant and playfully holding the hands of a man behind her—stands a few feet from Shipp and Smith's bodies with a mass of living bodies moving in the space between them. The men to the left of the frame are mostly smiling and gazing at Beitler's camera, while the men to the right are blurred but looking up at the bodies. In the center, a man with Chaplin's moustache—or shall we call it Hitler's?—points at Smith's body, which was stripped from the waist down and covered with a makeshift toga. Smiles are visible in the crowd. Cropped to display only the crowd—an editorial choice made by *New York World*—the photograph seems to show a community in their town square enjoying the presence of friends as they watched fireworks on the Fourth of July. "None in the crowd seems embarrassed or angry," James. H. Madison argues, "All are so ordinary, even banal. Few could have imagined the place in history they earned that night by posing for Lawrence Beitler's camera. It was their shameless faces and everyday gestures as much or more than the limp bodies that . . . keep the photo alive long after" their deaths (Ibid., 115). Smiling pregnant women and country swains in the photograph do much to build an illusion of consensus, as Shawn Michelle Smith has argued, while drawing a color line in Marion that integrated the lynchers in the image with the larger structure of white supremacy (Apel and Smith 2007, 15–17). Yet, textual meaning can shift until the photograph can provoke Meeropol's protest and Beitler's entrepreneurism, while serving as my roadmap to the lawn on which the watchers once paced.

When we arrive in Marion, James Cameron has been dead for two years and Shipp and Smith for seventy-eight. Without difficulty, we find the location where Shipp and Smith hanged for nearly seven hours as the town went about the business of the day. Beitler's iconic photographic of their crime does not show the surrounding territory—certainly not enough to guide our steps—but the street lights, now mounted on taller poles, are nearly identical. The place where they died now has smaller trees, brightly-colored mulch, and wagonloads of scant gravel, the landscaping features of bureaucracies and municipalities. If I replicated Lawrence Beitler's pose and position today, I would see not two tortured bodies and a crowd of pleased perpetrators, but a sparkling new method of containing and controlling the bodies of the Other. The curiously-named Grant County Complex and Security Center has the telltale tiny windows of a county jail and a name that reminds me of the exchange of liberty for security that has characterized the last decade of American life. Looking at Beitler's photograph now, I suspect the citizens of Marion's mob would recognize their country, even though its President is not white.

Writing in favor of prison abolition in the flagging days of Republican dominance in all three branches of government, Angela Davis argued that the presence of people of color in Bush's administration—and, indeed, the presence of women in the most iconic and violent images of Abu Ghraib—indicated that "the techniques of racism [can be] administered not only by white people, but by black, Latino, Native American, and Asian people as well. Today we might say that we have all been offered an equal opportunity to perpetuate male dominance and racism" (Davis 2005, 66). In the weeks after Barack Obama's election to the presidency, the comparative racialization of categories of prisoners—racially-marked domestic prisoners and international "enemy combatants"—was made more apparent by the debate over closing

Figure 5. The Grant County Security Center in Marion, Indiana.

Conclusion

Figure 6. The courthouse in Marion, Indiana.

the brig at Guatanamo Bay. The location, once used to contain persons with AIDS who had attained refugee status, now holds unindicted "evildoers" in a juridical state that might be described as permanent purgatory. The fervor of foreign policy hawks over Obama's executive order to close Guatanamo filled the twenty-four hour cable networks with panic about where the "worst of the worst" would be contained. Though the prisons of the United States have been deemed sound to hold ts prisoners—who constitute more than one percent of the total population, an exceptional space was required to hold the accused terrorists. Congressional Republicans, flogging away at the demonic San Francisco liberals of their fevered imaginations, threatened to reopen Alcatraz to bring the War on Terror to American soil ("Boehner Repeats Gitmo Recidivism Propaganda"). Presuming apocalyptic consequences in bringing the war home requires the paranoid populace to forget the proliferation of prisons in rural isolates like Albion and Attica in New York, and the specter of bloody death on the courthouse lawn in Marion. Thus, political discourse has banished the prisoner—who, because of the intimate connection between American prison economies and plantation slavery, Davis argues, is racialized as black regardless of his or her race—to the oubliette of the "security center" (Ibid., 97).

We walk the perimeter of the courthouse, looking at every one of its monuments for every one of America's wars, but the sights of public squares and marble memorials grew banal between a sweltering August in South Carolina and a frigid January in Indiana.

The public library, which doubles as a museum, tells us more about the town, home to an icon of middle American tastes: Jim Davis, the creator of *Garfield*. Gazing at the displays and faceless mannequins in nineteenth-century dress trapped behind glass, I want to flee.

Though the glass cases brag of James Dean and Cole Porter's births within city limits, they linger only briefly on telling information: their residencies within the town lasted only a few years, since Marion is a town for people of talent to escape. It is a town that etches whiteness onto its civil sites with a Daughters of the American Revolution-funded memorial—a few feet from the site of the lynching—in memory of Martin Boots, "the first white man to enter land in Marion"—and a display in its museum in honor of Mr. and Mrs. Nelson Conner, the "first white couple" married in the city. No comparable honors exist for indigenous landowners, or the first African-Americans to marry—or, least of all, Shipp and Smith. Indeed, I ask, why does Marion need another memorial when marble proliferates on the courthouse lawn? What would be fitting—more fitting than Dollar General or Kentucky Fried Chicken—in the place where two men died? After half a year of lynching travel, I am left wondering if the work of human hands can remember Shipp and Smith with the "visual embodiment of public affect" and "public archive of feeling" and "with the "archive of public effect" that Erika Doss defines as the impulse of memorialization (Doss 2007, 13). There are no more spectacle lynchings in American public squares, so a memorial like that in Oklahoma City—deemed necessary by then-president Bill Clinton to stand against domestic terrorism—is no longer an urgent need, but I feel, after all this driving, a craving for the sight of Shipp and Smith's names rendered in marble, demarcated as receptacles and avatars of feeling in a public memorial that awakened memory, rather than assuaging guilt.

In the shadow of unrelieved marble whiteness, I feel emboldened by the incomplete memories of Port Jervis and Greenville, trips that our co-traveler Burke described as "wading among public memorials while hunting for one that's conspicuously absent" (Scarbrough to Lightweis-Goff, personal correspondence, March 3, 2009). Motivated by an impulse to turn the trips and this memoir into the *ourobouros* for which studying narrative has taught me to yearn, I cajole Chip into asking the curator for the thing we seek, but she neither panics or refuses as the Pickens County Museum curator did. Indeed, Marion librarians are accustomed to such requests. As retired librarian Ruth Thomas testified to Cynthia Carr in 1998, scarcely a day went by without a visitor demanding information about the lynching, a nuisance that a curator in a more remote public building in a less populous town is likely spared (Carr 2006, 102).We are rewarded for our request with two three-ring binders of information, fat with photocopies of newspaper stories old and new. Entries for August 6 and 8 are in place, but no documents are dated August 7. No primary documents about Marion's homegrown lynching are included in the makeshift archive, though a bundle of pages about Cameron's role in ongoing memorialization debates is appended to the final binder. I find more about my own homespace in a story that detailed the lynching of a pardoned ex-convict named Allen Green for "putting on airs" in Walhalla, South Carolina, than about the land on which I am standing.

Though the archive does not name the city's offense, the land might soon mark it. The space between the jail where Shipp and Smith were abducted and the courthouse lawn where they were lynched has been the site of varying schemes for memorialization. The jail, which housed prisoners as late as 1981, was purchased by Marion native Rex Fansler in 1990 for $500; he moved into the sheriff's house behind the structure, and dreamed of turning the building, with its gothic turrets and leaded windows, into a bed and breakfast (Ibid., 33). For most of the 1990s, he searched for a buyer for the building, which needed much renovation and an owner willing to pay $17,000 in back taxes to Marion's municipal government. One potential buyer was James Cameron, who opened the Black Holocaust Museum in Milwaukee after a trip to Israel's Yad Vashem convinced him of the necessity of memorializing lynching in the way that the Shoah is memorialized in sites as various as the United States Holocaust Museum in Washington DC, the Holocaust Centre in the United Kingdom, the Cape Town Holocaust Centre in South Africa, the New Mexico Holocaust and Intolerance Museum, and the Candles Museum and Education Center in Terre Haute, Indiana. Though there are twenty-five Holocaust museums in the United States alone, no comparable drive to remember exterminationist violence against people of color has marked American public space—certainly not in the privileged space of memory that the District of Columbia has become. The Black Holocaust Museum, founded by Cameron and using his personal story as the centerpiece of its exhibition, has had a home in its founder's basement, a strip mall, and, ultimately, a fifteen-thousand square-foot building in Bronzeville, Milwaukee's historic black neighborhood. Since Cameron's death, the Museum has been plagued with financial problems and even shut its doors for six months; eventually, it was purchased by the city, which forgave $386,000 of debt and refurbished the building in an attempt to turn Bronzeville into an arts and entertainment district (Daykin 2008).

Arguing that the decommissioned jail should be a space of memory and the location of the museum, James Cameron attempted to buy the building in the 1990s and move his facility from Milwaukee. But the idea proved controversial; Mayor Ron Mowery told Fansler that he would "screw it up" with the power of city government if Cameron should raise the prohibitive $160,000 Fansler demanded, flouting the bank's assessment of a $10,000 value (Carr 2006, 241). At the time of my visit, the old jail had been converted into apartments—iron bars optional, one suspects. At the same time that Fansler and Mowery collectively jettisoned Cameron's plans, a white witness to the lynching named Howard Vermilion dreamed of placing a memorial on the courthouse lawn. As a five-year old boy, Vermilion's father had taken him to ee the lynching of Shipp and Smith; he remembered "bumper-to-bumper traffic around the square" and being "so frightened that he got down on the floor of the car" (Ibid., 319). Compelled to work toward reconciliation by his sense that the image was "follow[ing] through all [his] life," he held Concerts of Prayer, integrated revivals at which he preached. "And my prayer is that before I die, I will see this come to an end," he told Cynthia Carr. "I want to see this thing done" (Ibid.). As a memorial, he wanted a bronze statue of Willie Deeter, brother of the murdered Claude Deeter, embracing James Cameron in the exact site of the Shipp and Smith lynching, modeled from a real embrace featured in a BBC documentary titled *Unforgiven: Legacy of a Lynching* (Paul Sapin, 1995), which arranged a meeting between the two men (Ibid., 316). But the city again resisted.

In 2003, responding to a mixed-race commission that organized a "day of forgiveness" in which the "black community" apologized for the assaults on Deeter and Mary Ball, and the "white community" apologized for the deaths of Shipp and Smith, as well as the assault on Cameron, Grant County began debating the possibility of a memorial. The festival of apologies would conclude, with the cooperation of the city and county governments, on October 19, with the dedication of a simple plaque. Eventually, the county commissioners voted in favor of a plaque not at the site of the lynching, but inside of the courthouse, with the word *lynching* omitted from its text. The proposed plaque would have read:

Conclusion 171

> As citizens of Marion, Grant County, Indiana, we acknowledge that hatred, violence, and bigotry have scarred this community. We confess that this legacy touches all of us. We both seek and offer forgiveness. We commit ourselves to the pursuit of healing, unity, and peace. (Ibid, 458)

But the town—comprised of black and white citizens—resisted. In a public meeting of the county commissioners, Xen Stewart, a seventy-three year old African-American witness to the witness, pronounced the plan "sick" and not befitting a gesture of reconciliation. Tommy Shipp's niece Ruth Ann Nash collected more than five hundred signatures of African-American residents against the notion of a memorial, telling the commissioners that she "resent[ed] the implications that this act will bring closure" to the families of the lynched men, or African-Americans who had encountered prejudice in Marion. In response to a poll that indicated only 8 percent of Marion residents approved of a memorial (35 votes out of a 427-person survey), the county commissioners rescinded their vote to place a plaque at the courthouse (Ibid., 457–58).

On January 5, 2009, Chip and I spent a long afternoon photographing the courthouse grounds—covered, like Port Jervis, with memorials to Vietnam prisoners of war, veterans of two World Wars, and white settler colonialism. The ground where Shipp and Smith died was covered with a shoddily-constructed gazebo, where we took brief shelter against an ice storm. Wind howled and ice sluiced against the wood and our faces. If it whispered the names of the dead, I did not hear it. In Marion, they say that the man pointing at Shipp and Smith in Beitler's photograph died at the hands of their ghosts, who stood bleeding and noosed on the hood of his car one snowy night, driving it into a ditch; they say that the dome of the courthouse, which once contained a statue of "Lady Justice," crumbled thirteen years after the lynching because of the intervention of the supernatural (Ibid., 372). In lieu of a memorial, they choose ghost stories. As the sun went down, I chose to leave.

The Labor of Forgetting

Asking passersby, pedestrians, and public servants about the history of their communities at the sites of three lynchings, I encountered rage in the South, ignorance in the North, and avoidance in the Midwest. To wit: Get out, I don't know, and Are you finding everything you need? with politeness so acute that I felt ashamed to ask for more horror. Can I attribute these verbal denials to region? Are they motivated by the temporal distance from lynchings? Too far away for living memory in Port Jervis, the residents had little to offer in the way of revelation. Protective because of the closeness of the offense, they refused a word—potentially incriminating to their parents, aunts, and uncles—in Greenville. In Marion, a community accustomed to the tremendous attention paid to the lynching by journalist Cynthia Carr, historian James H. Madison, and lynching survivor James Cameron, gave me controlled access to very limited information in an uninviting, noncirculating library, where I was astonished by both the cordiality and elisions of the librarians. Perhaps we could attribute these differences to the ways we police our outsiders and insiders. The Pike's County Museum curator disciplined me like a disobedient family member shaming the clan. Port Jervis residents offered me tolerant misdirection, as you would to an outsider. And in Marion, where three documentaries and two books have brought a flood of outsiders to recount their communal pathology, they gave me just enough to stop the flood of questions. Each location, in word and deed, practiced for forgetting.

When I asked my friend Mark Theiling, a native Southerner and the ambivalent heir to generations that have lived within and honored Charleston, South Carolina's borders, history, and heritage, he attributed the silence and stonewalling to the desire to "forget an irrelevant negative," a claim of which I am skeptical (Theiling to Lightweis-Goff, personal correspondence, January 7, 2009). To turn out to a county commissioners' meeting with a speech against memorialization is not a failure of memory, but the labor that forgetting requires. As Ernest Renan argued, forgetting is a "crucial element in the creation of nations," a formulation I would extend to regions and communities (Renan 1996, 42). This is not easy task. The citizens who argue in favor of erasure would inevitably believe that remembering is hard work, but I think of it as an a priori relationship to our lived architecture, which becomes written and overwritten until we can no longer trust the outermost layer of the palimpsest, nor privilege any particular ring of meaning. Not *either/or*, but *both/all/always*.

It is difficult work to forget, to work toward seamless relationships between self and space, between nation and citizen, demarcated so often in public displays of patriotism. To place an ominous black-and-red obelisk in memory of prisoners of war a few feet away from a lynching site privileges certain memories and banishes others, remembering as it begs me to forget.

Conclusion 173

But I am no longer convinced that replacing the obelisks can answer the longings of James Cameron and Howard Vermilion or, for that matter, my traveling companions in Port Jervis. Dwight Eisenhower toured concentration camps so that no one could ever tell him that the Holocaust was a fiction, since the first deniers of atrocity are very often its perpetrators (Eisenhower 1997, 441). Yet, sixty years later, Holocaust photographs—bundles of acute angles, gassed, stiff, and stacked like wood—offer no certainty. Even a "liberal heart" gazing upon the image of bodies bulldozed into mass graves, Cynthia Ozick warns, quoting a wag who had lost his sensitivity to the violence, can yearn for a " 'bit of satire' " (Ozick 1999, 22).

So what can be done at the sites of lynching to jettison the "memorial mania" that has gripped the United States since September 11, to avoid the outpouring of "public affect" that inscribes national innocence on the landscape, divorcing contemporary American foreign policy from conditions of inequality in the Middle East (Doss 2007)? To what extent should builders

Figure 7. 'You are not forgotten,' reads the Vietnam POW/MIA memorial on the courthouse lawn where Shipp and Smith were lynched in 1930.

of memorials remember Lincoln's injunction at Gettysburg that "we cannot consecrate—we cannot hallow" ground that has seen so much death? How can memorial efforts avoid turning spectators into "tourists of history" who, through consumerism and militant patriotism, experience the marble as catharsis, as "mediated and reenacted experience" (Sturken 2007, 9)? How can contemporary citizens attentive to the publicness of lynching stage a public intervention in favor of memory without leaving hearts yearning for the satire in ironic detachment to the violence therein evoked and represented? Surely, even those who feel no satiric longing at Holocaust photographs have felt just that toward the presumed consensus expressed in flags waving on the Fourth of July, or pyrotechnic versions of the national anthem performed at the Super Bowl. How ought memorials bypass this false consensus, so close to that communicated by the smiling faces in lynching photographs?

To answer these questions, I would revise the previous paragraph—however belatedly—to diminish its abstraction, as I ask these questions as much of my own eye as I do that of the imagined citizen. To prevent these gestures of catharsis, innocence, peace, and guiltlessness on the ground where people died, I propose—in response and with caution—that lynching memorials should be anti-mimetic and denaturalizing, refusing somatic figures of identification for spectators and disrupting public space so that they problematize their relationship to synthetic space. Though Ozick argues that the battle of memory is won with images rather than words, I emphasize the latter above the former in the interests of diminishing the experience of voyeurism at the lynching site. In the previous chapter on Kara Walker and James Allen, I argue that gallery exhibitions can replicate the experience of the lynch mob for audiences in the interests of consciousness raising. At the sites of lynching, the space—rather than the spectacle—ought to be the emphasis, because the critique of publicness and consensus disrupts the tourist's relationship to the ground on which he is standing, or the resident's relationship to the community in which he is embedded.

When a memorial mimetically represents trauma—like Eric Fischl's "Tumbling Woman" (2002), which reproduced the moment of impact on a female body that fell from the World Trade Center—it is often grossly prurient. Fischl's sculpture was removed from the lower concourse of Rockefeller Center because it was thought too graphic, disturbing, without beauty or art (*Time Magazine Blogs* 2007). As much as a statue of hanging bodies in Marion would disrupt and interpellate at the site of lynching, I am squeamish for the same reason that I reject Howard Vermilion's desire to reproduce Deeter and Cameron's embrace on the courthouse lawn, as it offers a too-easy analog for the spectator—a body without risk looking at a body in peril, demanding an image of reconciliation that offers closure for the very open, very present trauma of racism.

A possible alternative is the model of the negative memorial, like the Hamburg Memorial Against Fascism. A forty-foot column was erected in Hamburg, Germany in 1986, and was lowered slowly into the ground over five years, until only the base was visible. Passersby could inscribe the soft lead exterior with memories of those who died at the hands of the Nazi horror; in a city rife with neo-Nazism, it recorded the hatred that inspired that crime, as well as its bloody result. Day-by-day, the column disappeared; the still-present base forcefully disrupts the pleasure one might feel walking the city sidewalks on a cool and sunny German morning, as questions crack and unsettle certainty (Forty and Kuchler 2001, 6). On the border between Greenville and my home counties in South Carolina, just such a monument—a disruption in spatial and temporal identification—could point to the violence that can colonize and coexist with beauty. Because the culture and its ideologies are neither static nor stable, our relationship to organic and synthetic landscapes should be able to evolve without overdetermined interventions in the forms of tumbling women or the hypermartial Washington Monument. But the interior, the submerged, the hidden, must remain. Though I dream of demolishing racism in the democracy yet to come, I cannot imagine conditions under which its pernicious foundations will become irrelevant.

In Port Jervis, I repeated to Chip, Katie, and Burke the state motto of South Carolina—*dum spiro spero* (while I breathe, I hope)—in a moment of yearning for a plaque, an empty space, a demarcation of Robert Jackson Lewis. But I cannot forget that the motto was written when more than half of the state's population lived hopelessly in bondage, just as I cannot forget that the cornerstone of this Republic is masoned by inspirational, eloquent words penned by people who owned people. But I suspect that the pause I feel upon reading these words is the good news, rather than the bad, because vigilance against ease is how I avoid the mania of public affect, the possibility of becoming a tourist of history, and, yes, the desire for satire at the sight of horror. Yet I know that my response was not automatic, but rather a refusal of repeated entreaties to become an unreconstructed citizen of the South, the nation, and white supremacy enabled not by my agency, but by the repetitions of power. Judith Butler writes of these matrices of acculturation in *Gender Trouble* (1990):

> Power rather than the law, encompasses both the juridical (prohibitive and regulatory) and the productive (inadvertently generative) functions of differential relations. Hence, the sexuality that emerges

> within the matrix of power relations is not a simple replication or copy of the law itself, a uniform repetition of a masculinist economy of identity. The productions swerve from their original purposes and inadvertently mobilize possibilities of "subjects" that do not merely exceed the bounds of cultural intelligibility, but effectively expand the boundaries of what is, in fact, culturally intelligible. (Butler 2006, 40)

Just as the gendered subject cannot escape the matrix of relationships and repetitions by which she is acculturated, she cannot become a perfect copy of the abstract woman, a perfect template for the law that governs the body and its performance of identity. Neither can the repetitions and rituals of herrenvolk democracy create a perfect citizen. The repetitions of the landscape—my car on the highway in Greenville, my feet on the sidewalk in Marion, my eyes on the steeple in Port Jervis—can be interrupted with matter out of place that resists seamless replication: the plaque we never notice until the day we notice nothing else.

This condition, which I call the "performative pause," is the goal of my memory project: disruptions of landscape that open a gap between the spectator and the law, between the witness and whiteness. It can be interrupted with a detail out of place that resists seamless replication: the plaque we never notice until the day we notice nothing else. The pause should not only make the witness aware of the gap between the risk of the lynched man and the safety of their own body, since having one's privilege delineated often results only in a sigh of helplessness. Gaps between the witness and his predecessor—the lyncher—should also be underscored in the act of memorialization. Just as I wish for the abolition of torture, lynching, the hate crime, and, along with Angela Davis, the prison, the poet Philip Larkin dreamed of the abolition of religious faith in his poem "Church Going" (1954):

> A serious house on serious earth it is,
> In whose blent air all our compulsions meet,
> Are recognised, and robed as destinies.
> And that much never can be obsolete,
> Since someone will forever be surprising
> A hunger in himself to be more serious,
> And gravitating with it to this ground,
> Which, he once heard, was proper to grow wise in,
> If only that so many dead lie round. (Larkin 1989, 97–98)

Imagining a world where churches have fallen into disuse, in which they are sought for solace, Larkin posits the power of seriousness, the impulse to determine where one resides in relationship to the past, a vigilant self-correction that the resistant citizen cannot forsake. For contemporary white spectators of lynching memorials, struggling to find a more productive relationship than so-called "white guilt," a memorial on serious earth asks them to unsettle their relationship to home, their certainty that white privilege is "robed as destiny." For spectators with an experience and history of racial oppression, the memorial desanctifies the once sacred, once holy ritual of racial violence. In a reversal of Larkin's formation of the atheist stumbling upon once-hallowed ground, Jack Santino theorizes that memorials "display death in the heart of social life. These are not graves awaiting occasional visitors and sanctioned decorations. Instead of a family visiting a grave, the grave comes to the family—that is, the public. All of us" (Santino 2006, 13).

Borrowing terminology from W. E. B. DuBois, Angela Davis posits a vision of abolition democracy, a struggle to destroy the institutions that have benefited from oppression in a quest for a new world. The longed-for society will exist when white supremacy is remote, when the institutions that have benefited from racism have disappeared. But such a victory cannot be achieved only at the level of institutional change. The abolition citizen must aid the process by divesting himself of the most pervasive form of privilege: the tyranny of experiential and emotional empiricism. This is the assertion that what one can see and feel—an affective relationship to home, to nation, to citizenship—overwrites the histories, the pasts, and the memories of others. After the "sensual turn" of public culture, in which sentiment is martialed in a process rationalized by committed relativisms but deployed in favor of conservatism, Lauren Berlant advocated theory as a "critical realm of the senses . . . [that] encompasses what the senses do empirically; what feelings are made out to mean; and which forces, meanings, and practices are magnetized by concepts of affect and emotion" (Berlant 2004, 446).

With Berlant's injunction in mind, I began this book with a meditation on my own experience and affective connections to the landscape and culture of the South, and began this travelogue in my own hometown: the place where I spent twenty-three years of my life, met and fell in love with my partner, and maintain connections to friends and family. But I cannot mistake my libidinal attachments to the town, the region, and the nation for the nature of any of the three. I traveled to three lynching towns with very beloved people, but the pleasures I felt there were only the outermost layer of the palimpsest; I cannot deploy the dogma of empiricism to "presume the clarity of the senses and their phenomenological and historical place in world building" (Ibid., 448). In this fragmentation of vision, I imagine the project of Noel Ignatiev's *Race Traitor* (1996) returning from the ghetto of recherché activism in which so much theory has placed it; the distrust that I assign to seamless visions of home and citizenship is the beginning of "treason to the white race" (Ignatiev 1996, 10). The abdication of homespace—with its fraught relationship to public acts of racial violence—and the willing embrace of psychic nomadism might begin the process of abdicating whiteness in the attendant knowledge that home is nowhere, a curse and blessing shared by Ida Wells-Barnett and Richard Wright. In this book, I have aspired to nothing teleological, nor a stunning and complete divestiture of white supremacy: only to the pause that precedes them and the democracy to come.

Notes

Introduction

1. On the 2002 album *Unleashed*, Toby Keith and Willie Nelson's duet on "Beer for My Horses," in which the narrator tells of his "grandpappy" recommending lynching as a general remedy for criminality. The song's lyrics provoke the reader with a repeated "you," who is told to "saddle up [the] boys" and "draw a hard line" against "bad boys" who should "hang . . . high in the street." Bizarrely, the song was adapted into a film—*Beer for my Horses* (Michael Salomon, 2008)—starring Toby Keith and Rodney Carrington, who "take justice into their own hands" to save the former's girlfriend (Claire Forlani) from an evil Mexican drug dealer (Greg Serano) who kidnaps her.

2. As Jeffory Clymer has argued, "citizenship becomes an ideologically weighted term" for lynch mobs and the activists who militated against their violence (129). Because of the value and contestation of citizenship in the period of Reconstruction, both the mob and their opponents shaped their rhetoric around this subject of debate. For Ida B. Wells-Barnett, this resistance emerges in the construction of lynching as a "peculiarly national crime" that reveals that its mobs were " 'wedded' to the 'revolting' violence of political disenfranchisement" (Clymer 2003, 130).

3. On February 18, 2010, white computer engineer Joseph Stack flew a small plane into an Austin, Texas Internal Revenue Service building, after burning down his own home and authoring a tax-resisting manifesto. Despite the similarities to 9/11, as Brian Stelter argued in the Media Decoder blog of *The New York Times*, the major cable networks evinced a studied refusal to call the act "terrorism" without the qualifier "domestic," a reticence they did not demonstrate when US Army Major Nidal Malik Hasan opened fire at the military base at Fort Hood (Stelter 2010).

4. "A catalyst for the women's club movement," biographer Mia Bay writes, "Wells could never become a long-term club member herself" because she came from a working-class background, began her work in isolation from the social networks of powerful male leaders, and espoused radical, rather than moderate, political positions (119). Urging armed self-defense and carrying a pistol in her purse, as black women

began to mobilize for political and social action—she was an unlikely club woman—who nonetheless offered a powerful model of leadership (Bay 2010, 118–22).

5. Both Thomas Holt and Paula Giddings have compellingly argued that Wells-Barnett was ostracized and marginalized by the intra-racial community of the civil rights establishment. Giddings describes the coup inside of the NAACP that replaced Wells-Barnett with Celia Woolley, a white ally of Booker T. Washington's with a reputation for fractious and patronizing relationships with black women (Giddings 2001, 8). Holt attributes the loss of support within the journalistic community, the NAACP, and the black women's club movement as results of Wells-Barnett's autocratic and uncompromising politics and personality (Holt 1982, 59). Jacqueline Goldsby discusses accusations of "harlotry," vanity, and sexual malfeasance against Wells-Barnett by both the white press and black community (Goldsby 2006, 59).

Chapter One

1. Gaines M. Foster defines the political ideology of the Lost Cause as "support for states' rights, white supremacy, and the Democratic party." In the early twentieth century, the Lost Cause became "a civil religion [that] rendered southerners a people set apart by a special sense of mission" (Foster 1989, 1134). The term was coined in 1966 by Edward A. Pollard, who wrote one of the first histories of the Civil War. During the nadir of race relations (1880–1920), the term was deployed to legitimize a Confederate public culture, the chief evidence of which is Richmond, Virginia's Monument Avenue and the shocking proliferation of United Daughters of the Confederacy monuments, placed even in states that did not exist in 1861. The landscape of the South is littered with UDC monuments that police the borders of Southern identity, standing at the site of the Free States of Jones with a tribute to the Confederate cause, lest current inhabitants grow too utopian about the potential for racial justice, and free counties across Kentucky and Missouri to dislocate their Unionist past (Loewen 1999, 104–105).

2. In *The Country and the City* (1973), Raymond Williams prefigured both Luce Irigiray's claim of universal manhood from "This Sex Which Is Not One" and the founding notion of unmarked racial identity in whiteness studies by delineating marked regions and unmarked nationhood. "The life and people of certain favored regions are seen as essentially general, even perhaps normal," he writes, "while the life and people of certain other regions are, well, regional" (Williams 1973, 199).

3. Because of the reliable liberalism of African-American voters, they have attained the same mystified status in Republican circles as the so-called Red States now have among liberals. Conservative columnist Ann Coulter has, as ever, been the most hyperbolic in her rhetoric. "Here's the deal on politics and race in America: Republicans don't need black voters, but they want them. Democrats don't want black voters, but they need them." Though Coulter lists no evidence of the above claim,

she was right in predicting three weeks before the 2004 election, that Bush would significantly expand his voting base among African-Americans—from 7 percent in 2000 to 12 percent in 2004 (Lopez. May 2005, 5, http://civicyouth.org/PopUps/FactSheets/FS_04VotingRace.pdf).

    4. For analysis of these electoral shifts, Kari Frederickson's *The Dixiecrat Revolt and the End of the Solid South, 1932–1968* (2000) and Dewey W. Grantham's *Life and Death of the Solid South* (1992) are quite illuminating. Recent Democratic attempts to restore the South to its past Democratic solidity have often ignored the racial implications of that fictional solidity, which was accomplished through voter suppression and state-level electoral colleges that weighted influence and power in predominantly white districts. Virginia Senator and former Republican Jim Webb, a self-identified "Jacksonian Democrat" and strategist for the 2008 election, is the foremost advocate of renewing the party's traditional influence in the South ("What It Means to Be a Democrat").

    5. In this matter and others, Wright dramatically differs from his friend, fellow expatriate and frequent critic James Baldwin. In "Equal in Paris," Baldwin recounts the experience of being jailed for over a week in a country where he had "nothing in the bank, and no grasp whatever of the French language." The past, Baldwin suggests, weighs heavily upon the French, for whom a glorious history "impl[ies] . . . present fatigue . . . and paranoia." Shocked by the experience of imprisonment in a country he regarded as freer than America, Baldwin's essay treats diaspora—musing on the distance he feels from his North African cellmates—and the weight of the past, concluding that "no people come into possession of a culture without having paid a heavy price for it" (Baldwin 1998, 102). The cost of cultural cohesion, it seems, is xenophobia and racism. Because this essay is so seldom treated by Baldwin scholars, I certainly needed an introduction to it. As such, I am grateful for the lively discussion about it at the James Baldwin: Life and Legacies Conference at Queen Mary University in London in June 2007, where Quentin Miller presented "Separate and Unequal in Paris," an examination of Baldwin's relationship to law and imprisonment.

    6. Since public burning did not require the close range for spectatorship of a firing squad or a hangman, it was a popular method of spectacle lynching that enabled the fifteen spectators of Washington's lynching and the four thousand of Hose's. Yet, the broad range for spectatorship, the carnivalesque atmosphere of the crowd, and the historical echo of witch burnings meant that lynchings by fire ran the risk of bringing community disapproval down upon the mob. The burning of Jessie Washington was, in fact, a key factor in public opposition to the "Waco Horror," as it was called. The symbolism of the fire—associated with both witch hunts and ritual sacrifice—turned the community against Washington's lynchers, leading them to disavow the perpetrators as exceptional cases. "If only they had just hung him," NAACP field researcher Elizabeth Freeman was told, "they felt that would have been all right, but the burning—the dragging of the charred torso through the streets is so much worse than [the murder of which he was accused]" (Dray 2002, 218).

Chapter Two

1. Though a political opponent of Nazism, Schuyler hoped that World War II would provide traditionally colonized nations with a chance for national liberation through the exhaustion of Western resources and military might, which would weaken the imperial stranglehold in Africa and Asia. He was sympathetic in particular to the Japanese interventions in the Pacific theatre of the war, which he read as "chickens coming home to roost" against the Western powers. When combined with his stated resistance to black enlistment until the end of segregation in the Armed Forces, these positions make him "the most radical voice in the black press during World War II," a voice that migrated toward conservatism as he embraced proto-McCarthyite anti-Communism (Ferguson 2005, 25–27).

2. The connections here, though of my own making, were first suggested by Jeffrey B. Ferguson's *The Sage of Sugar Hill*, in which he notes that DuBois and Schuyler shared "northern origin[s] and fatherless upbringing[s]" (Ferguson 1995, 226). Henry Louis Gates's review essay of Schuyler's black internationale and black empire relies on the metaphor of fragmentation to explain Schuyler's politics and place him within the DuBoisian paradigm of doubleness. Gates argues that Schuyler "play[ed] out his ambivalent feelings . . . by literalizing DuBois's famous metaphor . . . [and] dividing himself into two: conservative, colored G.S. Schuyler and militant, black Samuel I. Brooks," the pen name under which he wrote in the 1930s (Gates 1992, 42).

3. Though the hard sciences and medicine in particular are the targets of his sharpest attacks, the social sciences are also prodded in the representations of Beard and Bonds, two "race men" whose revelations of the consequences of racism are laughably predictable. "Most of the data were highly informative," Schuyler writes, "revealing the amazing fact that people went to jail oftener than rich ones; that most of the people were not getting enough money for their work; that strangely enough there was some connection between poverty, disease, and crime" (Schuyler 1999, 71). Whether the older, more conservative Schuyler looked back on the familiar rhetorics of liberal apologias with chagrin is a matter about which I cannot testify, though the relevance of his satire of the unsurprising revelations of social science has not diminished with the passing of eight decades.

4. The Atlanta Riots, as Phillip Dray argues, were caused by social and economic problems operating in tandem to inflame already-existing white hostilities against African-Americans. Just as many "rootless young black men" were moving to the city from the country, Atlanta's newspaper "drummed up" a "ravishment crisis, prey[ing] on whites' powerful anxiety that the earth was shifting beneath their feet." The ground shifted even further when increasingly prosperous black Atlantans formed an "urban demimonde of saloons, pawnshops, billiard halls, and brothels along Decatur Street." In the summer before the riot, a hotly-contested gubernatorial campaign between Hoke Smith and Clark Howell created a climate of irresponsible and partisan

journalism that touted "a steady flow of 'Negro Beast' and 'Black Brute' " stories in *The Atlanta Journal* and its chief rival *The Atlanta Constitution*, two papers that were consolidated into the current *Atlanta Journal-Constitution* in 1982 (Dray 2002, 162–67).

5. In the eponymous essay in *Publics and Counterpublics*, Michael Warner defines the paradigmatic counterpublic in response to Jurgen Habermas's idealized salon of public debate. At the same time that the coffee houses and literary journals of eighteenth-century Europe were taking form and giving rise to public sphere democracy, "the public places and stranger sociability of London were also giving rise to clubs of all kinds . . . including the so-called molly houses where something like modern homosexual culture was developing" (Warner 2005, 112). Similarly, the Harlem Renaissance had a public identity—printed protest literature addressed to socially-conscious "Negrotarian" whites—and a counterpublic sphere of Harlem nightlife, where interracial queer desire and other outrages of respectability were the norm. Because the public sphere is not a quantifiable space, but an audience invoked by discourse, we might also imagine African-American lifeways—barbershops, churches, women's clubs—as counterpublics to dominant white spatial relations.

6. Samuel R. Delany claims that the lynching of Buggerie and Snobbcraft "simply use[s] accounts of actual lynchings of black men at the time, with a few changes in wording" (Delany 2000, 384). Whether he refers to Matthew Williams's lynching is not apparent in his essay, but he does recount a family story of a pregnant cousin lynched because her pale skin, in juxtaposition to her darker husband's, made a mob believe that their relationship was interracial. "Her husband's body was similarly mutated [to Snobbcraft and Buggerie's]," Delany writes. "And her child was no longer in her body when their corpses . . . were returned in a wagon to the campus of the black Episcopal college where my grandparents were administrators" (Ibid., 385). The mutilation and the quest into the interior space of the womb for verification of the fetus's race can be read as a quest for essence that functions like pseudoscience.

Chapter Three

1. Because of these themes, he has been paired in recent critical readings with fellow Nobel Laureate Toni Morrison, whose writing is similarly dominated by representations of racial violence. See Erik Dussere's *Balancing the Books: Faulkner, Morrison, and the Economies of Slavery* (2003), Philip M. Weinstein's *What Else But Love? The Ordeal of Race in Faulkner and Morrison* (1996), Carol A. Kolmerten and Stephen M. Ross's *Unflinching Gaze: Morrison and Faulkner Re-envisioned* (1997), and Morrison's own work on whiteness and the literary imagination productively suggest this connection.

2. In 1911, thirteen years after this dismissive pronouncement, Booker T. Washington was assaulted for allegedly catcalling a white woman on West 63rd

Street in New York City. Albert Ulrich, the woman's husband, beat Washington with a cane and pursued him to the perimeter of Central Park, where several other white men joined him in the pummeling. While convalescing with seventeen stitches in his head, Washington told the press that he was meeting Daniel C. Smith, a Tuskegee associate, at the apartment building where Ulrich encountered him. Rumors reached W. E. B. DuBois that Washington was actually visiting a brothel in the city, but the rival was circumspect, and discreetly avoided a reminder of the "Wizard's" earlier pronouncement on the morality of lynched men in his statements of condolence (Dray 2002, 186–89).

3. It is worth noting, as Anne Goodwyn Jones has, that the reader is left not knowing if Minnie Cooper makes the accusation against Will Mayes. With regards to gender, Jones argues, Faulkner is best known for what he does not include, like the absent narration of Caddy Compson in *The Sound and the Fury*. "The absences are critical," Jones writes of "Dry September." "We are never shown a scene of Will Mayes's lynching, nor are we given a scene either of Minnie Cooper's being accosted by a 'Negro' or of her inventing a story to that effect. Yet critics almost invariably conclude that some of these at least are 'facts. . . .' For many readers, that story is antiracist but still sexist: Minnie did it, not Will Mayes" (Jones 1995, 145). To assume that Minnie Cooper is simply a Delilah who, in the contemporary parlance, "cries rape," is to ignore the history of punishing consensual interracial intimacy, and containments and regulations of the white female body under white supremacy.

4. Hoke Perkins reads the scenes with Mannie's ghost as interrupting the narrator's omniscience with the "everyday miracle of shared vision, the leap of imagination applied to the objects Mannie saw, and Rider sees" that communicates their interdependency, love, and the fragmentation of the senses that Rider experiences at the loss of a sensory and sensual partner (Perkins 1987, 229).

5. Even when they avoided undercounting the numbers of natives in their midst, Europeans thanked God for their absence. Plague preceded Pilgrims to Plymouth, decimating the indigenous population. William Bradford wrote that it "pleased God to afflict these Indians with such a deadly sickness that out of 1,000, over 950 of them died" (Bradford 1909, 258). The purpose of this logic is, as sociologist James Loewen has argued, to "mak[e] the present . . . inevitable," and therefore, unresponsive to ethical claims against the genocide and violence that enabled expansion in the colonial period and early Republic (Loewen 1995, 126).

6. Critic Richard Gray has read the death of Joe Christmas as a far more affirmative moment for its spectators. The silence of the witnesses "define[s] the limit of speech acts, any attempt to turn experience into a communal language, by seeking deliverance and redress in a nonverbal world." The vomit of the witness, Gray argues "helps us take the measure of this act of violence . . . [and] helps us to locate it . . . as a possible act of transformation." The ambiguity of the look—and the ambiguity of Joe Christmas's racial status—"anticipate[s] the possibility that history may generate new directions in language, voice, and vision: new habits of meaning and action" (Gray 2002, 67). I would be compelled by this claim were that

racial ambiguity not presented as a source of tremendous anxiety and motivator for violence by Christmas and Hines.

    7. This omission provokes Don H. Doyle's claim that "the killing of Joe Christmas . . . is not [a lynching]" because the lynching posse under the leadership of Percy Grimm are "legally deputized agents of the law and technically chased and killed a fugitive who had escaped and resisted arrest" (Doyle 1999, 239). As Neil McMillen has argued, distinctions between "popular violence and the formal administration of law" were narrower in Mississippi, not because the law was disregarded, or the white population anarchic, but because white communities "shared a more expansive view of [law] . . . that embraced such cultural codes as community tradition, family pride, personal vengeance, feminine virtue, male honor, and white supremacy" (McMillen 1990, 240).

Chapter Four

    1. According to Saidiya Hartman, the replacement of the black subject with the sympathetic white spectator has a long history in antiracist praxis that "efface[s] the horrors" suffered under racist regimes. Reading the letters of Abolitionist John Rankin, who mitigates the unrepresentability of the pain of the enslaved person by replacing black subjectivity with his own, in a written fantasy of his own flogging, sale, and separation from his family, Hartman argues that he "begins to feel for himself rather than for those whom this exercise in imagination presumably is designed to reach"—the enslaved African. Within regimes of sentiment and sympathy, the white spectator "becomes a proxy" for another's person pain, "yet by virtue of this substitution the object of identification threatens to disappear" (Hartman 1997, 19). In order to raise consciousness against slavery, Hartman fears, the Abolitionists diminished racial particularities of captive suffering.

    2. Much like *Without Sanctuary*, the 1935 exhibition An Art Commentary on Lynching attracted unexpected crowds and controversy in New York City. The exhibition culled representations of lynching by emerging artists—including John Stewart Curry, Peggy Bacon, Thomas Hart Benton, Paul Cadmus, and the remarkable Isamu Noguchi, whose metal sculpture of a burning body was denounced by art critic Henry McBride as sensationalistic and "just a little Japanese mistake." Though Noguchi's *Death (Lynched Figure)* remains on display at the Noguchi Museum in New York City, much of the art—thought of as ephemeral political interventions—no longer exists. Margaret Vendryes's essay on the subject rescued this exhibition and much of the lost art displayed there from obscurity (Vendryes 1997, 153–76).

    3. For Saidiya Hartman, Douglass's reproduction of this scene, and "the ease with which such scenes are usually reiterated" in literature and criticism bypasses outrage and instead encourages a familiarity that dramatizes the suffering of African-Americans, making both voyeurs and witnesses out of readers (Hartman 1997, 3).

The critical impetus of her study tasks the readers with "illuminat[ing] the terror of the mundane and quotidian rather than the shocking spectacle" of scenes of suffering on the plantation, the minstrel stage, and the lynching site (Ibid., 4). Though I agree with Hartman's figurations of the violence of everyday life, I nonetheless reproduce Douglass's account—as well as the accounts of lynching at other moments in this project—because I imagine these violences as part of everyday life—functions of the quotidian nature of white supremacy, rather than occlusions of it.

Conclusion

1. Throughout this final chapter, I develop a personal voice designed to challenge the critical convention of disinterest, as well as the conception that lynching is a topic that has reached its saturation point within the academy. In the years that I wrote and researched this book, I often heard other academics claim that the subject of lynching was truly "done" after the flood of publications on the subject that followed *Without Sanctuary*. Despite these claims, the world outside of the academy was bereft of the memorialization work that academicians considered accomplished.

Writing and research are collaborative efforts, and this general condition is more, rather than less, true of the memoir and travelogue that follow. I am grateful to those who traveled with me—Chip Lightweis-Goff, Burke Scarbrough, and Katie Van Wert. Though I challenge the drive to proceduralism in academic labor, it is not my intention to replace that convention with an enthronement of the researcher as singular hero or rugged individual. As such, I maintain the texture of collaboration by including the letters, emails, conversation, and voice mails that we wrote by way of reminding ourselves and each other of the powerful absences we had encountered. These references function much like the field notes of an ethnography. Though the totality of my experience at lynching sites is not available to my readers, I hope that these snapshots provide useful signposts and mile-markers.

As we traveled, Chip and I also sustained ourselves with the love and support of Patricia and Alan Lightweis, Keith Davis, Carole Morgan, and Phillip Goff, Sr. For their willingness to be drafted into temporary (and unwelcome) labor as unpaid research assistants, I am also grateful to Steven Clodfelter, Mark Theilling, and his parents, Dale and Nancy Theiling.

2. I am grateful to Patricia Lightweis—my indomitable mother—for this very valuable insight. She would have me inform readers that it is influenced by a ghost story she heard during summers spent with her grandparents Sarah Gibson and Russell Endicott in Jim Thorpe, Pennsylvania. Cell 17 of the city's Old Jail Museum contains a bloody handprint on the wall, pressed into the brick by Alexander Campbell, a member of the Molly Maguires—a miners' union that was broken by the interventions of the industrial bosses—who proclaimed his innocence of the murder of mine boss John P. Jones. The handprint, which is now a major tourist attraction,

is said to have remained and reappeared on the wall despite scrubbing, painting, and replacement of the brick (http://www.theoldjailmuseum.com/).

    3. When journalist Cynthia Carr moved to Marion for a year to recover living memory of the lynching, and the concomitant history of the Ku Klux Klan in Grant County, she was astonished to discover how unpopular Cameron was among Marion's very small African-American community, in which some argued that his near-lynching was an error, since he was in jail for "stealing chickens," rather than the assault of Ball and Deeter. The historical record, which attests to Cameron's 1930 trial, sentencing, 1934 parole, and eventual pardon by Governor Evan Bayh in 1995, contests this local legend (Carr 2006, 345).

Bibliography

Ackerman, Diane. *A Natural History of the Senses*. New York: Random House, 1991.

Adams, Timothy. "Richard Wright: Wearing the Mask." In *Richard Wright's Black Boy (American Hunger): A Casebook*, edited by L Andrews and Douglas Taylor, 171–90. New York: Oxford University Press, 2003.

Allen, James, Jon Lewis, Leon F. Litwack, and Hilton Als. *Without Sanctuary: Lynching Photography in America*. Santa Fe, New Mexico: Twin Palms Publishing, 2000.

Althusser, Louis. "Ideology and Ideological State Apparatuses: Notes Toward an Investigation." In *Lenin and Philosophy and Other Essays*, 85–126. New York: Monthly Review Press, 2001.

Anderson, Benedict. *Imagined Communities: Reflections on the Origin and Spread of Nationalism*. New York: Verso Books, 1991.

Apel, Dora. "On Looking: Lynching Photographs and Legacies of Lynching After 9/11." *American Quarterly*. 55, no. 3 (2003): 457–78.

Apel, Dora and Shawn Michelle Smith. *Lynching Photographs* (Defining Moments in American Photography). Berkeley, CA: University of California Press, 2007.

Apess, William. "An Indian's Looking-Glass for the White Man." In *On Our Own Ground: The Complete Writings of William Apess, A Pequot*, edited by Barry O'Connell, 155–61. Amherst, MA: University of Massachusetts Press, 1992.

Aravamudan, Srinivas. *Tropicopolitans: Colonialism and Agency, 1688–1804*. Durham, NC: Duke University Press, 1999.

Arendt, Hannah. *Eichmann in Jerusalem: A Report on the Banality of Evil*. New York: Penguin Classics, 2006.

Bache, W. B. "Moral Awareness in 'Dry September.'" *Faulkner Studies* 3 (Summer 1954): 53–57.

Baker, Houston A. "Critical Memory and the Black Public Sphere." In *The Black Public Sphere: A Public Culture Book*, edited by Black Public Sphere Collective, 5–38. Chicago: University of Chicago Press, 1995.

———. *Turning South Again: Re-Thinking Modernism, Re-Reading Booker T.* Durham, NC: Duke University Press, 2001.

Baker, Houston A. Jr. and Dana D. Nelson. "Preface: Violence, the Body, and 'The South.'" *American Literature*. 73, no. 2 (June 2001): 231–44.

Baldwin, James. "Equal in Paris." In *Collected Essays*, 101–116. New York: Library of America, 1998.

Baldwin, W. O. "Tribute to the Late James Marion Sims, November 1883." In *The Story of My Life*, edited by H. Marion-Sim. New York: Appleton and Company, 1886.

Bataille, George. "Chinese Torture." In *Tears of Eros*, 205–213. San Francisco, CA: City Lights Books, 1989.

"Battle of Central Re-Enactment Canceled." *The Anderson Independent-Mail*. April 17, 2009, www.independentmail.com/news/2009/apr/17/battle-central-re-enactment-canceled-organizers-sa/.

Bay, Mia. *To Tell the Truth Freely: The Life of Ida B. Wells*. New York: Hill and Wang, 2010.

Bederman, Gail. " 'The White Man's Civilization on Trial': Ida B. Wells, Representations of Lynching, and Northern Middle-Class Manhood." In *Manliness and Civilization: A Cultural History of Gender and Race in the United States, 1880–1917*, 45–76. Chicago: University of Chicago Press, 1995.

Benn Michaels, Walter. "Autobiography of an Ex-White Man." *Transition*. 73 (1997): 122–43.

———. *Our America: Nativism, Modernism, and Pluralism*. Durham, NC: Duke University Press, 1995.

———. *The Trouble With Diversity: How We Learned to Love Identity and Ignore Inequality*. New York: Holt Paperbacks, 2007.

Benn Michaels, Walter and Donald Pease, eds. *The American Renaissance Reconsidered*. Baltimore, MD: Johns Hopkins University Press, 1989.

Berlant, Lauren. "Critical Inquiry, Affirmative Culture." *Critical Inquiry* 30, no. 44 (Winter 2004): 5–51.

———. "Notes on Diva Citizenship." In *The Queen of America Goes to Washington City: Essays on Sex and Citizenship*, 221–46. Durham, NC: Duke University Press, 1997.

———. *The Queen of America Goes to Washington City: Essays on Sex and Citizenship*. Durham, NC: Duke University Press, 1997.

Berlant, Lauren and Michael Warner. "Sex in Public." In *Publics and Counterpublics*, edited by Michael Warner, 187–208. New York: Zone Books, 2005.

Bhabha, Homi K. "The Postcolonial and the Postmodern: The Question of Agency." In *The Location of Culture*, 171–98. New York and London: Routledge, 1994.

Blight, David. *Race and Reunion: The Civil War in American Memory*. Cambridge, MA: Belknap Press, 2002.

Blotner, Joseph. *Selected Letters of William Faulkner*. New York: Random House, 1977.

"Boehner Repeats Gitmo Recidivism Propaganda." January 25, 2009, http://videocafe.crooksandliars.com/david/boehner-repeats-gitmo-recidivism-propaganda.

Bogues, Anthony. "The Radical Praxis of Ida B. Wells-Barnett: Telling the Truth Freely." In *Black Heretics, Black Prophets: Radical Political Intellectuals*, 47–67. New York: Routledge, 2003.

Bone, Martyn. "New Southern Studies and the Race-Sex-Gender Spiral." *Southern Literary Journal*. Volume 39, no. 1 (Fall 2006): 119–27.
Bordo, Susan. "Reading the Male Body." *Michigan Quarterly Review* 32, no. 4 (Fall 1993): 696–737.
Bowles, Juliette. "Extreme Times Call for Extreme Heroes." *International Review of African-American Art*. 14, no. 3 (Summer 1998): 3–16.
Bradford, William. *Of Plimoth Plantation*. Edited by Valerian Paget. New York: McBride Press, 1909.
Bragdon, Allen. *Can You Pass These Tests?* New York: Harper and Row, 1987.
Brooks, Cleanth. *William Faulkner: Toward Yoknapatawpha and Beyond.* Baton Rouge, LA: Louisiana State University Press, 1990.
Brooks, Gwendolyn. "The Chicago Defender Sends a Man to Little Rock." In *Selected Poems*, 68–70. New York: Harper Perennial Modern Class, 2006.
Brown, John Fed. "Dr. Hamilton's Experiments Upon Me. My Master Dies and I Again Change Hands." In *Slave Life in Georgia: A Narrative in the Life of John Brown*, edited by L.A. Chamerovzow, 45–61. Freeport, NY: Books for Libraries Press, 1971.
Brown, John. *Slave Life in Georgia*. The Black Heritage Library Collection. Manchester, NH: Ayers Company Publishing, 1977.
Brundage, Fitzhugh. *Lynching in the New South: Georgia and Virginia, 1880–1930*. Urbana, IL: University of Illinois Press, 1993.
Burroughs, William S. "A Thanksgiving Prayer." In *Dead City Radio*. Fontana Island Records, 1990.
Butler, Jack. "Still Southern After All These Years." In *The Future of Southern Letters*, edited by John W. Lowe and Jefferson Humphries, 33–40. New York: Oxford University Press, 1996.
Butler, Judith. "Endangered/Endangering: Schematic Racism and White Paranoia." In *The Judith Butler Reader*, edited by Sara Salih and Judith Butler, 204–211. New York: Wiley Blackwell, 2004.
———. *Excitable Speech: A Politics of the Performative*. New York: Routledge, 1997.
———. *Gender Trouble: Feminism and the Subversion of Identity*. New York: Routledge, 2006.
Bynum, Victoria. *Free State of Jones: Mississippi's Longest Civil War*. Chapel Hill, NC: University of North Carolina Press, 2002.
Carothers, James B. "Faulkner's Short Story Writing and the Oldest Profession." In *Faulkner and the Short Story*, edited by Evans Harrington and Ann J. Abadie, 38–61. Jackson, MS: University Press of Mississippi, 1992.
Carr, Cynthia. *Our Town: A Heartland Lynching, A Haunted Town, and the Hidden History of White America*. New York: Crown Publishing Group, 2006.
Christian, Barbara. "Race for Theory." *Feminist Studies* 14, no. 1. (Spring 1998): 67–79.
Ciner, Elizabeth J. "Richard Wright's Struggle With Fathers." In *Richard Wright: Myths and Realities, edited by* James Trotman, 125–36. New York: Garland Publishing Inc., 1988.

Ciner, Elizabeth J. "Richard Wright's Struggle with Fathers." In *Richard Wright's Black Boy (Bloom's Modern Critical Interpretations)*, edited by Harold Bloom, 117–126. New York: Chelsea House Publishers, 2006.

"Closing Arguments Today in Texas Dragging-Death Trial." February 22, 1999, www.cnn.com/US/9902/22/dragging.death.03/.

Clymer, Jeffory A. "The United States of Terrorism: The Political Economy of Lynching and Citizenship in Thomas Dixon and Ida B. Wells." In *America's Culture of Terrorism: Violence, Capitalism, and the Written Word*, 100–133. Chapel Hill, NC: University of North Carolina Press, 2003.

Collins, Patricia Hill. *Black Feminist Thought: Knowledge, Consciousness, and the Politics of Empowerment*, 2nd ed. New York: Routledge, 2000.

Cosmides, Leda and John Tooby. "Evolutionary Psychology: A Primer." Center for Evolutionary Psychology at University of California at Santa Barbara, 1997, www.psych.ucsb.edu/research/cep/primer.html.

Coulter, Ann. "40 Excuses and a Mule." October 28, 2004, www.jewishworldreview.com/cols/coulter102804.asp

Crane, John K. "But the Days Grow Short: A Reinterpretation of Faulkner's 'Dry September.'" *Twentieth Century Literature* 31, no. 4 (Winter 1985): 410–20.

Cullen, John B. and Floyd C. Watkins. *Old Times in the Faulkner Country*. Chapel Hill, NC: University of North Carolina Press, 1961.

Curtis, Brian. "NASCAR's Silent Majority." February 16, 2004, www.slate.com/id/2095592/.

Daly, Mary. *Gyn/Ecology: The Metaethics of Radical Feminism*. Boston: Beacon Press, 1990.

Davis, Angela. *Abolition Democracy: Beyond Empire, Prisons, and Torture*. New York: Seven Stories Press, 2005.

Davis, James C. " 'Stage Business' as Citizenship: Ida B. Wells at the World's Columbian Exposition." In *Commerce in Color: Race, Consumer Culture, and American Literature, 1893–1933*, 64–85. Ann Arbor, MI: University of Michigan Press, 2007.

Davis, Simone W. "The 'Weak Race' and the Winchester: Political Voices in the Pamphlets of Ida B. Wells-Barnett." *Legacy* 12, no. 2 (1995): 77–97.

Day, Ken Gonzales. *Lynching in the West, 1850–1935*. Durham, NC: Duke University Press, 2006.

Daykin, Tom. "Plan to Buy Former Black Holocaust Museum Passes City Committee." December 9, 2008, www.jsonline.com/news/milwaukee/35815459.html.

"Death by Lynching." *The New York Times*. March 16, 2000, www.nytimes.com/2000/03/16/opinion/death-by-lynching.html.

DeGraw, Sharon. *The Subject of Race in American Science Fiction*. New York: Routledge, 2007.

Delany, Samuel R. "Racism and Science Fiction." In *Dark Matter: A Century of Speculative Fiction from the African Diaspora*, edited by Sheree R. Thomas, 383–97. New York: Time Warner Books, 2000.

Deleuze, Gilles and Felix Guattari. *Kafka: Toward a Minor Literature*. Minneapolis, MN: University of Minnesota Press, 1986.

Derrida, Jacques. *Archive Fever: A Freudian Impression*. Chicago: University of Chicago Press, 1995.

Dickinson, Stephanie. "A Lynching in Stereoscope." In *The Best American Nonrequired Reading 2005*, edited by Dave Eggers, 96–111. New York: Mariner Books, 2005.

Dickstein, Morris. "Ralph Ellison, Race, and American Culture." In *Ralph Ellison's Invisible Man: A Casebook*, edited by John F. Callahan, 125–48. New York: Oxford University Press, 2004.

Dippie, Brian W. *The Vanishing American: White Attitudes and U.S. Indian Policy*. Lawrence, KS: University Press of Kansas, 1991.

Dixon, Annette, ed. *Kara Walker: Pictures from Another Time*. Ann Arbor, MI: University of Michigan Museum of Art, 2002.

Doss, Erika, *Memorial Mania: Public Feeling in America*. Chicago: University of Chicago Press, 2007.

Douglass, Frederick. *Autobiographies*. Edited by Henry Louis Gates. New York: Library of America, 1994.

Doyle, Don H. "Lynching." In *The William Faulkner Encyclopedia*, edited by Robert W. Hamblin and Charles A. Peek, 238–40. Westport, CT: Greenwood Publishing Group, 1999.

Doyle, William. *An American Insurrection: The Battle of Oxford Mississippi, 1962*. New York: Doubleday, 2001.

Drake, James David. *King Philip's War: Civil War in New England, 1675–1676*. Amherst, MA: University of Massachusetts Press, 2000.

Dray, Philip. *At the Hands of Persons Unknown: The Lynching of Black America*. New York: Modern Library, 2002.

Dsb, "Is Hatred Part of Our Human Heritage?" Without Sanctuary: Lynching Photography in America, February 6, 2008, <http://withoutsanctuary.org/phpbb2/viewtopic.php?t=653>.

DuBois, W. E. B. "Richard Wright Looks Back: Harsh, Forbidding Memories of Negro Childhood and Youth." In *Richard Wright's Black Boy (American Hunger): A Casebook*, edited by William L Andrews and Douglas Taylor, 33–36. New York: Oxford University Press, 2003.

———. *The Souls of Black Folk: A Norton Critical Edition*. New York: Norton, 1999.

Durden, Richard F. *The Gray and the Black: The Confederate Debate on Emancipation*. Baton Rouge, LA: Louisiana State University Press, 2000.

Dworkin, Andrea. "Intercourse in a Man-Made World." In *Intercourse*, 3–79. New York: Basic Books, 2006.

Eisenhower, Dwight David. *Crusade in Europe*. Baltimore, MD: Johns Hopkins University Press, 1997.

Elkins, Stanley. *Slavery: A Problem in American Institutional and Intellectual Life*. Chicago and London: University of Chicago Press, 1959.

Ellison, Ralph. *Going to the Territory*. New York: Vintage Books, 1995.

———. *Invisible Man*. New York: Vintage Books, 1995a.

———. "Richard Wright's Blues." In *Richard Wright's Black Boy (American Hunger): A Casebook*, edited by William L Andrews and Douglas Taylor, 45–60. New York: Oxford University Press, 2003.

———. *Shadow and Act*. New York: Vintage Books, 1995b.

Fabre, Michel. *The Unfinished Quest of Richard Wright*. Urbana, IL: University of Illinois Press, 1993.

Fanon, Frantz. *Black Skin, White Masks*. Trans. Richard Philcox. New York: Grove/Atlantic Press, 2008.

Faulkner, William. *Collected Stories*. New York: Vintage Books, 1995.

———. *Essays, Speeches, and Public Letters*. Edited by James B. Meriwether. New York: Modern Library, 2004.

———. *Go Down, Moses*. New York: Vintage Books, 1990a.

———. *Light in August*. New York: Vintage Books, 1990b.

Ferguson, Jeffrey B. *The Sage of Sugar Hill: George S. Schuyler and the Harlem Renaissance*. New Haven, CT: Yale University Press, 2005.

Forty, Adrian and Susanne Kuchler. *The Art of Forgetting*. Munich: Berg Publishers, 2001.

Foster, Gaines M. "The Lost Cause Myth." In *Encyclopedia of Southern Culture*, edited by Mary L. Hart, Charles Reagan Wilson, William Ferris, and Ann J. Adadie, 1134–35. Chapel Hill, NC: University of North Carolina Press, 1989.

Fowler, Doreen. "Faulkner's Return to the Freudian Father." *Modern Fiction Studies* 50, no. 2 (2004): 411–34.

Francisco, Edward, Robert Vaughan, and Linda Francisco, eds. *The South in Perspective: An Anthology of Southern Literature*. New York: Prentice Hall, 2000.

Frank, Thomas. *What's the Matter With Kansas? How Conservatives Won the Heart of America*. New York: Henry Holt and Company, 2004.

Freud, Sigmund. *Group Psychology and the Analysis of the Ego*. New York: The Norton Library Standard Edition, 1959.

———. "The Unconscious." In *The Standard Edition of the Complete Psychological Works of Sigmund Freud*, vol. 14, ed. and trans. by James Strachey, 159–215. London: The Hogarth Press and the Institute of Psychoanalysis, 1957.

Frost, Robert. *The Poetry of Robert Frost: The Collected Poems, Complete and Unabridged*. Edited by Edward Connery Lathem. New York: Henry Holt and Company, 1969.

"Fuck the South," www.fuckthesouth.com.

Fuss, Dianna, *Essentially Speaking: Feminism, Nature, and Difference*. New York: Routledge, 1989.

Garrett, Shawn-Marie. "Return of the Repressed." *Theatre Journal* 32, no. 2 (2002): 26–43.

Gastner, Michael, Cosma Shalizi, and Mark Newman. "Maps and Cartograms of the 2004 US Presidential Election Results," www-personal.umich.edu/~mejn/election/.

Gates, Henry Louis. "A Fragmented Man: George Schuyler and the Claims of Race." *New York Times Book Review* 31 (September 20, 1992): 42–43.

Giddings, Paula. "Missing in Action: Ida B. Wells, the NAACP, and the Historical Record." *Meridians: Feminism, Race, Transationalism* 1, no. 2 (Spring 2001): 1–17.

Gilman, Sander. "Confessions of an Academic Pornographer." In *Kara Walker: My Complement, My Enemy, My Oppressor, My Love*. Edited by Philippe Vergne. Minneapolis, MN: Walker Art Center, 2007.

Gilmore, Ruth Wilson. *Golden Gulag: Prisons, Surplus, Crisis, and Opposition in Globalizing California*. Berkeley, CA: University of California Press, 2007.

Ginzburg, Ralph. *100 Years of Lynching*. Detroit, MI: Black Classic Press, 1996.

Goldfield, David R. *Black, White, and Southern: Race Relations and Southern Culture, 1940 to the Present*. Baton Rouge, LA: Louisiana State University Press, 1990.

Goldsby, Jacqueline. *A Spectacular Secret: Lynching in American Life and Culture*. Chicago: University of Chicago Press, 2006.

Gossett, Thomas F. *Race: The History of an Idea in America*. New York: Oxford University Press, 1997.

Gray, Richard. "Inventing Communities, Imagining Places: Some Thoughts on Southern Self-Fashioning." In *South to a New Place: Region, Literature, and Culture*, edited by Suzanne W. Jones and Sharon Monteith, xiii–xxiii. Baton Rouge, LA: Louisiana State University Press, 2002.

———. "On Privacy: William Faulkner and the Human Subject." In *Faulkner and Ideology*, edited by Donald Kartiganer and Ann J. Abadies, 45–69. Jackson, MS: University Press of Mississippi.

Gregory, James N. *The Southern Diaspora: How the Great Migrations of Black and White Southerners Transformed the Nation*. Chapel Hill, NC: University of North Carolina Press, 2007.

Griffin, Farah Jasmine. *"Who Set You Flowin'?" The African-American Migration Narrative*. New York: Oxford University Press, 1995.

Griffin, Larry J. and Ashley B. Thompson. "Enough About the Disappearing South, What About the Disappearing Southerner?" *Southern Cultures* (Fall 2003): 51–65.

Gunning, Sandra. "Black Women and White Terrorism: Ida B. Wells, David Bryant Fulton, Pauline E. Hopkins, and the Politics of Representation." In *Race, Rape, and Lynching: The Red Record of American Literature*. New York: Oxford University Press, 1996. 77–107.

Gurganus, Allan. *Oldest Living Confederate Widow Tells All*. New York: Vintage Books, 2001.

Gussow, Adam. "Shoot Myself a Cop: Mamie Smith's 'Crazy Blues' as Social Text." In *Seems Like Murder Here: Southern Violence and the Blues Tradition*, 159–94. Chicago: University of Chicago Press, 2002.

Guthrie, Woody. "Woody's Artist Friend Paints Lynch Scene." *Daily Worker* 22 (April 1940): 7.

Hair, William Ivy. *Carnival of Fury: Robert Charles and the New Orleans Race Riot of 1900*. Baton Rouge, LA: Louisiana State University Press, 1976.

Hale, Grace Elizabeth. "A Horrible, Beautiful Beast." *Southern Spaces: An Interdisciplinary Journals About the Regions, Places, and Cultures of the American South*. (March 6, 2008), www.southernspaces.org/contents/2008/hale/1a.htm.

———. "Untitled" *Journal of American History* 89, no. 3 (December 2002): 989–94.

Harris, Trudier. "Lynching." In *The Companion to Southern Literature*, edited by Joseph M. Flora, Lucinda Hartwick MacKethan, and Todd W. Taylor, 462–64. Baton Rouge, LA: Louisiana State University Press, 2002.

"Hannity on Obama's Pastor." *Media Matters*, http://mediamatters.org/items/200712200007?f=s_search.

Hartman, Saidiya. *Scenes of Subjection: Terror, Slavery, and Self-Making in Nineteenth-Century America*. New York: Oxford University Press, 1997.

Haslam, Jason. " 'The Open Sesame of a Pork-Colored Skin': Whiteness and Privilege in *Black No More*." *Modern Language Studies* (Special Issue on The "White Problem": The Critical Study of Whiteness in American Literature) 32, no. 1 (Spring 2002): 15–30.

Hobson, Fred. "Of Canons and Culture Wars: Southern Literature and Literary Scholarship After Midcentury." In *The Future of Southern Letters*, edited by Jefferson Humphries and John Lowe, 72–86. New York: Oxford University Press, 1996.

———. *Tell About the South: The Southern Rage to Explain*. Baton Rouge, LA: Louisiana State University Press, 1998.

Holt, Thomas C. "The Lonely Warrior." In *Black Leaders in the 20th Century*, edited by John Hope Franklin and August Meier, 39–61. Urbana, IL: University of Illinois Press, 1982.

Holtzman, Dinah F. " 'Save the Trauma for your Mama': Kara Walker, the Art World's *Beloved*." In *Revisiting Slave Narratives II/Les Avatars contemporains des recits d'esclaves II*, edited by Judith Misrahi-Barak, 377–404. Montpelier, France: Universite Paul Valery, 2007.

hooks, bell. *Yearning*. Boston: South End Press, 1990.

Horowitz, David. "Ten Reasons Why Reparations Are for Black is a Bad Idea for Blacks—and Racist Too." January 3, 2001, www.frontpagemag.com/Articles/ReadArticle.asp?ID=1153.

Horwitz, Tony. *Confederates in the Attic: Dispatches from the Unfinished Civil War*. New York: Vintage Departures, 1998.

"How a 1947 Greenville Nightmare Changed South Carolina." February 13, 2007, http://hnn.us/roundup/comments/35962.html.

Howe, Irving. *William Faulkner: A Critical Study*. Chicago: University of Chicago Press, 1951.

Hull, Gloria T., Patricia Bell Scott, and Barbara Smith, eds. *But Some of Us Are Brave: Black Women's Studies*. New York: The Feminist Press at CUNY, 2003.

Hutchinson, George. *The Harlem Renaissance in Black and White*. Cambridge, MA: Belknap Press of Harvard University Press, 1995.
Ignatiev, Noel. *Race Traitor*. New York: Routledge, 1996.
"I'll Make Me a World." Dir. Denise Green and Samuel Pollard. Public Broadcasting Service. 1999, www.imdb.com/title/tt0184123.
Jackson, Mark Allan. "Dark Memory: A Look at Lynching in American Through the Life, Times, and Songs of Woody Guthrie." *Popular Music and Society* 28, no. 5 (December 2005): 663–75.
Jefferson, Thomas. *Notes on the State of Virginia*. Edited by David Waldstreicher. The Bedford Series in History and Culture. Boston: Bedford/St. Martins, 2002.
Jenkins, Candice M. *Private Lives, Proper Relations: Regulating Black Intimacy*. Minneapolis, MN: University of Minnesota Press, 2007.
Jensen, Robert. *Getting Off: Pornography and the End of Masculinity*. Cambridge, MA: South End Press, 2007.
John R, "The Duke Lax Case: An Example of Black Injustice To Whites." Without Sanctuary: Lynching Photography in America. 25 February 2007. <http://withoutsanctuary.org/phpbb2/viewtopic.php?t=580>.
Johnson, Richard with Paula Froelich, Bill Hoffman, and Corynne Steindler, "Trying Day for N-Word Comic," February 16, 2007, www.nypost.com/p/pagesix/trying_day_for_word_comic_IWc0gtDAz2ZgwAbVckwLSM.
Johnson, Walter. "On Agency." *Journal of Social History* 37, no. 1 (2003): 113–24.
Jones, Anne Goodwyn. "Desire and Dismemberment: Faulkner and the Ideology of Penetration." In *Faulkner and Ideology*, edited by Donald Kartiganer and Ann J. Abadie, 129–71. Jackson, MS: University Press of Mississippi, 1995.
Jones, Suzanne W. "I'll Take My Land: Contemporary Southern Agrarians." In *South to a New Place: Region, Literature, and Culture*, edited by Suzanne W. Jones and Sharon Monteith, 121–46. Baton Rouge, LA: Louisiana State University Press, 2002.
Kaplan, John. "Charles Moore: The Life Magazine Civil Rights Photographs, 1958—1965." 1998, www.viscom.ohiou.edu/oldsite/moore.site/Pages/About-Moore.html.
Kantrowitz, Stephen. *Ben Tillman and the Reconstruction of White Supremacy*. Chapel Hill, NC: University of North Carolina Press, 2000.
Kapsalis, Teri. *Public Privates: Performing Gynecology From Both Ends of the Speculum*. Durham, NC: Duke University Press, 1997.
Karem, Jeff. " 'I Could Never Really Leave the South': Regionalism and the Transformation of Richard Wright's *American Hunger*." *American Literary History*. 13, no. 4 (Winter 2001): 694–715.
Kartiganer, Donald M. " 'Listening to the Voices': Public and Fictional Language in Faulkner." *Southern Quarterly*. 45, no. 2 (Winter 2008): 28–44.
King, Richard H. *A Southern Renaissance: The Cultural Awakening of the American South, 1930–1955*. New York: Oxford University Press, 1980.

Kinney, Arthur F. *Go Down, Moses: The Miscegenation of Time*. New York: Twayne Publishers, 1996.

Kirkpatrick, Jennet. *Uncivil Disobedience: Studies in Violence and Democratic Politics*. Princeton, NJ: Princeton University Press, 2008.

Kovel, Joel. *White Racism: A Psychohistory*. New York: Columbia University Press, 1984.

" 'Kramer's' Racist Tirade—Caught on Tape" (video), www.tmz.com/2006/11/20/kramers-racist-tirade-caught-on-tape/.

Kreyling, Michael. "Toward 'A New Southern Studies.' " *South Central Review* 22, no. 1 (Spring 2005): 4–18.

Kuenz, Jane. "American Racial Discourse, 1900-1930: Schuyler's *Black No More*." *Novel: A Forum on Fiction* 30, no. 2 (Winter 1997): 170–192.

Ladd, Barbara. "Dismantling the Monolith: Southern Places—Past, Present, and Future." In *South to a New Place: Region, Literature, and Culture*, edited by Suzanne W. Jones and Sharon Monteith, 44–57. Baton Rouge, LA: Louisiana State University Press, 2002.

———. *Nationalism and the Color Line in George W. Cable, Mark Twain, and William Faulkner*. Baton Rouge, LA: Louisiana State University Press, 1996.

Laqueur, Thomas. *Making Sex: Body and Gender from the Greeks to Freud*. Cambridge, MA: Harvard University Press, 1990.

Larkin, Philip. "Church Going." In *Collected Poems*, 97–98. New York: The Noonday Press of Farrar, Straus, and Giroux, 1989.

Levy, Ariel. *Female Chauvinist Pigs*. New York: Free Press, 2005.

Lewis, C. S. *Mere Christianity*. New York: MacMillan, 1952.

Lightweis-Goff, Jennie. "Against Agency: A Polemic." Paper presented at the Cornell School of Criticism and Theory Participant Colloquia. Ithaca, NY. June 10, 2006.

———. " 'Blood at the Root': Lynching, Memory, and Freudian Group Psychology." *Psychoanalysis, Culture, and Society*. 12, no. 3(September 2007): 288–95.

Lightweis-Goff, Phillip. "Voice Note." *Email to Jennie Lightweis-Goff*. November 21, 2008.

Lipsitz, George. *The Possessive Investment in Whiteness: How White People Profit from Identity Politics*. Philadelphia, PA: Temple University Press, 1998.

Litwack, Leon F. "Hellhounds." In *Without Sanctuary: Lynching Photography in America*, edited by James Allen, 3–32. Santa Fe, NM: Twin Palms Publishing, 2000.

Loewen, James. *Lies Across America: What Our Historical Sites Get Wrong*. New York: Touchstone Books, 1999.

———. *Lies My Teacher Told Me: Everything Your American History Textbook Got Wrong*. New York: Touchstone/Simon and Schuster, 1995.

———. *Sundown Towns: A Hidden Dimension of American Racism*. Touchstone Publishing. Austin, Texas, 2006.

Lopez, Mark Hugo. "Voting Patterns of Young People by Race and Ethnicity, 1988 to 2004." CIRCLE: The Center for Information and Research on Civic Learning and Engagement, accessed in May 2005, http://civicyouth.org/PopUps/FactSheets/FS_04VotingRace.pdf.

"Lynched at Port Jervis: Robert Jackson, a Colored Man, Hanged by a Mob." *The New York Times*. June 3, 1892, http://query.nytimes.com/mem/archive-free/pdf?_r=1&res=990DE1DD1538E233A25750C0A9609C94639ED7CF.

MacKinnon, Catharine A. *Only Words*. Cambridge, MA: Harvard University Press, 1996.

Madison, James H. *A Lynching in the Heartland*. New York: Palgrave MacMillan, 2001.

Mann, Brian. *Welcome to the Homeland: A Journey to the Heart of America's Conservative Revolution*. Hanover, NH: Steerforth Press, 2006.

"Maps and Cartograms of the 2004 Election." http://www.cscs.umich.edu/~crshalizi/election/.

Marriott, David. *On Black Men*. New York: Columbia University Press, 2000.

Marx, Karl. "The Eighteenth Brumaire of Louis Napoleon." In *Selected Writings*, 2nd ed, edited by David McLellan, 329–55. New York: Oxford University Press, 2000.

Matthews, John T. "Shortened Stories: Faulkner and the Market." In *Faulkner and the Short Story: Faulkner and Yoknapatawpha, 1990*, edited by Evans Harrington and Ann J. Abadie Jackson, 3–37. Jackson, MS: University Press of Mississippi, 1990.

McCarthy, Mary. "Portrait of a Typical Negro?" Ed. William L Andrews and Douglas Taylor. In *Richard Wright's Black Boy (American Hunger): A Casebook*. New York: Oxford University Press, 2003. 41–45.

McMillen, Neil. "Judge Lynch's Court." In *Dark Journey: Black Mississippians in the Age of Jim Crow*, 224–56. Urbana, IL: University of Illinois Press, 1990.

McMillen, Neil R. and Noel Polk. "Faulkner on Lynching." *Faulkner Journal* 8 (Fall 1992): 3–14.

McPherson, Tara. *Reconstructing Dixie: Race, Gender, and Nostalgia in the Imagined South*. Durham, NC: Duke University Press, 2003.

Melville, Herman. *Moby-Dick Or, The Whale*. New York: Modern Library/ Random House, 1992.

Meriwether, James B. and Michael Millgate. *Lion in the Garden: Interviews with William Faulkner, 1926–1962*. New York: Random House, 1968.

Miller, Perry. *Errand Into the Wilderness*. Cambridge, MA: Belknap Press, 1956.

Minh-Ha, Trinh T. "Of Other Peoples: Beyond the Salvage Paradigm." In *Discussions in Contemporary Culture Number 1*, edited by Hal Foster, 140–42. Washington: Bay Press.

———. *Framer Framed: Film Scripts and Interviews*. London: Psychology Press, 1992.

Mohanty, Chandra Talpade. *Feminism Without Borders: Decolonizing Theory, Practicing Solidarity*. Durham, NC: Duke University Press, 2003.

Moore, Marianne. "The Student." In *Complete Poems*, 101–102. New York: Penguin Books, 1994.

Morgan, Stacy. " 'The Strange and Wonderful Workings of Science': Race Science and Essentialism in George Schuyler's *Black No More*." *CLA Journal*. 42, no. 3 (1999): 331–52.

Morrison, Toni. *Playing in the Dark: Whiteness and the Literary Imagination*. New York: Vintage Books, 1993.

Mulvey, Laura. "Visual Pleasure and Narrative Cinema." In *Film Theory and Criticism*, 5th edition, edited by Leo Braudy and Marshall Cohen, 833–44. New York: Oxford University Press, 1998.

Murnighan, Jack. *The Naughty Bits: The Steamiest and Most Scandalous Scenes from the World's Great Books*. New York: Three Rivers/Random House Books, 2001.

Nelson, Dana. *National Manhood: Capitalist Citizenship and the Imagined Fraternity of White Men*. Durham, NC: Duke University Press, 1998.

Olney, James. "Autobiographical Traditions Black and White." In *The Future of Southern Letters*, edited by Jefferson Humphries and John Lowe, 134–42. New York: Oxford University Press, 1996.

Ong, Walter J. "World as View and World as Event." *American Anthropologist*. 4, no. 1 (1969): 634–47.

Ozick, Cynthia. "The Rights of History and the Rights of Imagination." *Commentary Magazine*. March 1999, 22–27.

Pease, Donald E. "Melville and Cultural Persuasion." In *Ideology and Classic American Literature*, edited by Sacvan Bercovitch and Myra Jehlen, 384–417. New York: Cambridge University Press, 1986.

Perkins, Hoke. " 'Ah Just Cant Thinking': Faulkner's Black Razor Murders." In *Faulkner and Race*, edited by Doreen Fowler and Ann J. Abadie, 222–35. Jackson, MS: University Press of Mississippi, 1987.

Piepmeier, Alison. "The Supreme Right of American Citizenship." In *Out in Public: Configurations of Women's Bodies in Nineteenth-Century America*, 129–71. Chapel Hill, NC: University of North Carolina Press, 2004.

Pizzato, Mark. *Theatres of Human Sacrifice*. Albany, NY: State University of New York Press, 2005.

Polsgrove, Carol. "William Faulkner: No Friend of *Brown v. Board of Education*." *The Journal of Blacks in Higher Education*. 32 (Summer 2001): 93–99.

"The Port Jervis Lynching: Foley, Charged with Being the Negro's Accomplice, Arrested." *The New York Times*, June 4, 1892, http://query.nytimes.com/mem/archive-free/pdf?res=9802E4DC1538E233A25757C0A9609C94639ED7CF.

Povinelli, Elizabeth. (2005) "A Flight from Freedom." In Cooper and Chrisman, *Postcolonial Studies and Beyond*, edited by Ania Loomba and Suvir Kaul, 145–65. Durham: Duke University Press.

Powell, Timothy B. *Ruthless Democracy: A Multicultural Interpretation of the American Renaissance*. Princeton, NJ: Princeton University Press, 2000.

Priestly, John. *A Course of Lectures on Oratory and Criticism*. London: Printed for J. J. Johnson, 1777.

R, John. "The Duke Lax Case: An Example Of Black Injustice To Whites." Without Sanctuary: Lynching Photography in America. February 25, 2007, accessed on March 29, 2009, http://withoutsanctuary.org/phpbb2/viewtopic.php?t=580.

Raper, Arthur Franklin. *The Tragedy of Lynching*. New York: Courier Dover Publications, 2003.

Rayson, Ann. "George Schuyler: Paradox among "Assimilationist" Writers." *Black American Literature Forum*. 12, no. 3 (Autumn 1978): 102–106.

Reed, Ishmael. "Introduction." In *Black No More: A Novel*, ix–xiii. New York: The Modern Library, 1999.

Reid, Richard M. "Review of *The Heart of Confederate Appalachia* by John C. Inscoe and Gordon B. McKinney." *Journal of Southern History* 67, no. 4 (November 2001): 871–72.

Renan, Albert. "What is a Nation?" In *Becoming National: A Reader*, edited by Geoff Eley and Ronald Grigor Suny, 42–57. New York: Oxford University Press, 1996.

Rice, Anne P. "Dangerous Memories: Lynching and the U.S. Literary Imagination." PhD diss. City University of New York, 2005.

Richardson, Riche. *Black Masculinity and the U.S. South: From Uncle Tom to Gangsta*. Athens, GA: University of Georgia Press, 2007.

Roberts, Paul Craig. "Delegitimizing the West." September 7, 2001, www.townhall.com/opinion/columns/paulcraigroberts/2001/09/07/165616.html.

"Robinson on O'Reilly." *Media Matters of America*. September 27, 2007, http://mediamatters.org/items/200709270005.

Romine, Scott. "Where is Southern Literature? The Practice of Place in a Postmodern Age." In *South to a New Place: Region, Literature, and Culture*, edited by Suzanne W. Jones and Sharon Monteith, 23–43. Baton Rouge, LA: Louisiana State University Press, 2002.

Rosenbaum, Ron. *Explaining Hitler: The Search for the Origins of His Evil*. New York: Random House, 1998.

Rutledge, Gregory E. "Futurist Fiction and Fantasy: The *Racial* Establishment." *Callaloo* 24, no. 1 (2001): 236–52.

Saltz, Jerry. "Ill Will and Desire." *Flash Art* 29, no. 191 (November/December 1996): 82–86.

Sammons, Jessie Lee. "Statement, Greenville, S.C., February 19, 1947." In *Lynching in America: A History in Documents*, edited by Christopher Waldrep, 249–53. New York: New York University Press, 2006.

Santino, Jack. "Performative Commemoratives: Spontaneous Shrines and the Public Memorialization of Death." In *Spontaneous Shrines and the Public Memorialization of Death*, edited by Jack Santino, 5–16. New York: Palgrave MacMillan, 2006.

Scarbrough, Burke. "PoJe? PorJer? P-Jizzle?"*Email to Jennie Lightweis-Goff*. March 3, 2009.

Schechter, Patricia A. "Unsettled Business: Ida B. Wells Against Lynching or, How Antilynching Got Its Gender." In *Under Sentence of Death: Lynching in the*

South, edited by W. Fitzhugh Brundage, 292–317. Chapel Hill, NC: University of North Carolina Press, 1997.

Scherer, Michael. "Teammates: Allen Used N-Word in College," www.salon.com/news/feature/2006/09/24/allen_football/index.html.

Schneider, Elizabeth. "The Violence of Privacy."*Connecticut Law Review* 23 (1990): 973–99.

Schuyler, George S. *Black and Conservative: The Autobiography of George S. Schuyler.* New Rochelle, NY: Arlington House Publishers, 1966

———. *Black No More: A Novel.* New York: The Modern Library, 1999.

———. "The Negro-Art Hokum." In *Voices from the Harlem Renaissance*, edited by Nathan Irvin Huggins, 309–12. New York: Oxford University Press, 1995.

Shaw, Gwendolyn DuBois. *Seeing the Unspeakable: The Art of Kara Walker.* Durham, NC: Duke University Press, 2004.

Shear, Michael D. and Tim Craig. "Allen Denies Using Epithet to Describe Blacks." *Washington Post.* Tuesday, September 26, 2006, B01, www.washingtonpost.com/wp-dyn/content/article/2006/09/25/AR2006092500558.html

Sims, James Marion. *The Story of My Life.* Edited by H. Marion-Sims. New York: D. Appleton and Company, 1886.

Skei, Hans H. *William Faulkner, The Short Story Career.* New York: Columbia University Press, 1981.

Smith, Dave. "Speculations on a Southern Snipe." In *The Future of Southern Letters*, edited by Jefferson Humphries and John Lowe, 143–54. New York: Oxford University Press, 1996.

Smith, Lillian. *Killers of the Dream.* New York: W. W. Norton and Company, 1994.

Smith, Mark M. *How Race is Made: Slavery, Segregation, and the Senses.* Chapel Hill, NC: University of North Carolina Press, 2006.

———. *Listening to Nineteenth Century America.* Chapel Hill, NC: University of North Carolina Press, 2001.

Smith, Jon and Deborah Cohn. "Introduction: Uncanny Hybridities." In *Look Away! The U.S. South in New World Studies*, edited by Jon Smith and Deborah Cohn, 1–19. Durham, NC: Duke University Press, 2004.

Smith, Vernon E. and Jon Meacham. "The War Over King's Legacy." *Newsweek*, www.washingtonpost.com/wp-srv/national/longterm/mlk/legacy/legacy.htm.

Sontag, Susan. *Regarding the Pain of Others.* New York: Farrar, Straus, and Giroux, 2003.

"Southern Partisan: Setting the Record Straight." Fairness and Accuracy in Reporting, January 12, 2001. www.fair.org/index.php?page=1880.

Spillers, Hortense J. " 'All the Things You Could Be By Now if Sigmund Freud's Wife Was Your Mother': Psychoanalysis and Race." *Critical Inquiry* 22, no. 4 (Summer 1996): 710–34.

Stelter, Brian. "In Plane Crash Coverage, Networks Use the Word 'Terrorism' With Care." *New York Times Media Decoder.* February 18, 2010, http://mediadecoder.blogs.nytimes.com/2010/02/18/in-plane-crash-coverage-networks-use-the-word-terrorism-with-care/?src=twt&twt=mediadecodernyt.

Stephens, Alexander. "The Cornerstone of the Southern Confederacy." March 12, 1861, http://teachingamericanhistory.org/library/index.asp?document=76.

Strauss, Leo. *Natural Right and History*. Tulsa, OK: University of Oklahoma Press, 2008.

Sturken, Marita. *Tourists of History: Memory, Kitsch, and Consumerism from Oklahoma City to Ground Zero*. Durham, NC: Duke University Press, 2007.

Szabo, Julia. "Kara Walker's Shock Art." *New York Times Magazine*, March 23. 1997, 49.

Talalay, Kathryn. *Composition in Black and White: The Life of Philippa Schuyler*. New York: Oxford University Press, 1995.

Tate, Allen. *Collected Poems, 1919–1976*. New York: Farrar, 1977.

———. "The New Provincialism." In *Essays of Four Decades*, 535–55. Chicago: Swallow, 1968.

Tate, Claudia. *Psychoanalysis and Black Novels: Desire and the Protocols of Race*. New York: Oxford University Press, 1998.

Time Magazine Blogs. "9/11 Art." September 12, 2007. http://lookingaround.blogs.time.com/2007/09/12/911_art/.

Thaddeus, Janice. "The Metamorphosis of Richard Wright's *Black Boy*." In *Richard Wright's Black Boy (American Hunger): A Casebook*, edited by William L Andrews and Douglas Taylor, 63–80. New York: Oxford University Press, 2003.

Theiling, Mark. "An Irrelevant Negative." Chat with Jennie Lightweis-Goff. January 7, 2009.

Thomas, Michael. "An Old Man and a Black Boy: Reimagining Two Richards." *Richard Wright Newsletter* 12, nos. 1 and 2 (Fall/Winter 2004, Spring/Summer 2005). 1–16.

Tolnay, Stewart E. and E. M. Beck. *A Festival of Violence: An Analysis of Southern Lynchings, 1882–1930*. Urbana, IL: University of Illinois Press, 1995.

Toomer, Jean. *Cane: A Norton Critical Edition*. New York: Norton, 1987.

Tompkins, Jane. *Sensational Designs: The Cultural Work of American Fiction, 1790–1860*. New York: Oxford University Press, 1986.

"Trying Day for N-Word Comic." *New York Post*. February 16, 2007, 12.

Tucker, Cynthia. "Stark Photos of Past Horrors Promote Healing." *Atlanta Journal Constitution*, April 28, 2002, F10.

Tucker, Jeffrey A. "Can Science Succeed Where the Civil War Failed? George S. Schuyler and Race." In *Race Consciousness: African-American Studies for the New Century*, edited by Judith Jackson Fossett and Jeffrey A. Tucker, 136–152. New York: New York University Press, 1997.

Tulloch, Hugh. *The Debate on the American Civil War*. Manchester, UK: Manchester University Press, 2000.

Van Wert, Katie. "A Sentence or a Series of (Ugh) Adverbs." *Letter to Jennie Lightweis-Goff*. February 27, 2009.

Vendryes, Margaret. "Hanging on Their Walls: An Art Commentary on Lynching, The Forgotten 1935 Exhibition." In *Race Consciousness: African-American Studies for the New Century*, edited by Judith Jackson Fossett and Jeffrey A. Tucker, 153–76. New York: New York University Press, 1997.

Vickery, John B. "Ritual and Theme in Faulkner's 'Dry September.' " *The Arizona Quarterly* 18 (Spring 1962): 5–14.
Waldrep, Christopher, ed. *Lynching in America: A History in Documents*. New York: New York University Press, 2006.
Wallace, Maurice O. *Constructing the Black Masculine: Identity and Ideality in African American Mens Literature and Culture, 1775–1995* (A John Hope Franklin Center Book). Durham, NC: Duke University Press, 2002.
Warner, Michael. *Publics and Counterpublics*. New York: Zone Books, 2005.
Washington, Harriet. *Medical Apartheid*. New York: Harlem Moon/Doubleday Books, 2008.
Weinstein, Philip M. "Marginalia: Faulkner's Black Lives." In *Faulkner and Race*, edited by Doreen Fowler and Ann J. Abadie, 170–91. Jackson, MS: University Press of Mississippi, 1987.
Wells-Barnett, Ida B. *Southern Horrors and Other Writings: The Anti-Lynching Campaign of Ida B. Wells 1892–1900*. Edited by Jacqueline Jones Royster. Boston: Bedford Books, 1997.
West, Cornel. "Dr. Cornel West." *The Tavis Smiley Show*, January 12, 2007, Transcript available at http://www.pbs.org/kcet/tavissmiley/archive/200701/20070112_west.html#.
West, Rebecca. "Opera in Greenville." In *Lynching in America: A History in Documents*, edited by Christopher Waldrep, 253–55. New York: New York University Press, 2006.
Wexler, Laura. *Fire in a Canebrake: The Last Mass Lynching in America*. New York: Scribner, 2003.
"What It Means To Be a Democrat: Jim Webb, Jacksonian Democrat," www.npr.org/templates/story/story.php?storyId=6777795.
White, Hayden. *The Content of the Form: Narrative Discourse and Historical Representation*. Baltimore, MD: Johns Hopkins University Press, 1990.
Williams, John A. "Foreword to *Black Empire*." In George Schuyler, *Black Empire*. Boston: Northeastern Library of Black Literature, 1993.
Williams, Raymond. *The Country and the City*. London: Chatto and Windus, 1973.
Williamson, Joel. *New People: Miscegenation and Mulattos in the United States*. New York: Free Press, 1980.
———. "Wounds Not Scars: Lynching, the National Conscience, and the American Historian." *Journal of American History*. 83, no. 4 (March 1997): 1221–53.
Willmott, Keven. *CSA: Confederate States of America*. DVD. Lawrence, KS: Hodcarrier Films, 2004.
Woodward, C. Vann. *The Burden of Southern History*. Baton Rouge, LA: Louisiana State University Press, 1993.
Wright, Richard. "Between the World and Me." *Partisan Review* 2 (July–August 1935): 19.
———. *Black Boy*. New York: Harper and Brothers Publishers, 1945.

———. *Black Boy: The Restored Text Established by the Library of America*. New York: Harper Perennial, 1993.

———. *Twelve Million Black Voices*. New York: Basic Books, 2002.

X, Malcolm. "Black Nationalism Can Set Us Free." n.d. (Audio recording), www.marxists.org/reference/archive/malcolm-x/index.htm.

Yaeger, Patricia. *Dirt and Desire: Reconstructing Southern Women's Writing, 1930–1990*. Chicago: University of Chicago Press, 2000.

Yan, Haiping. "On Theatricality." Paper presented at Cornell School of Criticism and Theory. Ithaca, New York. July 20, 2006.

Zizek, Slavoj. "Eastern Europe's Republics of Gilead." *New Left Review* 183 (September/October 1990): 50–62.

———. *The Plague of Fantasies*. New York: Verso Books, 1997.

———. *Violence*. New York: Picador Books, 2008.

Index

Abu Ghraib, 116
Ackerman, Diane, 110–111
Adair, Ellie, xii
Afghanistan, 3
African-American conservatism, 63–64
Agency, 9, 22, 116, 127–135; of the enslaved, 121, 129–135
Albion Correctional Facility, 167
Alcatraz Prison, 167
Ali, Muhammad, 162
Allen, George, 8
Allen, James, xi, 5, 11-12, 25, 27, 113–127, 153, 162, 174
Althusser, Louis, 90
Anderson, Benedict, 39–40
Apel, Dora, 69, 113, 114–115, 122, 123, 126, 143, 165
Apess, William, 100–102, 105
Aravamudan, Srinivas, 130
Arendt, Hannah, 164
Armstrong, Karen, 48
Arnold, Roger, xii–xiii
The Assassination of Jesse James by the Coward Robert Ford (Andrew Dominik, 2007), 42
Association of Southern Women for the Prevention of Lynching (ASWPL), 87–88
Atlanta, Georgia, 31, 69, 75, 78
Atlanta Riots (1906), 69, 182
Attica Correctional Facility, 167

Auburn, Alabama, 143, 162
Aunt Jemima, 23, 128

Bache, William B., 94, 96
Bacon, Peggy, 185
Baker, Houston, 10, 40
Baldwin, James, 31, 49, 103, 114, 181
Baldwin, W.O., 81
Ball, Hoot, 163
Ball, Mary, 163–164, 170, 187
Ball, Sol, 164
Bamonti, Patricia, xii
Baraka, Amiri (LeRoi Jones), 131
Barnett, Pamela, xi
Bataille, George, 122
Battle of Central (Pickens County, South Carolina), 46
Bavarian Motor Works (BMW), 152
Bay, Mia, 19, 179
Bayer, Betty, xii
Bayh, Evan, 187
Beck, E.M., 77
Bederman, Gail, 14
Beer for My Horses (Michael Salomon, 2008), 179
Benavidez, David, xii
Benton, Thomas Hart, 185
Beitler, Lawrence, 11, 164–165, 171
Benn Michaels, Walter, 33, 40, 60, 66–67, 80
Berlant, Lauren, 3, 4, 22–23, 61, 177

Black Arts Movement, 131
Bhabha, Homi, 123–124, 130
Black Holocaust Museum, 164, 169
Birmingham Civil Rights Institute, 164
Birth of a Nation (D.W. Griffith, 1914), 44
Blagg, David, xiv
Bleich, David, xi
Blight, David, 22, 144
Blotner, Joseph, 84, 86
Bragdon, Allen, 43-44
Blue Ridge Mountains, 28, 32
Boas, Franz, 64
Bob Jones University, 152
Bogues Anthony, 14
Bohn, Aimee Senise, xii
Bone, Martyn, 34–35
Book of the Month Club, 49–51
Booth, John Wilkes, 45
Boots, Martin, 168
Bordo, Susan, 117, 122
Boston, Massachusetts, 156
Bowles, Juliet, 128, 137–138, 139
Brent Sikkema Gallery, 141
Brooks, Cleanth, 95
Brooks, Gwendolyn, 123
Brown v. Board of Education of Topeka, 86–87
Brown, John, 21, 128
Brown, John "Fed," 80
Brown, Thomas W., 146–147
Bruce, Lenny, 38
Brundage, Fitzhugh, 15, 142–143
Bryan, William Jennings, 69
Buchberger, Glenn, xii
Buffy the Vampire Slayer, xiii
Burns, Ken, 43
Burroughs, William, 101–102
Butler, Jack, 41
Butler, Haas, 146–147
Butler, Judith, 5–6, 24, 120, 175–176
Butler, Octavia, 63

Bush, George W., 180–181
Byrd, James, 5, 7, 151–152

Cadmus, Paul, 185
Caldwell, Erskine, 90
Calhoun, John C., 145
Candles Museum and Education Center, 169
Calhoun, John C., 145
Cameron, James, 161–171, 172, 173
Campbell, Alexander, 186
Cape Town Holocaust Centre, 169
Carothers, James B., 88
Carr, Cynthia, 28, 170, 172, 187
Carrington, Rodney, 179
Cartwright, Samuel, 73
Castleberry, Kristi Janelle, xii
The Chamber (James Foley, 1996), 165
Chaplin, Charles, 165
Charleston, South Carolina, 58, 64, 146
Chicago Defender, 164
Chicago, Illinois, 51–58, 65, 143, 153
Christian, Barbara, 46
Ciner, Elizabeth J., 57
Citizenship, 3, 4, 14, 19-20, 22, 24, 69–70, 90, 143, 175–178
Civil Rights Movement, 5, 90, 130, 144
Civil War, 4, 22, 32
Clark-Taylor, Angela, xii
Clemson University, xi, 146
Clinton, Bill, 168
Clodfelter, Steven, 186
Clymer, Jeffory A., 14, 179
Cogdell, Josephine, 75
Cohn, Deborah, 41, 46
Cold War, 86–87
Collective responsibility, 95–96, 139–140
Collins, Patricia Hill, 29
Columbia, South Carolina, 146
Communist Party, 15, 49, 182

Confederacy, 13, 32, 41
Confederate Knights of America, 152
Confederate Myth of Reconstruction, 44
Conklin, James, 156
Conner, Nelson, 168
"Cornerstone of the Confederacy," 45–46
Cosmides, Leda, 71–72
Coulter, Ann, 180–181
Crabill, Jessie, xii
Crane, John K., 96
Crane, Stephen, 154
Crane, William Howe, 154
Creadick, Anna, xii
The Crisis, 164
CSA: The Confederate States of America (Kevin Willmott, 2004), 43
Cunningham, Erin, xii
Cuddlebackville, New York, 154
Cullen, John B., 107, 109–110
Curry, Stewart, 185

Dahmer, Jeffrey, 122, 127
Dahlonega, Georgia, 31
Daly, Mary, 29
Daniell, Beth, xi
Dash, Julie, 137
Davis, Angela, 166–167, 176, 177
Davis, James C., 23
Davis, Jefferson, 44, 47
Davis, Jim, 168
Davis, Keith Wayne, xiii, 162, 186
Davis, Ossie, 137
Davis, Simone, 18–19
Dawson County, Georgia, 69
Day, Ken Gonzales, 4
Daykin, Tom, 170
Dean, James, 168
Deeter, Claude, 163–164, 170, 174, 187
Deeter, Willie, 170
DeGraw, Sharon, 63–68

Delany, Samuel R., 183
Deleuze, Gilles, 99
Deliverance (John Boorman, 1971), 31, 152
Demorest, Georgia, 31
Derrida, Jacques, 145
Detroit, Michigan, 143
Detroit Institute of Arts, 128
Dickens, Charles, 61
Dickinson, Stephanie, 125, 142
Dickstein, Morris, 102
DiStefano, Molly, xii
District of Columbia, 157
Dixon, Annette, 137
Doolen, Andy, xi
Doss, Erika, 168, 173
Douglass, Frederick, 46, 132–133, 144, 185
Doyle, Don H., 87, 185
Drake, James David, 101
Dray, Phillip, 5, 11, 12, 89, 181, 182, 183, 184
DuBois, W.E.B., 2, 11, 24, 50, 55, 64, 66, 93–94, 177, 182, 184
Duke, David, 10
Duke Power, 152
Duke University Lacrosse Scandal, 113–114
dum spiro spero, 175
DuSable Museum, 164
Dussere, Erik, 183
Dworkin, Andrea, 116
Dylan, Bob, 20
Dyson, Michael, 113
Dworkin, Andrea, 117

Earle, Willie, 145–153
Eisenhower, Dwight, 173
Elections (2004–2008), 36–39
Elkins, Stanley, 121, 128–129
Ellison, Ralph, 27, 49, 51, 85, 100, 105, 131

Emancipation, 8
Empty land (*terra nullius*), 101, 150–151
Endicott, Russell, 186
Equal Employment Opportunity Commission, 143
Evans, David, 114
Evers, Medgar, 10, 24
Evolutionary psychology, 71–72

Fanon, Frantz, 12, 64
Fansler, Rex, 169
Fantasy, 59–62, 76
Faulkner, William, 6, 26-27, 34, 79, 83–111, 183–185; *Absalom, Absalom!*, 91; "Dry September," 94–97, 184; *Go Down, Moses*, 92, 83; letters on lynching, 87–92; *Light in August*, 98, 103–106, 109, 123; "Pantaloon in Black," 97–100; *Sanctuary*, 91, 109; *The Sound and the Fury*, 184
Feminism; and models of the gaze, 116–121; as interventionist scholarship, 28–29
Ferguson, Jeffrey B., 65, 76, 79, 182
Fetchit, Stepin (Lincoln Perry), 109
Fetish, 122–123
Fleming, Amanda Mary, xii
Finnerty, Collin, 114
Fischl, Eric, 174
Foley, Peter, 20
Forest, Nathan Bedford, 11
Forlani, Claire, 179
Forsyth County, Georgia, 69
Fort Pillow Massacre, 11
Forter, Gregory, xi
Forty, Adrian, 175
Foster, Gaines M., 180
Foster, Stephen, 161
Fowler, Doreen, 91–92
France, 78
Frank, Jamie, xii

Frank, Leo dedication, xi, 12
Frank, Thomas, 44
Frederickson, Kari, 181
Freedom, 129–130
Free-Soil Revolt, 21
Free State of Jones, 32, 180
Freeman, Elizabeth, 181
Freud, Sigmund, 10–14, 36, 51, 61–63, 93
Frey, James, 49
Frost, Robert, 150–151
"Fuck the South" (2004), 36
Fugitive Slave Law, 161
Furman University, 152
Fuss, Diana, 57

Garland, Campbell, xii
Garrett, Shawn-Marie, 135
Gates, Henry Louis, 136–137, 182
Gaze, 92–94, 100–106, 126; Mulveyian gaze, 104, 117, 126–127; and fantasy 59, 80–81
Genovese, Eugene, 121, 128
George, Rex, 164
Gettysburg Address, 173–174
Gibson, Sarah, 186
Giddings, Paula, 180
Gilman, Sander, 127–128
Gilmore, Ruth Wilson, 3, 88–89
Gilroy, Paul, 24
Gilstrap, J.E., 147
Ginzburg, Ralph, 4
Glass-Steagall Act, 142
Goff, Phillip Calhoun, xiv, 186
Goldfield, David R., 23–24
Goldhagen, Jonah, 95
Goldman, Morton, 26, 83, 85–86, 100, 110–111
Goldsby, Jacqueline, 7–8, 17, 19, 70, 122, 123, 126, 152, 153–154, 180
Gone With the Wind (1936), 35–36
Gossett, Thomas F., 71–72

Governor's Island, New York, 66
Grant, Madison, 63
Grantham, Dewey W., 181
Gray, Richard, 40, 184–185
Great Barrington, Massachusetts, 66
The Great Debaters (Denzel Washington, 2007), 152
Great Migration, 15–20, 25, 33, 35, 41, 48–58, 65
Green, Allen, 169
Green, Nancy, 23
Greene, Libby, xii
Greenville, South Carolina, 28, 145–153, 176; Pickens County Museum, 145–148; intersection of Old Bramlett and Gethsemane Roads, 148; Greenville County Historical Society, 152; Greenville County Library, 152; Southern Provisions Company, 28, 147–151
Gregory, James N., 48
Griffin, Farah Jasmine, 14–15
Griffin, Larry J., 39
Griffith, D.W., 44
Grimke, Angelina, 86
Grushevksy, Anna, xii
Guantanamo Bay, 167–168
Guattari, Felix, 99
Gunning, Sandra, 18
Gurganus, Allan, 42
Gurliacci, Michael, 156
Gussow, Adam, 68
Guthrie, Woody, 20, 124–125
Guenther, Genevieve, xi

Hale, Grace Elizabeth, 113–115, 119, 126, 133
Hallman, Allyson, xiii
Hamburg Memorial Against Fascism, 175
Hamilton, Thomas, 80
Harlem, 74, 78

Harlem Renaissance, 33, 183
Harris, Joel Chandler, 93
Harris, Trudier, 84, 85
Hartman, Saidiya, 25, 120, 130, 131–133, 141, 185–186
Hasan, Nidal Malik, 179
Haslam, Jason, 79, 81
Hearing, 92–93, 107–111
Henking, Susan, xii
Henry, Kyvaughn, xii
Hitler, Adolf, 95, 144, 165
Hobart and William Smith Colleges, xii, 29
Hobbes, Thomas, 3
Hobson, Fred, 33–34, 58
Holliday, Billie, 5, 164
Holocaust, 129, 141
Holocaust Centre in the United Kingdom, 169
Holt, Thomas, 180
Holtzman, Dinah, 135
Homespace, 177–178
Honea Path, South Carolina, 31
hooks, bell, 9, 123–124, 144
Horowitz, David, 95, 133–134, 143
Horton, Seward B., 154
Horwitz, Tony, 44–45, 48
House Un-American Activities Committee (HUAC), 24
Howe, Irving, 96
Howe, Russell, 86
Howell, Clark, 182–183
Howell, Matthew, 156
Hudnut, William H., 158
Hummer, T.R., 42–43

Ice T. and Body Count, 68
Ignatiev, Noel, 178
Imus, Don, 8
Invisibility, 100–107
Iraq, 3
Irigiray, Luce, 180

Jackson, Mark Allan, 124
Jackson, Stonewall, 43
Jacobi, Martin, xi
James, C.L.R., 50
James, W.H., 87–90
Jefferson, Thomas, 26, 72–73, 79, 89
Jena, Louisiana, 143, 152
Jensen, Robert, 119, 121
Jim Crow, 8, 11, 15, 69, 73, 142–144, 160
Jim Thorpe, Pennsylvania, 186
Johnson, Else, 86
Johnson, James Weldon, 78, 93
Johnson, Walter, 130–131
Jones, Anne Goodwyn, 184
Jones, Bill T., 137
Jones, John P., 186

Kantrowitz, Stephen, 146
Kapsalis, Teri, 81
Karem, Jeff, 50
Kartiganer, Donald M., 91–92
Keith, Toby, 3, 179
Kennedy, John F., 43
Keyes, Alan, 63
King Phillip's War, 45, 101
King, Adrean, 156
King, John William, 150–151
King, Martin Luther, 10, 43
King, Richard H., 33–35
King, Rodney, 120
Kirkpatrick, Jennet, 5
Kokomo, Indiana, 163
Kolmerten, Carol A., 183
Kovel, Joel, 69–70
Kowalcyzk, John, xii
Ku Klux Klan, 11, 64, 187
Kuchler, Susanne, 175
Kuenz, Jane, 63
Kurtz, Shawn, 156

Ladd, Barbara, 9

Larkin, Philip, 176–177
Laskey, Erin, xii
Ledbetter, Huddie ("Leadbelly"), 124
Lee, Rachel, xii
Lee, Robert E., 43
Lee, Spike, 137
Lewis, C.S., 159
Lewis, Robert Jackson, 15, 20, 28, 153–161, 175
Levi, Primo, 141
Levy, Ariel, 117
Li, Stephanie, xi
Lightweis, Alan, xiii, 1, 186
Lightweis, Bryan, xiii
Lightweis, Karen, xiii
Lightweis, Patricia, xiii, 1, 2, 186
Lightweis-Goff, Phillip Calhoun, xiii, xiv, 149–150, 153–161, 169, 171, 177, 186
Lincoln, Abraham, 173–174
Lipsitz, George, 37
Littlefield, John, 113
Litwack, Leon, 11, 104
Loewen, James, 9, 32, 44, 180
Loney, George, 142
Lopez, Mark Hugo, 181
Looking, 59, 92–94, 100–106
Lost Cause, 44
Lynching Photographs, 113–127; and contemporary memory, 145–178; as evidence, 115; attempted, of James Cameron, 161–171, 187; in the space of the museum gallery, 113–27; of Abram Smith, 118, 161–171; of Frank Embree, 118, 121–127, 136; of John Richards, 125; of Laura Nelson, 120, 121–127; of Leo Frank, 125; of Jesse Washington, 118; of Thomas Shipp, 11–12, 161–171; "using" vs. "looking," 119–120
Lynching; and Christianity, 12; and hate crimes, 6; and the phallus,

122–123; and the motifs of empty land, 150–153; as capital punishment, 77; and 9/11; 28, 116, 155; and surveillance, 7, 115; commercial zoning, 160–161; in Moore's Ford, Georgia, 15; of Elwood Higginbotham, 27, 86; of Frank Embree, 106–107; of Jesse Washington, 57, 181; of Laura Nelson dedication, xi, 27, 141–142; of Lawrence Nelson, 124–125, 142; of Frazier Baker, 160; of Matthew Williams, 80, 183; of Melby Dotson, 68–69, 75; of Michael Donald, 15, 143; of Nelse Patton, 27, 86, 107–111; of Robert Charles, 68–69; of Robert Jackson Lewis, 15, 20, 28, 153–161, 175; of Sam Hose, 11, 57, 93, 181; of Thomas Moss, Calvin McDowell, and William Stewart, 16; of Willie Earle, 145–153; on regional specificity, 9, 17, 20, 25, 36, 48–49, 54, 148; public memory of, 145–178
Lynching sites; Greenville, South Carolina, 145–153, 168; Port Jervis, New York, 153–161, 168, 176; Marion, Indiana, 161–171, 176, 187

MacKinnon, Catherine, 118–119, 126
Macoby, Hyam, 159–160
Madden, Ed, xi
Maddox, Lester, 10
Madison, James H., 164, 165, 172
Malcolm X, 41
Male body; racially marked, 118–121
Mann, Brian, 37–38
Manomet, Massachusetts, 156
Mapplethorpe, Robert, 122, 127
Marion, Indiana, 28, 161–171, 176, 187; Grant Count Courthouse, 163–165; Grant County Security Center, 166–168; Marion Machine Foundry, 163; Vietnam Prisoners of War obelisk, 172–173
Marimekko, 160
Marked identity, 36–37
Marriott, David, 122, 127
Marx, Karl, 52–53, 56
Mason-Dixon Line, 45
Massachusetts Colony, 101, 184
Matthews, John T., 84
Mayer, John, 8
McCarthy, Mary, 51
McCue, Jess, xii
McMahon, Lena, 20, 154
McMillan, Mattie, 107
McMillen, Neil, 87–91, 94, 111, 163, 185
McNally, Susanne, xii
McPherson, Tara, 20, 34–35, 47–48
McVeigh, Timothy, 45
Meconi, Honey, xii
Meeropol, Abel, 114, 164–165
Melville, Herman, 85, 101–103, 105
Memorials, 145–178; as disrupters of spatial identification, 171–178; as places of public mourning, 171–178; and legislation, 169–171; post 9/11, 156–157; comparisons to lynching photographs
Memory, 145–178; and development, 150–151, 160–161; as a "performative pause," 175–176; and museums, 145–148; and nationhood, 172
Meriwether, James B., 86
Middle Passage, 134–135
Miller, Quentin, 181
Millgate, Michael, 86
Milwaukee, Wisconsin, 164
Minh-ha, Trinh T., 41
Missinewa River, 163
Mitchell, Margaret, 10
Mohanty, Chandra Talpade, 45
Molly Maguires, 186

Montgomery County, Kentucky, 108
Moore, Marianne, 160
Morgan, Annie, 69
Morgan, Carole, xiv, 186
Morgan, Stacy, 63, 65
Morrill Land Grant Act, 146
Morrissey, Lee, xii
Morrison, Toni, 102, 161, 183
Morton, Samuel George, 73
Mowery, Ron, 170
Moynihan Report on the Negro Family, 142
Mulvey, Laura, 104
Murnighan, Jack, 59–60
Museum of Tolerance, 164
Myrtle Beach, South Carolina, 146

Nash, Ruth Ann, 171
Nast, Thomas, 44
Natchez, Mississippi, 20, 36
National Association for the Advancement of Colored People (NAACP), 5, 15, 48, 64, 116, 143, 164, 180, 181
Nazism, 86–87, 95, 129, 144, 182
Nelson, Dana D., 40, 101
Nelson, Laura dedication, xi, 27, 141–142
Nelson, Willie, 179
Neversink River, 154
New Mexico Holocaust and Intolerance Museum, 169
New Orleans, 20, 31, 36, 58, 68
New Social History, 8
New York City, 1, 15–16, 25, 65, 152, 155–156, 184
Nigro, Julianne, xii
Niu, Greta Aiyu, xi
Nixon, Richard M., 60
Noguchi, Isamu, 185
Norton, Holly, xiii
Nott, Josiah, 73

Nuremberg Trials, 129
N.W.A. (Niggas wit Attitude), 68

O'Halloran, Julia, xii
O'Riordan, Heather, xii
Obama, Barack, 3, 38, 166–168
Oconee County, South Carolina, 146
Okemah, Oklahoma, 124–125, 142
Oklahoma City Bombing, 168
Olney, James, 53
Ong, Walter, 92–93
Oxford, Mississippi, 27, 105–111
Ozick, Cynthia, 173, 174

Page, Thomas Nelson, 40
Pain, 113–121
Painter, Nell Irvin, 33
Palin, Sarah, 156–157
Paniccia, Michela, xii
Parks, Rosa, 24
Pascagoula, Mississippi, 31
Pascal's Wager, 158
Paul, Catherine, xi
Pease, Donald, 33, 102
Pequod War, 45, 101
Percy, William Alexander, 34
Perkins, Hoke, 99, 184
Perry, Lincoln (Stepin Fetchit), 109
Philadelphia, Pennsylvania, 155
Photography, 113–127
Piepmeier, Alison, 23
Pizzato, Mark, 120
Plantation; problem of comparing with concentration camp, 129; and agency, 133–135; and Kara Walker, 128, 141–142
Plessy, Homer, 93
Polk, Noel, 87–91, 94
Pollard, Edward A., 180
Polsgrove, Carol, 87
Pornography, 116–120; and anti-pornography, 117–119; as evidence,

118; as false mimesis, 127; and lynching, 116–120
Port Allen, Louisiana, 68
Port Jervis, New York, 15–16, 20, 28, 153–161, 176; Blue Parrot Restaurant, 153; Delaware House Hotel, 154–155; Erie Hotel and Trackside Manor, 154–157; First Presbyterian Church, 157–159; First Baptist Church, 158–159; Immaculate Conception Catholic Church, 153; Northern Metroline Railroad, 153; Orange Square, 157
Porter, Cole, 168
Postcolonial studies, 41–47
Post-Raciality, 59, 114
Povinelli, Elizabeth, 129–130
Powell, Timothy B., 102
Primal scenes and "the primal (un)scene," 92–94, 110–111
Prisons, 2, 3, 166–168
Privacy, 13, 68–70, 80, 99–100, 108, 111
Providence, Rhode Island, 65–66
Pryor, Richard, 135–136, 162
Psychoanalysis, 10–14, 26, 49, 59–63, 70–73, 130
Public Spheres and Public Spaces, 3, 6, 68–70, 78–80, 91–94, 104, 108, 145–178, 186–187
Purdin, Bethany, xiii
Putin, Vladmir, 159

Racial science, 67–68, 70–73, 79–82, 139
Ragusa, Gina, xii
Randolph, Innes, 42
Rankin, John, 185
Rape, 11, 16–20, 92, 107, 131–133, 142, 146, 164, 184
Rayson, Ann, 66
Reagan, Ronald, 145

Reconstruction, 26
Regional boundaries, 31–33, 161–164, 171
Renan, Ernest, 172
Reynolds, Joshua, xii
Rice, Anne P., 108–109, 111
Richards, Michael, 8
Richmond, Virginia, 157, 180
Ridgefield, Connecticut, 156
Riefenstahl, Leni, xi, 144
Robertson, Ben, 146
Robeson, Paul, 24
Robinson, Cedric, 50
Roe, Kyle, xii
Rogers, George-Tom, xii
Roots (Chomsky and Ehrman, 1977), 8, 142
Rosenbaum, Ron, 95
Rosenblat, Herman, 49
Ross, Stephen M., 183
Roth, Andrew, 113
Roth Horowitz Gallery, 25, 113, 141
Runner, Jeffrey, xii
Rush, Benjamin, 73
Rutledge, Gregory, 67

Saab, A. Joan, xi
Saar, Betye, 128, 137, 139
Saint Severin, 162
Salisbury, Maryland, 80
Saltz, Jerry, 128
Saluda River, 28, 147, 152–153
Sammons, Jesse Lee, 147
San Diego, California, 65
Santino, Jack, 177
Sapin, Paul, 170
Savannah, Georgia, 58
Sbriglia, Russell, xii
Scarbrough, Burke, xiii, xiv, 153–161, 168, 186
Schlink, David, xii
Schmidt, Bonnie Lightweis, xiii

Schmidt, Phillip, xiii
Schneider, Elizabeth, 13
Schuyler, George, 6, 26, 60–82, 182–183
"Scopophilia," 127
Scottsboro Boys, 114
Seligmann, Reade, 114
Seneca, South Carolina, 1, 3, 31, 46, 156
Serano, Greg, 179
Shannon, James, 148
Shaw, Gwendolyn DuBois, 131–134, 136, 139–141, 144
Shelton Laurel Massacre, 46
Shephard, Matthew, 5, 7
Sherman Anti-Trust Measures, 142
Sherman, William Tecumseh, 146
Shilstone, Fred, xii
Shipp, Thomas, 11-12, 161–171
Signifying Monkey, 136–138
Sims, James Marion, 80–82
Simpson, O.J., 7
Skei, Hans, 85, 94–95
Slavery; Atlantic Slave Trade; and agency, 127–135; and Jim Crow, 142–144
Smith, Abram, 11-12, 161–171
Smith, Daniel C., 184
Smith, Hoke, 182–183
Smith, Jon, 41, 46
Smith, Lillian, 34, 90, 109
Smith, Mark M., 73, 97, 100–101
Smith, Mamie, 68
Smith, Shawn Michelle, 165
Smithsonian Folkways Collection, 124–125
Social Darwinism, 71–72
Sontag, Susan, 115–116, 142
South Bend, Indiana, 162–163
Southern Diaspora, 48
Southern Partisan, 45
Southern Renaissance, 33
Sowell, Thomas, 63

Spectatorship, 113–127
Spencer, J. Morgan, 87
Spillers, Hortense J., 70
Stack, Joseph, 179
Stampp, Kenneth, 121, 128
Steele, Shelby, 63
Stelter, Brian, 179
Stephens, Alexander, 45–46
Stewart, Xen, 171
Stoddard, Lothrop, 63
Storey, Susan, xii
Stoutenburgh, Angela, xii
Stowe, Harriet Beecher, 161
Sturken, Marita, 174
Strauss, Leo, 95
Subjectivity; and agency, 106–107, 124, 129–135; of photographed subjects, 124; and subjection, 58, 129–30, 135
Sullivan, W.V., 107, 109
Susan B. Anthony Institute, xii
Swenson, Leah, xii
Sympathy, 12, 49, 89, 115–116, 184
Syracuse, New York, 65–66, 113
Szabo, Julia, 141

Talalay, Kathryn, 75
Tate, Allen, 27, 41, 108
"Teflon slaves," 121
Terre Haute, Indiana, 169
Terrorism, 13, 179
Theiling, Dale (Sr.), 186
Theiling, Dale (Jr.), xiii
Theiling, Mark, xiii, 172
Theiling, Nancy, 186
Thomas, Clarence, 7, 63
Thomas, Sheree, 63
Thompson, Ashley B., 39
Thurmond, Strom, 89
Till, Emmett, 87, 109
Tillman, Ben ("Pitchfork"), 146
Tolnay, Stewart E., 77
Tooby, John, 71–72
Toomer, Jean, 6, 26, 59–61, 74

Towns County, Georgia, 69
Trail of Tears, 45
Triumph des Willens (Leni Riefenstahl, 1935), 144
Tucker, Cynthia, 113–114
Tucker, Jeffrey, xi, 60, 63–68
Tulloch, Hugh, 121
Tulsa Race Riots, 12
Turbeville Correctional Institute, 3
Turner, Nat, 21

Ulrich, Albert, 184
Union County, Georgia, 69
United Daughters of the Confederacy, 180
United States Holocaust Museum, 169
University of Kentucky, 152
University of Notre Dame, 161–163
University of Rochester, xi, 153
University of South Carolina, xi–xii, 2
Unmarked identity, 7, 19, 29, 101, 125, 134–35, 180

Van Wert, Katie, xiii, xiv, 153–161, 186
Vermilion, Howard, 170, 173, 174
Vickery, John B., 94, 96
Voyeurism, 2, 115, 121–127; and resistance, 121–124; and desire, 126–127
Victimization, 7, 8, 42–45, 113–115, 119–121, 129–135

Waldrep, Christopher, 160
Walhalla, South Carolina, 169
Walker, Alice, 10
Walker, Kara, 6, 27, 115, 121, 127–142, 174; *Cut,* 121, 140–143; art as self-portrait, 141
Wallace, Maurice O., 103
Ward, Lester F., 71–72
Warner, Michael, 61, 74, 183
Washington, Booker T., 89, 180, 183

Washington, Harriet, 81–82
Washington, Jesse, xi
Washington Monument, 175
Watkins, Floyd C., 109
Weatherford, Kayce, xiii
Webb, Jim, 181
Weems, Carrie Mae, 135
Weinstein, Philip M., 99, 105, 183
Weisberg, David, xii
Wells-Barnett, Ida, 13–20, 25, 114, 178, 179–180
West, Cornel, 124
West, Rebecca, 153
West Baton Rouge, Louisiana, 68
Wexler, Laura, 15, 204
Whitehurst, Joseph, xiii
Whiteness, 29, 56, 102–103; and femininity, 18, 59, 69; and "lenticular logics," 35–36, 75–76
White, Hayden, 126
Williams, John A., 61
Williams, Raymond, 180
Williamson, Joel, 40, 142–143
Wilson, Woodrow, 89
Winfrey, Oprah, 49
Wise, Rosemary, 145–146
Without Sanctuary: Lynching Photography in America, 113–127, 143, 144, 152, 162, 185
Woodward, C. Vann, 41
Woolley, Celia, 180
Worth's Museum of New York City, 154
Wright, Richard, 6, 24, 25, 48–58, 90, 93, 178, 181

Yad Vashem (Holocaust Martyrs' and Heroes' Remembrance Authority), 169
Yan, Haiping, 9
Yee, Catherine, xii

Zizek, Slavoj, 12, 40, 76